This is not a book about Gandhi, Mother Teresa, King and Mandela. It is rather a book about a thread or theme that runs through their stories, and which you can weave into yours.

That thread is a common concern for others, for putting people first. Their actions, clarity of purpose, focus, and moral stature transformed the 20th century. Your actions can transform the 21st century.

Every century opens with promise and opens ever wider because of great leaders. Not political, economic, or institutional leaders but moral leaders. People with the competence and capability to lead in business, government and society; and who possess the moral courage to refuse to be a bystander, the moral imagination to paint a picture of what could be, and the moral stature to draw people to follow them toward that better vision.

Mahatma Gandhi
2 October 1869 – 30 January 1948

Gandhi's commitment to non-violence and change influenced not just his fellow citizens, but other great agents of change who have followed in his footsteps, including Martin Luther King Jr and Nelson Mandela. He led India to independence, and perhaps led us all to independence of thought. Through his example we grasp the power of gently and persistently standing up for what is right.

Martin Luther King Jr
15 January 1929 – 4 April 1968

Martin Luther King Jr could have lived out his life as an academic, but chose to respond to the needs of his people in the USA's South, knowing that to do so put his life at risk. He was inspired by the example of Gandhi in overcoming oppression and adopted, embraced, and in the face of great violence, preached non-violent response.

He brought freedom to African Americans, and his 'I have a dream' speech with its call to 'let freedom ring' reverberates in the hearts and minds of leaders who find courage and inspiration in King's example.

He was awarded the Nobel Peace Prize in 1964 for his work in civil rights and social justice.

Mother Teresa
26 August 1910 – 5 September 1997

Mother Teresa was a Catholic nun of Albanian origin who, working as a teacher and headmistress in a school in Kolkata, became increasingly unsettled by the poverty that confronted her every day. Her response was not to tell others what to do, but to do something herself. Mother Teresa set out to help each person she came across in the slums of Kolkata, one person at a time. She devoted her life to alleviating suffering, sickness and poverty wherever she found it, eventually establishing hospices, orphanages and health clinics, and leaving a legacy which asks us about our response to those who suffer and who have less. Her example invites us to look beyond who stands in our way to the person who stands before us.

She alleviated the suffering and pain of the poor and the marginalised and continues to draw followers from all over the world.

She was awarded the Nobel Peace Prize in 1979.

Nelson Mandela
18 July 1918 – 5 December 2013

Nelson Mandela transformed from a terrorist to a world leader as I grew from a child to an adult. From 27 years in prison emerged a man radiating grace and wisdom, focused on reconciliation and renewal.

He brought an end to apartheid in South Africa, and his legacy invites us into the political arena, asking questions about the way power is wielded, the way people are treated by the state, and the injustice we choose not to see.

He was awarded the Nobel Peace Prize in 1993.

People are searching for a new form of leadership, the kind embodied in Gandhi, King, Mother Teresa and Mandela. These leaders all put people first. All responded to the needs of other human beings, and made their difference.

They were human-centred leaders who changed the 20th century.

You can be a human-centred leader who changes the 21st century.

Resource scarcity, climate change, deepening inequality—all of the challenges facing modern society and businesses mean we need to fundamentally reinvent the way we think about leadership. Results-centred leadership is no longer enough. *Humanise* is crucial reading for business leaders at the vanguard of change in a world that's crying out for leadership with a human purpose. Anthony Howard's delightful storytelling decodes the dilemmas facing leaders today and provides superb insight into how we can change leadership styles for future-fit growth. Great leadership is not about doing things the way they've always been done before and this book truly shakes up thought-leadership in this field.

—**Osvald Bjelland**, Chairman and CEO, Xyntéo
Vice Chairman, The Performance Theatre
Oxford University Business Fellow

In his latest work, Anthony Howard addresses a growing disconnect between corporate objectives and people-friendly practices that undermines the best interests of both parties. He focuses on a leadership vacuum at the highest levels that is leaving corporations aloof, adrift, and unable to capitalise on their most valuable resource: their own employees. *Humanise* is a critical reminder that all business is driven by people and meant to serve people; Howard's personal and accessible style makes this lesson resonate.

—**Ian Bremmer**, Founder and Chairman, Eurasia Group
Author of *Every Nation for Itself*

This book provides a powerful foundation to being the best person you can, and is essential reading for anyone in leadership, or on the path to leadership, who wants to leave their organisation and world in a better place. Anthony Howard's thinking about Human-Centred Leadership, and its relevance and application to contemporary leadership challenges, is an important insight for this time. There is much to consider and much to keep coming back to in this very practical book.

—**Dame Alison Carnwath**, Chairman Land Securities plc

Reading this book drives home just how inhuman so many organisations have become, in the demands and stresses they place on people. It also makes it clear that there is no reason to accept this status quo. Anybody can set off on the path towards a more human-centred business life, and as the book argues, if you can, you have a responsibility to do so. This is a liberating message — read this and act now!

— **Diane Coyle**, Vice Chair BBC Trust
Professor of Economics, University of Manchester
Founder of Enlightenment Economics

This book contributes considerably to the leadership debate:

- One can never stop learning leadership lessons. They are a vital constituent to the government of this increasingly fractious world. *Humanise* lays out the important lessons in simple and appealing terms.

- As communication becomes more sophisticated, leaders are more in the global eye and need to have a complete grasp of sound principles, and live by them. *Humanise* helps identify and then confirm these principles.

- As the media becomes more inquisitive, it is even more important to live decent lives, with clear values and standards. The imperative for leaders is to focus on people first and foremost, to take an interest in and care for them, to respect the community, to be an example to others. These are all the critical basics. *Humanise* shows how this is done.

- *Humanise* explains that whilst leadership is personal and dependent on circumstances, it is based on enduring principles.

With a deep commitment, sound judgement and a steady self control … you can lead in your chosen field.

—**Major General Arthur Denaro, CBE DL**

Anthony takes some seemingly 'old fashioned' and 'non-corporate' concepts, terms and values such as morality, virtue, humility, and justice, and weaves them into a coherent framework through which to consider one's own motivations, responses and journey through corporate and wider life. This creates a powerful mirror to look into but also a powerful window to look out on to what might be.

—**Gary Dransfield**, Chief Executive, Vero Insurance New Zealand

In a world dominated by technological change, it is easy to overlook the common humanity that binds us all. In his new book, Anthony Howard calls on leaders to integrate the intellectual, emotional, and spiritual dimensions of work. *Humanise* lays out a clear business case for re-humanising corporate life, and provides a useful reminder that, more than any other factor, a company's fate is determined by its people.

—**Serge Dumont**, Vice Chairman, Omnicom Group Inc.

Anthony Howard reminds us that a leader's true role is to serve the people who follow them and that good leaders reflect deeply on their purpose and the morality they bring to their role. He puts the view in a compelling way that it is not only appropriate for leaders to care deeply about the people they lead—it's an imperative. If you are looking to grow and become a better leader, you need to read this book.

—**Craig Dunn**, Chief Executive Officer (retired), AMP Limited

This is not a typical management textbook, rather a thoroughly thought-provoking narrative that is reminiscent of the path Anthony took me on when I was at a very difficult crossroads in my career. His insights and understanding of the human spirit are clearly demonstrated throughout the journey he will take you on as you read this book. Will you be a better person and a better leader for having read *Humanise*? I most certainly was after having worked with Anthony, and now you can get the benefit of his insights from reading and reflecting on the wisdom in these pages.

—**Eric Ford**, Non-executive director, Compass Minerals International
Former Chairman, Peabody Energy Australia
Former Executive Vice President, Office of the CEO, Peabody Energy

I have observed Anthony Howard's rare ability to get face to face with influential leaders, allow them to talk about their innermost thoughts and deepest leadership challenges, and then provide guidance and wisdom from his own unique background. In *Humanise* he outlines both the philosophy on Human-Centred Leadership and its application to contemporary and emerging challenges. The book offers page after page of usable insights, gleaned from his years of thinking about leadership, talking about leadership, and being a leader. His vision of aligning your own purpose with your organisational purpose, and then finding where that touches the world—in order to change the world—is truly inspiring. I would recommend this book both to those in leadership, and those contemplating leadership in the future.

—**Andrew Kakabadse**, Professor of Governance and Leadership,
Henley Business School, University of Reading
Emeritus Professor of International Management,
Cranfield University School of Management

During my business career I have learned that happy staff make happy customers make happy shareholders. In this book Anthony Howard explains why that is true. The world is crying out for leaders with strong moral compasses that care about people during the short, medium and long term. This book explains how you can build your own moral compass and provides insight about how you could be one of those leaders the world needs.

—**John Stewart**, Chairman, Legal & General plc.
Chairman, Guide Dogs for the Blind
Member of the Court of Directors of the Bank of England

Humanise could transform you from a reader to a leader. In this work Anthony Howard helps you restore your key settings, regain your footing and recharge your key values and virtues to cultivate truly Human Centred Leadership, so you can lead confidently and ethically.

The evenly paced narrative is strewn with unique insights drawn from Anthony's amazing life, accompanied by a roadmap and tools to help you unlock your hidden potential and get the most out of your journey.

Anthony has absorbed the experiences of many truly remarkable leaders and individuals whose powerful vision and input he shares with you in a step-by-step tale to help you achieve the moral heights that are needed for human-centred leaders in business, government and society.

No moralising or preaching, just a book to nudge you softly in the direction of something infinitely good and rewarding, where each step allows you to reflect on where you are and where you can go, shape your conscience and cultivate good habits and virtues to secure the foundation of your character. Anthony explains why we are experiencing a lack of great leaders today and why it is imperative for you to become one. *Humanise* explains how you can get there using your moral compass to stay the course to your true north.

— **Anatoly Yakorev**, Center for Ethical Business & Compliance,
International University in Moscow

humanise

humanise

WHY
HUMAN-CENTRED LEADERSHIP
IS THE KEY TO THE 21ST CENTURY

anthony howard

WILEY

First published in 2015 by John Wiley & Sons Australia, Ltd
42 McDougall St, Milton Qld 4064
Office also in Melbourne

Typeset in 12/15 pt Adobe Garamond Pro

National Library of Australia Cataloguing-in-Publication data:

Creator:	Howard, Anthony, author.
Title:	Humanise: why human-centred leadership is the key to the 21st century / Anthony Howard.
ISBN:	9780730316640 (pbk.)
	9780730316657 (ebook)
Notes:	Includes index.
Subjects:	Leadership — Social aspects.
	Executives — Conduct of life.
	Executives — Attitudes.
	Total quality management.
	Personnel management.
	Quality of work life.
Dewey Number:	658.409

Quotes from Nelson Mandela on p. 120, p. 123 and p. 171 reproduced with permission from the Nelson Mandela Foundation.

Cover design and illustrations by Wiley

10 9 8 7 6 5 4 3 2 1

Disclaimer

For Giovanna

Contents

About the author

Anthony Howard has a vision to build a more human world one leader at a time. He believes Human-Centred Leadership is the key to success in business, government and society. He is an entrepreneur, CEO, philosopher and writer who has made a life out of questions.

He has spent much of the 21st century capturing insights from people who shape and influence history, and applying those insights with leaders at the strategic apex of organisations. During a 10-year dialogue with global leaders he has interviewed more than 150 influencers from the business, academic, military and social sectors.

Anthony founded The Confidere Group, which consults to top-tier leaders working in complex and demanding environments. Known colloquially as the 'CEO Whisperer', he is a confidant to leaders in the US, the UK, Asia and Australia across sectors that include banking, insurance, retailing, advertising, mining, funds management and construction.

He is a 'sense-maker' whose services are based on the search for new questions as people seek new insights. Whether he is advising a board, acting as a confidant to a CEO, delivering a keynote presentation, or helping an executive team navigate uncharted waters, his approach starts in the unknown, using a unique search process that blends creativity, philosophy and navigational theory to help people gain clarity, focus and momentum.

Anthony writes and speaks extensively on Human-Centred Leadership. He is a guest lecturer at the School of Business (Sydney) and The University of Notre Dame Australia; speaks on radio, at conferences and company boardrooms; writes for the popular press; and has been published in the *Journal of Management Development*.

Acknowledgements

I would like to thank the many men and women who have participated in conversations with me over the past 10 years. Some of their stories and insights are captured in these pages. All of their stories and insights have influenced these pages. All of them have been very generous with their time.

I have lost track of the number of times I have made the long-haul flight from Australia to the Northern Hemisphere in pursuit of ideas, insights and perspectives. This is made easy by my love of travel and the privilege of meeting fascinating people in fascinating places. However, it's made possible by the patience, love and support of my family at home, for whom I am enormously grateful. I thank them, and also my parents, who are wonderful models of virtue and service.

I would also like to thank the clients who have trusted me with their time and thinking about themselves and their firms as they lead them in and through turmoil and change. I have learned much from these men and women who, while working at the strategic apex of their organisation, endeavour to be the best person they can be and to apply the principles of Human-Centred Leadership. They are an outstanding source of encouragement and inspiration.

Humanise would never have come to be without the influence of Andrew Kakabadse, Professor Emeritus at Cranfield University, who provided early encouragement and opportunities to write about the lessons learned from my interviews and who has been a very helpful sounding board; Katie McMurray, of KatieMac Publicity, who helped shape my thinking and writing in a way that aligns with my passion and purpose; and Kristen

Hammond, Executive Commissioning Editor at Wiley, who sponsored and supported the book. Thank you all.

Humanise is actually a collaborative effort. Although my name is on the cover, it really is the joint work of a number of people who have devoted considerable time, in the midst of their own busy lives, to reading and commenting on the drafts, and sitting down over coffee to pull apart the ideas. These individuals, spread across the globe, include Sven Atterhed, Christina Donatelli, Ileana Facchini, Professor Bill Jeynes, Ruth McCance, Tony Hughes, Peter Scott, Kellie Stirling and Sverre Stoje. The hard work they put in has undoubtedly made the book more readable and accessible, and I am in their debt.

And lastly I would like to thank you for taking the time to read and reflect on these words. Please enjoy the journey...

Preface

My whole life has been a voyage of discovery fuelled by restless curiosity.

Over the past 10 years I have crisscrossed the globe to talk to more than 150 men and women who shape and influence their part of history, seeking out their insight and inspiration. It has been an enormous privilege to learn about their life, leadership and legacy. I doubt I can ever repay the gift of their time and their timeless wisdom.

While circumnavigating the world I have also enjoyed the trust of many high-level leaders who have asked me to help them along the path to becoming the best person they can be, building the best organisations they can build and finding their point of contribution in and to the world.

This combination of conversations and consulting helped shape a philosophy—Human-Centred Leadership. This is leadership that puts people first, and that integrates the technical and moral aspects of leadership. As such it has a profoundly moral dimension, and is grounded in the person and character of each individual leader.

This book explains how the concept of Human-Centred Leadership emerged, the principles of Human-Centred Leadership and how you can apply these principles in your leadership roles. It contains the key insights gleaned from the great leaders I have met.

It is my gift to you, as a thank you for the gifts I have been given.

An invitation
Please let me know about your own efforts to be a human-centred leader in your company and in your own life. Your feedback and comments will be invaluable in the continuing development of this approach to leadership. I

would be thrilled to hear about your world and to support your efforts to become a human-centred leader and to build human-centred organisations.

Please consider this your personal invitation to contact me and join the quest to become the best person you can be, to build the best organisation you can build — to become a human-centred leader and to humanise your enterprise.

Contact details:

Office:	+61 2 9275 8718
Mobile:	+61 414 659 591
Email:	anthony.howard@confideregroup.com or mail@anthonyphoward.com
Web:	confideregroup.com or anthonyphoward.com
About:	http://about.me/anthonyphoward
Twitter:	@anthonyphoward
LinkedIn:	http://au.linkedin.com/in/anthonyphoward/

Introduction: Discovering Human-Centred Leadership

Two kinds of leadership

'I left Corporate America because of the sense of alienation it created in my life and soul.'

ANONYMOUS

'Please forgive me for ignoring your emails for the last five years,' said Susan as she joined me for coffee. She had recently resigned from her job and now had more time available. It had been a long silence, but her gracious apology and charming personality quickly placated my feelings.

She described the convergence of work and family pressures — including a son with chronic asthma and a husband facing a serious health issue — and the impact of work on her health and relationships. Family and friendships suffered ... although the work got done. Why had she waited until now to resign, I wondered silently.

'I finally left because I was dehumanised,' she exclaimed, then sat back with one hand on her heart and the other over her mouth when told the title of this book. As I watched and waited in silence she began a scathing review of her former employer. Sadly, the kind of behaviour she described is not limited to this firm, and occurs every day in many, many organisations.

Results-centred leadership

Susan held a senior leadership position reporting to a divisional head in XYZCom (not its real name). She is a seasoned executive, with an organisational psychology background and has worked across multiple cultures, countries and industries. She brings a high level of intelligence and experience to her roles and is held in very high regard by executives, directors and board chairmen. Her observations are not the complaints of a disgruntled employee or disappointed graduate, but the serious reflections of a mature, respected, proven leader.

'XYZCom is the single worst example of dehumanisation I have seen,' she continued. 'One of my people suggested that the firm actually "creates cancer". When the two of us discussed this we realised there was more medical illness there than anywhere else we had worked.

'The organisational "system" cuts off emotional interaction and dehumanises people. It enforces a dis-integration of your intellect, emotions, and physical and spiritual self. Every moment is about work, work, work … which is about being busy but not necessarily doing what really matters. And then evenings are taken up trying to respond to emails.

'There is no time for exercise, and many people are seriously unwell,' Susan went on, before providing two brief examples.

The first was of an overweight man with chronic health problems. Constantly under immense pressure to be seen to be working in the office, he was unable to make time for a doctor's appointment.

She described another occasion when a manager failed to arrive for an executive meeting. A series of agitated phone calls established that he was in hospital having a broken arm fixed. The firm immediately arranged teleconferencing facilities so he could dial into the meeting in the midst of x-rays, diagnosis and the application of a plaster cast.

I listened in silent horror as Susan told this story of industrial serfdom. Although I knew about the dehumanising impact of some contemporary organisations, Susan continued to describe the stark reality via another experience:

'Sometimes I get Susan and Andrea mixed up,' said Susan's new boss jovially as he presented his executive team to the top 100 staff. Susan, with an Asian heritage, and Andrea, from Africa, exchanged puzzled glances as their boss continued to display his ignorance and insensitivity.

'And I often call Susan "sweetie",' he continued, unconcerned by the offensiveness of his remarks, and inviting an immediate public and vocal denial from Susan.

When she challenged her boss privately he dismissed her protest by insisting that he was merely being friendly and playful, and that she was too sensitive. Susan held her ground, however. She realised that change needed to happen at the very top of this highly results-focused organisation.

One day she noticed a senior executive discreetly leaving the office early to pick up his child from sport. Like so many others who often covered up the need to attend to a sick child or a family commitment he found it difficult to act openly. In XYZCom putting family before work, or even on a par with work, is unacceptable, so people tell lies or behave deceitfully in order to fulfil their family obligations.

I wondered aloud why Susan had stayed in such a toxic environment, and what was the 'straw that broke the camel's back'.

'One day I realised I was becoming dehumanised too,' she said, lowering her voice. 'I had to take my son to hospital when he was having trouble breathing. He asked me with tears in his eyes to stay with him. He wanted his mother. But I had to go to work.

' "Mum can't be here," I told my sick son, "but Dad is here with you". My husband said he would stay and understood I needed to get to work.

'I only realised later that day that he had cancelled his own medical appointment to stay with our son while I went to work,' she said as her voice trailed off to a whisper.

'When I got into the car I hung my head over the steering wheel and sobbed. I cried all the way to work. And when I got there I resigned,' she said with little emotion.

The vision, mission and values of this particular firm are clearly articulated on their website, but their noble aims and worthy values camouflage a toxic internal environment. XYZCom treats its thousands upon thousands of employees as machines to deliver a result for their employer. People are being damaged in unimaginable ways that include physical and emotional ill health and social and family breakdown.

'Why do some corporations, and systems, force people to quit work in order to stay human?' I wondered silently after listening to this harrowing tale.

Human-Centred Leadership

The conversation with Susan was even more striking because of its contrast with those I had with Paul, one of the most human-centred leaders I have had the privilege of working with. He 'gets it' in every part of his being. In our very first meeting it was evident that what mattered most to him was people. This focus continues unrelentingly, despite his heavy workload as a busy CEO. He argues passionately in defence of his people and their needs.

When we speak about strategy, he thinks about people: staff and their families, customers and their communities. When we speak about operational matters, he talks about people. He recognises them, celebrates with them, encourages them and is loyal to them.

A staff member telephoned Paul on a recent Saturday evening as he was relaxing at home. She apologised for interrupting him and was a little nervous about calling since she did not report directly to him. As Paul set her at ease she began to talk about the immense pressure she was under, how she was not coping with the demands of her role, and the negative impact this was having on her health. She had called to resign.

Paul could hear her distress, anxiety and sense of failure. 'She was on the edge,' he said, and felt that quitting was her only option.

What would you do? Would you accept the resignation? Would you wonder why this couldn't wait until Monday in the office? Would you even be paying attention, or thinking instead of your interrupted meal or TV program? Would you perhaps be wondering how she had got your hoe number?

Before you read on to hear Paul's response, take the time to consider what you would do. Not a brief thought, but a deeper reflection. Have you encountered situations like this? Were you Paul or the employee? What did you learn about yourself from that event?

Many CEOs would politely take the call, accept the resignation, and suggest the employee talk to their line manager and/or someone in the human resources department on Monday to sort out the details. Or some variation on this theme.

Because Paul's starting point is concern for his people he immediately gave the woman three months' paid leave, told her to focus on getting better and not to worry about work. By Monday morning he had a number of support mechanisms in place, including access to counselling and therapy, and had initiated a conversation with her line manager to address the workload and stress factors. When she returned in three months she was refreshed, renewed and ready for the new role Paul had created for her.

I have thought many times about this story, and heard variations of it when Paul talks about other members of his staff. I remember feeling incredulous when he first told me. 'Who gives people three months' paid leave when they offer their resignation?' I thought.

And there is only one answer to that question: leaders who genuinely care about their people.

I don't quite understand why all leaders are not like Paul, because it just makes such sense to look after one another and look after your staff. I do, however, have sufficient understanding of humanity to know we come in all shapes and sizes with all manner of strengths and weaknesses.

There is no excuse, however, for people or firms that damage and dehumanise people. Treating people as units of economic production, as assets whose purpose is to deliver financial value to a firm or a country, is completely unacceptable.

People will determine the fate of the world. People will determine the fate of your business. People will determine the fate of your society. So doesn't it make sense to put them first in everything? To care for them in every possible way? If so, how do you do that?

By becoming a human-centred leader.

Let me tell you how I arrived at that conclusion.

Get out and see the future

'Travel is fatal to prejudice, bigotry, and narrow-mindedness, and many of our people need it sorely on these accounts. Broad, wholesome, charitable views of men and things cannot be acquired by vegetating in one little corner of the earth all one's lifetime.'

MARK TWAIN, *THE INNOCENTS ABROAD*

The image of 'beautiful people' relaxing in a Swedish hot tub under a starry sky had always held a certain allure, but when the opportunity arose I wasn't sure I wanted to find out what it was really like.

It happened after dinner with Sven Atterhed and one of his friends, by the shores of Lake Siljan in Sweden. We had enjoyed a wonderful meal, enhanced by the location and stimulating conversation about the big issues confronting the world. If we hadn't solved them we had at least understood what everyone else needed to do. Sven suggested we continue the conversation in the hot tub that sat on the corner of his balcony.

'Very pleasant,' I thought as the midnight sun slipped toward the horizon. Imagine still water on a huge inland lake, surrounded by pine forests, crisp night air and only the occasional light from a remote cabin. I was caught up in the beauty ... before Sven jolted me back to reality.

'We don't wear any clothes in the tub,' he added casually, knowing very well that would be right out of my comfort zone.

A thousand thoughts went through my mind. (Well, just a few really, including 'You're an old guy' and 'I'm not in the best shape' and 'You have got to be joking' and 'I wonder who else will be joining us?')

'We understand your English modesty, and don't mind if you wear something,' he said with a laugh, setting me a little at ease.

But still, sitting with my naked host in a hot tub at midnight did not seem conducive to deep and meaningful conversation.

How wrong I was.

How did I come to be half a world away from home, searching out ideas and insights in Tallberg, a small village more than three hours by train north of Stockholm?

The story opens with Professor Gary Hamel, the leading management thinker, who had propelled me down this track 12 months earlier. At the time I was a regional CEO for Merryck & Co., one of the world's leading CEO mentoring firms, and we were hosting a two-day forum for a small group of executive clients from across the globe.

Professor Hamel had been invited to lead a conversation on strategy and change, pushing our thinking to new levels, immersing us in new concepts and ideas. At one point he noted that the increasing rate of change meant the change curve 'has gone vertical'. He suggested that a key aspect of the CEO's role is not just to stay awake to change, but to get ahead of that curve.

'You should spend three to four weeks every year getting out and seeing the future,' he advised the participants.

That comment changed my life.

'Someone somewhere is doing something that will change your world tomorrow, and you need to get out and see it,' continued Gary.

'*You* need to do it,' he emphasised. 'You cannot delegate this. You have a perspective as the CEO that others won't have.'

He recommended we go beyond our cultures and countries, our industries and insular worlds, and look for the future.

His words lit up my imagination, giving meaning and direction to my restless curiosity. I immediately resolved to 'get out and see the future' both for my own growth and development and to bring back what I found and give it to others. This single phrase gave energy and impetus to a 10-year quest in search of insight through what I ambitiously called my 'global leaders' dialogue'. It continues to power me forward today.

But where does one begin to discover the future?

Connecting with people and ideas

I have always had a deep curiosity about people, about who they are, the forces that have shaped them and where they might be heading. In this I had become a collector of relationships, since everyone's life and story held a fascination for me.

I contacted a number of these friends and asked who they thought I should meet, which led me to Sweden, Sven Atterhed and the naked spa. Sven lived in Gothenburg and since I intended to spend time in Europe I requested an hour of his time. His reply expressed how pleased he would be for us to meet, and how disappointed he was that he would be away at that time. Can you imagine my surprise to read in the next sentence an invitation to spend a weekend at his summer holiday cottage? And that's how I came to be in a hot tub at midnight in Tallberg eating strawberries under a starry evening sky. This was the start of discovering the future.

As the water foamed around us Sven continued with his stories and insights about leadership and management, gleaned not just from 40 years of work, but also from his own deep conversations with thinkers and doers. For many years Sven and his colleagues in The ForeSight Group have sought out thought leaders in management, arranging workshops and dialogues between them and top managers. There seemed to be no end to his wisdom, as we discussed numerous ideas and concepts that have influenced my professional practice since. He showed me the power of finding the right question to elicit deeper insights and breakthrough thinking.

Most of all, his generosity gave me the courage to continue making connections with new people, searching out ideas wherever they might be found. Although I have not found myself in another hot tub, I have sat in coffee shops and boardrooms, in airport lounges and business clubs, with outstanding leaders from across the military, academic, social, political and business sectors. Some of them are well known, some known only to a few, but all shape and influence events in their own way, and in sometimes quite profound ways that impact history.

The global conversations

With Gary Hamel's advice about 'seeing the future' ringing in my ears I began the early conversations by asking my hosts simple questions about their thinking on the issues of the day and the emerging challenges of tomorrow.

A frequent comment would point to the absence of true global leaders, a new or different type of leader to help navigate the present and whatever lay ahead in the future. Traditional leaders and leadership models had been found wanting and something—or someone—more was required.

People who seemed to be great leaders were themselves searching for great leaders, wondering where the next generation would come from. They were searching for the men and women who could stand head and shoulders above the day to day, and bring a different level of wisdom and insight, peace and harmony, to contemporary challenges—and who could do so because of their character rather than their title.

Where are the new Mandelas?

'Where are the new Mandelas?' is the way some people expressed this question. This was during the decade immediately after Mandela's presidency, when his impact was evident for all to see and he seemed to be the kind of leader who was needed.

Pamela Hartigan, managing director of the Schwab Foundation for Social Entrepreneurship at the time, first alerted me to this question as we enjoyed a stimulating afternoon of conversation in Geneva. As she described projects in remote parts of Africa the conversation turned to Nelson Mandela, the leadership he had shown with regard to reconciliation and forgiveness, and what we could learn from him. Many people were wondering who could follow in his footsteps and who could assume his exemplary influence on the world stage.

The seeds of the questions that shaped my research were sown:

- Where are the new Mandelas?

- Who are the new Mandelas?

- How does one become such a person (without spending 27 years in prison)?

These questions highlight the kind of model being sought—a leader of stature, vision and gravitas. A leader whose life demonstrates growth and development, and who has the humility to reflect and learn from their actions, and to constantly seek a better way. A leader of character and courage, a leader who brings out the best in others. A leader responding to, and driven by, the needs and concerns of their people. Someone we may call a 'moral leader' or a 'human-centred leader'.

My search for the new Mandelas began by trying to understand what people meant by this term. It was clearly different from technical leadership, strategic leadership or economic leadership. It was often explained as 'moral leadership'—leadership resting on some kind of a moral foundation.

The conversations turned to asking people about their own leadership foundation and vision. I repeatedly found people shaped by their upbringing who wanted to do good, to make a difference, to create a legacy, to live a life of significance, while struggling with the conflict between their vision, values and aspirations and commercial reality or community expectations.

Many people felt drawn to Mandela's example and were inspired to emulate him, even if on a small scale.

As the conversations turned toward values and morals, my own biases began to intrude. 'Would I work for this person?' became a simple test of trustworthiness, based on little more than feelings that caused me to filter what was being said.

'Yes, you are biased,' said Andrew Kakabadse, former Professor of International Management, and now Professor Emeritus, at Cranfield University in the UK, with barely a moment's reflection when I sought his advice. He bluntly agreed that my judgement was clouding the conversation and so limiting my ability to listen.

'Why don't you ask how they have resolved moral dilemmas?' he suggested, believing that this approach would provide deeper insights into people's leadership development journey.

This question launched a new line of enquiry, eliciting far deeper understanding of the forces and influences that have shaped leaders. And it has been central to every conversation since, giving me a unique perspective on how leaders have become the men and women they are today.

I have heard the most profound stories of courage and conviction, of doubt and anxiety, of struggle and sweat. I discovered that the way people have resolved moral dilemmas depends on a range of factors, including character and conscience, upbringing and environment. I realised that a particular combination of those factors contributed to creating an outstanding leader, a moral leader, a 'new Mandela'.

I also noticed that most people—even the great and outstanding—were looking for someone else to step up, feeling inadequate, embarrassed and perhaps unworthy to do so themselves. They too were looking for the new Mandela. It struck me that many people hoped someone would suddenly appear, like Joan of Arc riding a horse and wielding a sword, and say 'I'm here to save you'. Who was this person, this great leader, and where were they to be found?

Then one day I realised the answer was staring me in the face. I don't know if it became clear in a blinding flash of light, or whether it slowly emerged through the haze. But I now knew the answer to the question.

The new Mandela is looking at you in the mirror each morning.

It's you. *You* are the new Mandela.

Perhaps now would be a good time to put the book aside and ponder what that could mean. Write yourself a note, starting with 'I am the new Mandela...', and once you have overcome your natural resistance to such a grand claim, let your imagine run.

- What sort of person would you be?

- What impact would you have on the world?

- What big issues would you speak out about?

And then...

- What would you need to do to become the best version of yourself... the new Mandela?

It's easy to be a bystander and hope someone else will step in or step up, or a deity will intervene to right wrongs or destroy the enemy. Given the challenges before us in a complex connected world it's not enough to point to your colleagues or wait on providence.

You have a responsibility to lead—at a minimum in your immediate domain, and ultimately at your point of contribution. Don't follow history and look to others to lead. Advance the future by being a leader.

It is not an option to wait for someone else or to point to someone else. The only option is for you to respond, for you to do your bit, to play your part.

To change the world, first change yourself

It's important to recognise that Mandela wasn't always Mandela. The man we remember became that man through a series of events that shaped his life. The boy grew into a man, responding to the needs of his people. Each response built on the previous one, forming his personality and building his authority. He refused to be a bystander.

We don't know from where the next Nelson Mandela, Martin Luther King Jr, Mahatma Gandhi or Mother Teresa will emerge, although we do know that they emerge when someone has the courage to respond to the demands of the moment. You will be able to respond to those demands when you have laid a solid foundation and found your place of contribution.

None of us is a 'finished product'. You can grow and develop, change and transform yourself. You may not become another Nelson Mandela, and your name may not become synonymous with greatness, but you can certainly become someone who does great things in your sphere of influence. You may not become the President of South Africa, or any other nation, but you can respond to human need where you see it. You can respond to the next need you see. You can bring your goodness to bear in every moment to every challenge you encounter. And you can be sure of one thing: you were born to do great things.

Humanise is written as a guide to help you on that journey toward greatness, toward becoming and being a human-centred leader. I believe deeply that this will be a defining characteristic of the great leaders of the 21st century.

This book follows a very simple path:

Part I: The challenge facing human-centred leaders gives my perspective on five major technological and moral challenges, each of which dehumanises us in some way, putting the person after other concerns. I argue that the world needs leaders who put people first—human-centred leaders—to counteract the depersonalising aspects of these trends.

Part II: Foundations for human-centred leaders provides a map, process and principles that will enable you to become a human-centred leader. Whether you are starting out on the journey or have many years of experience, you will be able to use these ideas to build or supplement a powerful set of leadership skills.

Part III: Human-Centred Leadership in action provides a parallel map, process and principles to show you how to operate as a human-centred leader in leadership roles, whether in a company, a community or a country.

In conclusion, **Human-centred leaders change the world** explains the impact of aligning your purpose with an organisational purpose at the point of intersection with the needs of humanity, and the responsibility each of us has to act in this moment.

The world faces any number of challenges in the 21st century. In order to grow and flourish through this time we need to put people first in every way in every decision—in business, government and society.

This is why Human-Centred Leadership is the key to the 21st century.

PART I

The challenge facing human-centred leaders

A framework for future leadership

Part I provides a framework for thinking about the future and the kind of leadership required. I review five key changes that attract my attention because of their relevance to Human-Centred Leadership.

Chapter 1 introduces the sigmoid curve and the game-changer curve, two helpful models for thinking about the changes and transitions occurring at this time. I then propose that we live in a 'leaderless' world and lack the quality of leadership that is required to lead us into the future through these shifts. Technology trends, examined in chapter 2, demand profound shifts in our moral and leadership capacity, while we need to develop a new moral foundation for business, government and society (chapter 3). Chapter 4 reflects on the humanisation of machines and the mechanisation of humanity and suggests we are about to witness a crossover where one could dominate the other.

Given these kinds of shifts it is time to upgrade our moral capability to match our technological capability. The key to this will be human-centred leaders who put people first and who integrate the technical and moral aspects of life and leadership.

·

CHAPTER 1

The future and the future of leadership

A water taxi ride from Marco Polo airport across the lagoon into Venice is one of life's great experiences. A few minutes after landing on a flight from London I was sitting in the stern of a motorboat skimming across the sparkling water. While my watch advanced an hour, time unravelled in this historic crossroads of people and culture. As we approached the legendary Hotel Danieli, housed in a regal fourteenth-century palazzo, gondolas bobbed in the water, the gondoliers resplendent in their simple striped shirts. Tourists filled Piazza San Marco, ignoring the glare of the midday sun in order to spend a few moments being blinded by beauty.

As I strolled the quiet empty streets that night my thoughts turned again to the relentlessness of change. Venice helps us maintain perspective when we consider the transitions, trends and shifts confronting our world. Venice may be sinking, but slowly. The sea may be rising, but slowly. The passenger ships deliver new loads of tourists by their thousands each day, leaving the city to silence and local life each night.

Venice reminds us that people adapt in the midst of change. We generally get on with living, muddle through and find a way forward through all that shifts, often with considerably more resilience than we tend to recognise.

While Venetians face a remorselessly rising sea level, what do you face? What are the sea changes in your world that will change the way you go about your life? What forces are changing business, government and society, and how will they change us? How can we understand this change?

Two models for understanding change

Much of this book is about change and responses to change. These two models offer a way of understanding change and seeing where we may be on the change curve.

The sigmoid curve

'The only constant is change' has become a rather tired aphorism, trotted out as if change is something unique to this moment. Change, however, is a function of time—and vice versa. It has been with us since the spark of the Big Bang and will be with us until the universe fizzles out. It's unrelenting, unstoppable and often uncomfortable.

Twenty years ago Charles Handy, in his book *The Empty Raincoat*, explained the concept of the *sigmoid curve* as a way of understanding change.[1]

The sigmoid curve starts with a standard lifecycle curve (see figure 1.1), which shows a simple timeline: products are launched, grow to maturity, and then begin to decline and eventually disappear. Manufacturers, for instance, pay attention to this curve as they invest in R&D to bring new products to market, steadily build market share and then enjoy a period of healthy sales and margins. Over time sales begin to decline as the market becomes saturated, competitors enter the market or technology becomes outdated. Eventually the product fades from view. Take a short moment to reflect on products you have used over the years — to play music or contact friends perhaps — and you will recognise this cycle.

Figure 1.1: lifecycle curve

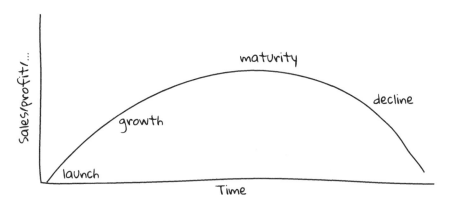

In order to avoid the inevitable decline, you need to rethink what you are doing — that is, innovate — as you approach the top of the curve, when everything appears to be going fabulously well. Doing this can sometimes lead to a temporary dip, for instance as profits decline due to increased R&D investment, although success will launch a new curve. This new upswing motion forms an inflexion point and creates the sigmoid curve (see figure 1.2, overleaf).

Figure 1.2: the sigmoid curve

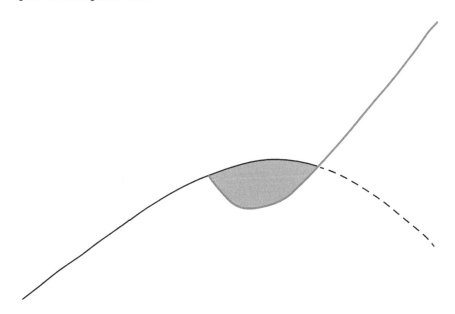

Changing direction when things are going well is not easy. In business sales are booming, profits are up, people enjoy working for a market leader, customers love you...In government the economy is strong, debt is being paid down, unemployment is low...In your personal life relationships are flourishing, communication is honest and frequent, the world seems radiant...This is often the calm before the storm, the comfort before the seven-year itch, the illusory satisfaction of supportive polls or market research.

Wise leaders take steps to prepare for the future, just as navigators know the sun does not shine forever and always keep a close eye on weather and water. They know a storm will roll in at some point and always maintain a state of readiness.

Looking away from what is successful at the moment to what could be successful in the future requires strong leadership. It requires courage to confront the chaos and confusion that marks inflexion points and to navigate the fog of uncertainty.

The game-changer curve

Many people sense that the change we are going through in the world at this time is in some way different from previous changes. When they talk about energy or the environment, the economy or society, governments or business, they talk about a 'gap' that separates today from tomorrow. This kind of change is not a transition along a continuum, such as on a sigmoid curve, but a transition from one continuum to another. In other words, a game-changing event causes a break or disruption in the curve (see figure 1.3, with thanks to Chris Bangle, former Chief of Design for BMW, who first alerted me to this concept).

Figure 1.3: the game changer

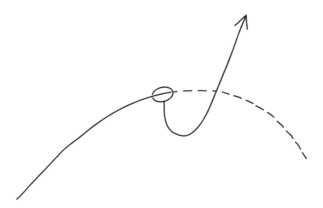

This concept of a disruptive, game-changing shift can help you understand why what is happening today feels more uncomfortable than previous changes. While some changes mark a journey from one place to another, as if following a winding road, contemporary changes are more like leaping across an abyss.

Digital disruption is one example of a game changer. Artificial intelligence is about to be unleashed on knowledge work, which will have a far greater impact than the computerisation of manufacturing jobs. Having been relatively passive observers as machines took over manufacturing, most people will be unwilling participants as machines take over intellectual jobs.

Governments and society are not equipped for the disruption that will occur as vast numbers of white-collar workers become unemployable, not because they are unskilled or lack digital savvy, but simply because their jobs will be performed by artificial intelligence. Tax and welfare systems, even the way we think about work and leisure, will change radically. And a raft of new industries and jobs that we cannot yet imagine will emerge. In this world your job will disappear with little warning, and no amount of training will bring it back. It will be gone forever.

Shifts, changes, transitions, uncertainty and the unknown…and tremendous possibility.

A future of unbounded possibility

Every moment is a meeting place of time and events flowing from choices made in the past. All history converges on you at this instant. The future, however, diverges. It's not a straight line forward. It opens rather than narrows, expanding into a range of possibilities (see figure 1.4). The future has both inevitability (elections are held on a predictable cycle) and possibility (who will be elected is unknown).

It's worth taking the time to think about that. This moment, right now, is the point at which your past meets the present, and your future opens out into unbounded, unlimited possibility…

Figure 1.4: a future of unbounded possibility

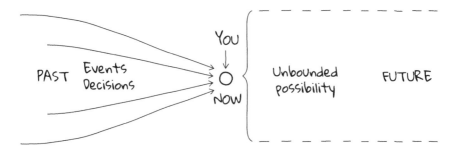

The future holds tremendous potential, limited only by your imagination and the choices you make. The choices made by people in positions of influence will have a profound effect on tomorrow's world. Hence, the character of leaders and the quality of their leadership is crucial.

A lack of leaders

The ultimate determinant of the shape of tomorrow's world will be the quality of leadership. Not social, technological, economic, environmental and political forces, but the force of leadership. While the five former forces will influence the world of tomorrow, it is leadership that will give it shape and definition.

What kind of leadership do you think may be required in the world of tomorrow? A world where ancient religious cultures clash with modern society, and advances in artificial intelligence clash with humanity. A world of national borders yet digital nations, in a constant state of flux, uncertainty and compounding complexity. Is it reasonable to suggest we will need a different kind of leadership from what we have today? Do we have the quality of local, national and global leadership we will need to effectively navigate this fast-moving world?

Ian Bremmer, the pre-eminent geopolitical strategist, writes in *Every Nation for Itself: Winners and Losers in a G-Zero World* that we are 'in a world without global leadership'.[2] He believes that the world is undergoing a 'tumultuous transition, one that is especially vulnerable to crises that appear suddenly and from unexpected directions ... Over the next decade and perhaps longer, a world without leaders will undermine our ability to keep the peace, to expand opportunity, to reverse the impact of climate change, and to feed growing populations. The effects will be felt in every region of the world—and even in cyberspace'.[3]

Who will lead us?

Ian then asks the question that is reiterated over and over, by observers of history and trends, by every leader I talk to, and in forums, conferences and conversations around the world: *'Who will lead us through?'* And to this question we will repeatedly return, because—and there's no getting away from it—the answer is *you*.

Take a moment to reflect on that ... *You* are the one the world is waiting for.

You may feel a sense of destiny and purpose and agree wholeheartedly with that statement. On the other hand, you may be doubtful that you could ever be called to greatness, and feel only fear and anxiety. If you are in this group you are not alone. Whether you feel a sense of destiny or doubt, this book is for you. Through its pages I will offer you both a roadmap and a toolkit for the journey, enabling you to start from scratch or to supplement and reinforce what you already possess.

Where will you lead us to?

'Who will lead us?' invites the further question: 'Lead us where?' Where is it we are going? What is it we are going through? Undoubtedly it involves upheaval, turmoil and tumult.

And that's why leadership, and Human-Centred Leadership in particular, is crucial, because you need to help your family and friends, your colleagues and staff, your neighbours and nation, through the disruptive changes ahead.

What are those changes? Many people look at change through a business, strategic or geopolitical lens. What might you see, though, if you look through a human lens? What might you see if you consider the impact of change and disruption on people and our relationships with one another?

As you look, I would like to draw your gaze toward five big shifts in particular.

Five big shifts revealed through a human lens

Curiosity has led me to seek out leaders and commentators and ask them for their perspective on trends, transitions and shifts. It's a fascinating area that helps us to build a map of the journey I think we are on. In global forums and private conversations over many years a small number of topics have appeared frequently.

Climate change is commonly first up, being front of mind for most people today, closely followed by globalisation in one form or another. Technology, with both its blessings and curses, is usually next, followed by the fragility of the economy and finally asymmetric warfare and the threat of religious wars. Woven within these themes are perennial questions about the distribution of wealth and power, food and water, oil and energy. There are many intelligent commentators writing in depth and detail about any and all of these subjects, as you can discover with a quick internet search. All are worthy of attention and discussion.

Looking at change through a human lens, however, reminds you that change involves people and impacts people. The changes I have noted influence where and how you live. They affect your work and leisure activities. They influence your personal, communal and national relationships. When you look through a human lens you encounter people who may be displaced because of climate change, people who are depersonalised by technology, people whose dreams were shattered by a financial crisis. And not just generic people, but people who have names. They are Mary and Bob, Alan, Anjila, Sanjay, Ola and Hanna. They are your parents, brothers, sisters, friends and colleagues.

Through all the changes, the person who thinks, acts and loves remains constant. This does not mean people don't change, or that they are always good and loving; it simply highlights that *change involves people*. It is always people who are driving change or being driven to change.

So looking through a human lens can provide a different perspective and lead to different insights and conclusions. In particular it reveals five shifts that touch the foundations of business, government and society, and that require a human-centred response. They are interwoven between people and machines, across the moral and technological domains, with considerable crossover and cross-fertilisation. Some are well developed while others are emerging and evolving, but each has the potential to change your world entirely.

The first three shifts inhabit the technological domain, the fourth is in the moral domain, and the last—and most pressing—involves a convergence of morality and technology. They are:

- technology: fragmented *and* connected
- technology: overwhelmed *and* underprepared
- technology: always on *and* never off
- moral drift
- convergence and crossover of 'man' and machine.

CHAPTER 2

Shifts 1–3: Technology

'Toto, I've got a feeling we're not in Kansas anymore.'
DOROTHY, IN *THE WIZARD OF OZ*

In the past half-century advances in technology have created a new world with entirely different social structures. These advances are built on hundreds of years of increasingly rapid technological development since the Renaissance and the Industrial Age. Technology has radically changed the way we live, work and relate to one another. Digital nations and communities of interest are replacing geographic nations and local communities. Deepening and broadening connectivity has spawned an exponential advance in social complexity.

My concern is that our 'choice making' capability, our moral capacity, is struggling to stay abreast of our technological capability, and it is about to fall even further behind at a time when it should be getting ahead. It is incredibly difficult for any one person or leader, or a traditional authority such as a government or religious institution, to remain current even in their chosen field, let alone other domains. It is bordering on impossible to create the time to think about, make sense of and integrate the overwhelming amount of disparate information we can now access.

Navigating this chapter

This chapter examines three shifts brought about by technology. This is neither a summary nor a critique of technological breakthroughs. It is my observation of three significant changes that call for profound shifts in our moral capability and our leadership capability. They impact on leadership because human-centred leaders recognise that technological change affects people, who require new levels of support in new and different social structures.

I have identified these technological shifts as:

1   fragmented *and* connected
2   overwhelmed *and* underprepared
3   always on *and* never off.

Shift 1: Fragmented *and* connected

While technology has spawned global interconnectivity and access, many people experience an increasing sense of isolation and feel as if things are coming undone. How can that be? What is going on?

Fragmented ...

Recent years have brought a growing concern about the idea of *fragmentation*, capturing as it does the concept of something breaking up, falling apart or dispersing. This phenomenon can be observed in multiple domains. Here are several examples.

The (Western) *political landscape* is less and less about red and blue, left and right, conservative and progressive, and more and more about Tea Parties and minor parties, pro-Britain and pro-America, or pro the way things used to be. In Europe anti-establishment and ultra-nationalist parties split votes once divided between socialists and democrats. Narrow issue parties focused on migration or motoring, guns or sex, have acquired legitimacy and a voice alongside the traditional parties. Global political groups and coalitions have fragmented, if not disintegrated.

The *media world* of broadsheets and broadcasts has fragmented in favour of browsing, tweeting and texting via a plethora of omnipresent devices seemingly wired into our brain. Deceptive headlines and click-baiting are replacing investigative journalism in a desperate competition for 'eyeballs' in a 24/7 world where attention spans seem inversely correlated to depth and detail. While we have unprecedented access to information, we can now select sources of news, knowledge or entertainment that reinforce our prejudices and bind us to an ever narrower social group that shares our views. Doing so fosters social division and accelerates social fragmentation.

The *business spectrum* stretches from massive, globally integrated enterprises whose balance sheets exceed the gross domestic product of many countries, to 'for cause' organisations whose vision exceeds that of most businesses. The incessant ebb and flow of downsizing, outsourcing and offshoring has fostered hub-and-spoke arrangements through which institutions enjoy rewards while shifting risk to ever smaller business units, such as a small marketing firm or a contract project manager. Most businesses today, whatever their size and scope, comprise a number of dispersed, disconnected and fragmented parts.

Other than those times of crisis when *communities* unite in the face of tragedies such as flood, fire or famine, we are largely disconnected from our immediate neighbours, and quite often disconnected from our immediate family. The wider community has fragmented into smaller and smaller tribes, while paradoxically we now find ourselves members of one or more global communities. We enjoy more global connections and less local community in a fragmented but fractal set of worldwide relationships. This, as I have suggested elsewhere, 'gives rise to a sense … of belonging in different places at the same time, of belonging to everywhere but nowhere, of feeling pulled in competing directions'.[1]

… and connected

Despite this splintering and dispersal we are more connected than ever in an incredibly complex set of relationships. Hence we are both fragmented *and* connected. Whether your passport is Australian or British or Japanese, there is a very good chance you identify more strongly with communities of interest on social media, are an active member of user groups associated with your professional or leisure activities, and consider yourself a citizen of a digital nation defined by your connections rather than your postcode.

Each advance in technology leads to an inevitable growth in social complexity—whether waterwheel or windmill, the industrial revolution or the explosive growth in digital connectivity over the past decade.[2] The technology that allowed manufacturing on an industrial scale, for instance, stimulated a series of seismic shifts in social relationships, within families and communities, between workers and employers, between one region and another. Relationships that were once localised to a village, for example, now extended to a far wider social group.

The internet has created unimaginable social complexity, with its new social structures and myriad ways of interacting in a dynamic set of global relationships. Compare for a moment the reach and complexity of relationships during your childhood with today.

I am a member of the generation that straddles the birth of the internet—I grew up without it and now cannot live without it. My early social structures were limited to immediate family and friends, a subset of the people who lived in our city—teachers, sports coaches and small business owners—and an extended family of relatives we saw infrequently. This was also true for my parents: proximate social relationships among family, friends and business people, and long-distance relationships maintained primarily by handwritten letters and occasional visits.

The social structures in my adult world are of a completely different order. They have compounded exponentially to include a 24/7 deep, and very rich, blend and complex interplay between family, friends, colleagues, clients and fellow travellers. They are not just local but global. Relationships are distributed across faiths (many and none), genders, political and sexual perspectives, social strata, race, culture and national heritage. We engage frequently via a combination of technology and touch—from written words exchanged at the speed of light, to spoken (and unspoken) words in coffee shops, conferences and conversations in the great cities of the world. With slight variations this will be the norm for the early years of the 21st century, until the next technological breakthrough generates another increase in social complexity.

One downside of connectivity and social complexity is that we can be immediately impacted by disparate and far-removed events as never before. The 21st century opened with the tragic events of 9/11, soon to be followed by the SARS bird flu outbreaks, a global financial crisis, and devastating floods, fires, hurricanes and tsunamis. Trauma, tragedy and disaster are nothing new. However, in a less connected world people who were not directly affected were largely quarantined by time and geography. As I've written elsewhere, 'Deep global linkages between people, organisations and nations now mean that our [part of the] world can change overnight because of the ripple effect of a single major event—even one which starts quite small. Economic shocks will become more frequent because of the complexity and connectivity of the system of which we are a part'.[3]

A fragmented and connected world where community can be broad but not deep, touching but not caring, needs human-centred leaders who promote depth and care in human relationships, who use technology to create inclusive communities, ensuring that those on the margins don't slip through the cracks.

Shift 2: Overwhelmed *and* underprepared

Gary Hamel is not alone in observing that the rate of change driven by technology has gone exponential. And it has accelerated so fast that many people struggle to adapt, lacking new capabilities and competencies by which they can be masters rather than servants of technology.

Overwhelmed...

In the relatively few years since a memo from Tim Berners-Lee launched the World Wide Web the volume of information at your fingertips has grown astronomically. And unless you have an almost inhuman capacity to resist the temptation to browse, it can rush in, overload your senses and overwhelm your soul.

Twenty years ago there was a handful of websites, mainly for connecting government departments or job seekers to work via bulletin boards. Now we are witnessing the emergence of a digital world in which ultimately everyone and everything will have a specific URL. Your digital address will be more important than your physical address, because you will always be home at your URL. In that world your physical home may become a retreat, where you can disconnect from the online world if you so wish.

The quantity of data in the world today is incomprehensible. Figures from 2011, although already outdated, provide an insight about the sheer scale. These show that the volume is comparable to sitting in front of your television for 47 million years to watch 200 billion high definition movies—giving an entirely new meaning to 'couch potato'—or enlisting everyone in the US to lobby the government by sending three tweets every minute for 26 976 years.[4]

If everyone in Ireland got to work downloading all this data it would take them 8205 days to complete the task.[5] During those 22+ years, however, the volume of data produced will increase exponentially,[6] so the finish line would keep receding for the overworked Irish. In the meantime rather than discovering fairies at the bottom of the garden, scientists may well have synthesised your digital twin with your DNA to fabricate fairies who can operate tiny space ships.[7]

It's all a bit overwhelming.

On a slightly more serious note, the sheer volume of data makes it impossible to keep up to date with everything that is published and relevant in your chosen field, let alone to keep abreast of all that is relevant in the wider world. In 2004 the global publisher Elsevier estimated that 1.2 million peer-reviewed papers were published each year in the science, technology and medicine arena.[8] The number is undoubtedly larger now. How many of these papers contain significant advances or breakthroughs in those fields? How can the overworked scientist or doctor know which ones? Is it any wonder we continue to do things the way we always have?

... *and* **underprepared**

While we struggle not to become overwhelmed by this overload, how do we prepare for tomorrow? While today's world is unbelievably different from the world of our childhood, the world of tomorrow is incomprehensible. This is tremendously exciting but also challenging.

- How do you maintain your humanity in the face of the digital deluge? It is easy to lose sight of the person behind and inside the words and images.

- How do you 'join the dots' to make sense of often disparate data? Sense-makers will become irreplaceable.

- How can you find the time and space to reflect and learn, when the volume of data input each day almost certainly exceeds your ability to assimilate it? It surely exceeds mine, many times over.

I commented in a paper some years ago that while 'we have unprecedented access to ever increasing information, [there is little] evidence of increased wisdom, or shared intelligence... We know more and more about less and less. The compounding intricacy of complexity increases exponentially as technology enables everyone to have a voice in every medium, continuing to saturate the world with "noise" ... As the fields of human knowledge accelerate, the issues requiring deep thinking and reflection will come thicker and faster. The tremendous changes we experience will escalate in their rapidity, requiring a huge psychological adjustment, which we have little time to do'.[9]

The problem is time—not a lack of it, but poor use of it. Increased social complexity, connectivity and access to unlimited information is overwhelming. At the very moment we need more time to reflect, we have less time than ever to do so.

Shift 3: Always on *and* never off

How often do you sit in a meeting and steal glances at your email or Twitter feed? Although you can switch your device to flight mode on those occasions where you want or need to 'switch off', you remain aware that you can access the digital world in an instant. While it remains ever on, it is becoming harder to take time out, and just sometimes turn off.

Always on ...

In one of the great paradoxes, technology has introduced a stream of time-saving devices, yet we seem to have less time than ever. 'We have become an "always on" society.'[10]

The relentless advance of technology, with its perpetual promise of labour-saving devices and increased leisure, has bound you ever more tightly to work. There are very few jobs that allow you to leave the office and your boss behind. Your smartphone is your office, enabling you to work anywhere at any time. Work is no longer a verb or a place but a way of life.

Your predecessors may have lugged a bulging briefcase home in order to work into the night, but they could park it silently in a corner by the door. The beep or blink from your smartphone is not as easy to ignore as it pings your curiosity. Your email and files are almost always within reach and rarely turned off, and the overwhelming urge to check in means you can become consumed in an instant.

Not only are you 'always on', but many employers expect you to be constantly available, at their beck and call. In their view, the good of the organisation outweighs your need for time off for rest and relaxation.

... *and* never off

It is extraordinarily difficult to turn these devices off and keep them off. The result is that you work at a relentless pace and don't take downtime for thinking and reflection, so you tend to react to events rather than take charge of events, to be acted upon rather than act. Because you are never off, you find it hard to get high-quality thinking time.

One of the most common complaints I hear from leaders is that they do not have enough time to think. Now you might suggest — and you could be right — that it is their fault for not *making* the time. The reality, however, is that the spaces that accommodated reflection time in the past — before 9 am, between meetings, when travelling, on weekends — are now filled with the devices by which you are wired into the world of work.

Many people have lost the capacity to create discretionary time, and when they do they don't use it well. When they find themselves with unexpected time on their hands — time that could fruitfully be spent thinking — they experience withdrawal symptoms and too readily fill the time with idle browsing.

This matters because if you don't find the time and space to think and reflect, you won't grow in self-knowledge and hence you won't become all you can be. While you may excel technologically, you risk falling short of your potential as a human being.

Occupying a position of leadership creates two obligations, one to yourself and one to your staff. Ensure you and they have adequate quality thinking time, and teach people to respect these gaps in their diaries, not fill them with tasks and meetings. Enjoy walking on a beach, gazing down from a mountain, or pondering over a coffee to give your brain space to turn thoughts over and reorganise its connections. You will be amazed what pops out. And lastly, if you are organising workshops, conferences or all-day meetings, build in time to think. Otherwise the experience will simply be overwhelming.

In short, create gaps. Avoid gridlock on the freeway of thought to ensure a steady flow of traffic.

* * *

Do you observe these three shifts in your world? Do you notice the fragmentation and yet the hyper-connectivity? Are you overwhelmed by the sheer volume of information, feeling underprepared for the present, let alone the future? Are you always connected, wired into a fast-moving grid, 24/7?

As already noted, innovation enables new ways of relating, whether on the production line during the manufacturing boom, or online during the internet explosion. How will we relate tomorrow? How will our children and their children relate to their friends and colleagues? Will they even have colleagues? What kind of leadership is required to manage increased technological change and social complexity? Although it has not yet fully emerged, I am confident that it will need to be human centred to be effective.

Your challenge, more than anything else, is to create the space and time to think—not about technology but about yourself, not about what is changing, but about what is unchanging, not about materiality but about humanity. We need to consider and begin to question the way we relate to one another, the way we make choices and the way we think about what it means to be human. Questions about people and choices open the gate to the field of morals and morality, where I believe we are experiencing another big shift.

CHAPTER 3
Shift 4: Moral drift

Adrift on a wide, wide sea

When I was a navigator on the ships of the British Phosphate Commissioners, we loaded raw phosphate at Christmas Island in the Indian Ocean and Nauru in the Pacific for shipping to various ports in Australia and New Zealand. Most journeys were relatively straightforward and uneventful, with the normal range of sunshine and cyclones, good weather and bad. But no-one looked forward to the 'drifting season' between November and February when monsoonal weather could play havoc with our plans.

Nauru does not have a safe harbour, so the ship carefully ties up to buoys fixed to the ocean floor far below, holding her from blowing onto reefs. When the ship is safely moored, huge cantilevers swing into position and discharge a continuous stream of phosphate into the gaping holds. As sunset approaches the massive vessel is released from the buoys and stands off the island through the night, before returning to complete loading the following day — if the weather allows.

When the weather turns against you, the ship cannot be safely moored so she spends the day with engines off, silent and almost lifeless, drifting aimlessly around the ocean. The ship creaks and groans as she rolls in the monsoon swell.

On the following day the crew turn out early and bring the ship up to the island, waiting and hoping for the signal to proceed. They are often turned back for another day of silent drifting.

This scenario can repeat itself for days and weeks. When water runs low you make a three-day dash to the Solomon Islands, fill up from a water pipe in the middle of Honiara Harbour and return to the end of an ever lengthening line of waiting ships. I once spent more than 20 days doing this, and had friends who endured nearly 40. And this is after a five-day passage to the island and then a week or more back to port with your cargo.

The uncertainty and delay play with your mind.

After just a few days of drifting, the crew starts getting anxious. After a week they start getting angry. When the conversation grows stale they become withdrawn. When the beer runs out they get aggressive. Day after day, night after night. Stuck, with little motion, to borrow from Coleridge's 'Rime of the Ancient Mariner'. Not knowing if the next day will prolong or bring an end to the aimlessness and indecision.

In this directionless, purposeless environment, cut off and adrift from the fixed points by which we navigate, reasonable people do unreasonable things. The honourable behave dishonourably, and the morally upright upend their morals. People said, 'It's all fun', but there many moments that seemed to border on anarchy.

By analogy, I believe contemporary society lacks a safe harbour and is adrift on a moral sea.

Navigating this chapter

This chapter proposes that Western society has drifted from its traditional roots and has failed to develop a new moral foundation for business, government and society, trusting markets or people to do the right thing. This moral drift has led to a separation of markets and morals, a trust deficit and an abdication of personal responsibility.

Moral drift and the separation of markets and morals

As Western cultures have drifted from their Christian roots they have failed to develop a sound moral foundation for business, society and government. We tend to assume altruism and place false hope in individuals and markets to 'do the right thing'. We assume people and amorphous markets will not act in ways that are ultimately not good for themselves or others. A moment's reflection on the power of greed should be sufficient to refute this notion. But the problem is not greed ... it's drift manifested as market creep.

Michael Sandel, the renowned Harvard philosopher, observes that in the past three decades 'market thinking' has permeated almost every element of society. The most fateful change, he says, 'was not an increase in the incidence of greed. It was the expansion of markets and of market values into spheres of life traditionally governed by non-market norms ... for example, the proliferation of for-profit schools, hospitals and prisons; the outsourcing of war to private military contractors ... the eclipse of public police forces by private security firms ...'[1]

'Without quite realising it,' he continues, 'without ever deciding to do so, *we drifted from having a market economy to being a market society.* The hope for moral and civic renewal depends on having that debate now.'[2]

As we drifted toward a market society we embraced a values-neutral society. We became hypersensitive to any possibility that someone might be trying to impose their values—simply because they mentioned values—and in the process we came adrift from our moorings. This book is a call not to embrace a particular set of values, but to have the disposition and courage to discuss moral meaning, values and principles in a respectful way. It is a call for the recovery of a moral consciousness that can place principles at the centre rather than the periphery of debate, discussion and action.

When market forces run ahead of, or away from, moral considerations, short-term results become the guiding principle, greed overshadows good, profits replace prudence and people become a means to an end. One of our most pressing challenges is to overcome this divorce between markets and morals, and to rediscover the person at the heart of business and society. Failure to find an effective reconciliation between markets and morals will inhibit our ability to build human-centred societies in which people flourish. Our challenge in the 21st century is not to go back to 'the good old days' but rather to upgrade our moral capability to create a brand new day.

Moral drift and a trust deficit

The implicit trust enjoyed by traditional institutions and their leaders has been undermined, fractured and perhaps irreparably damaged by scandals and poor behaviour. Lying and distorting the truth have become an accepted norm in this 'post-truth' age.[3]

It's a global problem, across geographies and domains.

In Spain 'politicians, parties and parliament, the government and the judiciary, the monarchy and the constitution, business and the unions... are all facing hostile scrutiny as never before'.[4] In the United States a mere 7 per cent of people have 'a great deal' or 'quite a lot' of confidence in Congress.[5]

I am always surprised when politicians campaign on a 'who do you trust' platform, claiming they are more trustworthy than their opponents. The reality is we don't trust any of them. When was the last time you had a conversation with friends who spoke highly of the honesty and trustworthiness of politicians?

There is a general distrust of church leaders too. In a poll commissioned by Britain's *Sunday Times* 40 per cent 'of those polled said they did not trust priests, vicars and other clergy to tell the truth, and overall doctors, teachers and judges were rated as more trustworthy. Fifty-four per cent believe the Church of England has struggled to give moral leadership'.[6] Scandal after scandal has rocked these institutions. Failure to measure up to community standards, let alone the higher standards to which churches aspire, appears endemic. Leaders of these institutions have been accused of covering up abuse, ignoring the plight of children and serving their own interests. Their actions imply a belief that they are above the law.

There is also a general distrust of business leaders. Too many stand accused of enriching themselves at the expense of their staff, customers and stakeholders. The size of executive pay packets and bonuses is incomprehensible to most people, particularly when the relationship between pay and performance lacks clarity, or indeed payouts seem inversely correlated to performance.

Greg Smith, a former employee of Goldman Sachs, wrote a very public letter about what he called a 'toxic and destructive' environment at the firm. He said, 'the interests of the client continue to be sidelined in the way the firm operates and thinks about making money … [The] decline in the firm's moral fibre represents the single most serious threat to its long-run survival'.[7]

Facebook, a merger of business and community, and currently the world's biggest digital nation, does not seem to appreciate the fragility of trust. In 2012 it manipulated the news feeds of more than 600 000 people — equivalent to the population of Oslo — to test their emotional response when fed a diet of positive or negative emotional content.[8] Imagine the outcry if the government of Norway had sponsored a secret social experiment to discover how the residents of Oslo responded to good or bad news? Facebook seems to have done just that, treating its customers with contempt, and showing scant regard for their privacy or emotional wellbeing. Researchers argued that this was legal, since users had agreed to their data being used for research. I doubt whether many users thought this extended to personally being used as a research subject.

While others can argue the legality or otherwise of Facebook's actions I see them as evidence of moral drift. I see no clear fixed point against which Facebook assessed the rightness or wrongness of its actions. 'We communicated really badly on the subject,' said Sheryl Sandberg, the Chief Operating Officer.[9] People don't want more effective communication. What they want is not to be treated with disdain, like unwitting guinea pigs in social experiments.

Many organisations fail to appreciate the impact of their actions and that human principles matter. They are all at sea in a moral drift. And when business, government and society are caught up in an aimless drift, many people have difficulty knowing how to act wisely and well, and often fail to accept full responsibility for their decisions and actions.

Moral drift and the abdication of personal responsibility

When institutional leaders and traditional guides fail to provide sound direction we tend to adopt the values and practices of our immediate social group—often in unacceptable ways.

Is it really wrong to take money from a bank?

While robbing a bank is illegal, is it wrong to accept money willingly—although erroneously—provided by an ATM? The answer is not as clear as it may seem.

Police had to guard a faulty Bank of Ireland machine after a Twitter user posted a photo of queues of people sharing in what looked like a giveaway.[10] The machine was happily playing 'double or nothing', with patrons getting double what they requested and the bank getting nothing. Since customers of other banks accessed the ATM the bank said they were unlikely to take action against those who had withdrawn excess funds. They did, however, apologise 'for any inconvenience caused'.[11]

Can you imagine the annoyance of queuing for 'free' money, and the difficulty of wrestling your conscience into submission? An apology seems quite fitting for people who surrendered their good judgement and sound reason and emptied the machine as fast as they could.

What would you have done?

What do you do when the shop assistant gives you excess change or the hotel billing system hasn't added today's breakfast to your final account? Do you speak up, or remain silent on the basis that it 'squares the ledger' for occasions when it has perhaps gone the other way?

A similar situation occurred when Westpac Bank in New Zealand approved a loan for NZ$10 900 … and then accidentally transferred NZ$10 000 000. In the face of such largesse the newly minted millionaire immediately moved the bulk of the money to an offshore account and embarked on an overseas holiday. In an electronic version of the 'finders keepers' principle the recipient told people he had 'won the Lotto' and proceeded to live a life of luxury.

The case 'hurled New Zealanders into the kind of moral maze that [the beneficiaries] appeared to have spent just a few seconds navigating before deciding to skirt around it altogether…'[12] Many people conceded that if the same thing happened to them they would trouser the money, preferring to 'live as wealthy fugitives than remain out of pocket but with a clear conscience'.[13] It seems that many people are more comfortable with a lump in their wallet than a lump in their conscience. The law eventually prevailed, and the perpetrator was given a few years' incarceration to contemplate his actions.[14]

How would you respond if three additional zeroes appeared unexpectedly in your bank account? Would you take the money and run, and deal with your conscience and the constabulary at some indeterminate point in the future? Although your temptation may not manifest as a banking error, it can manifest in many ways. Do you stand up to the Congress or the consultants who insist a proposed action is just, justifiable and irreproachable when you know otherwise?

Taking personal responsibility

Why does the law have to specify exact scenarios in order to make it clear to people that they are doing, or about to do, the wrong thing? Why is there an army of lawyers prepared to defend the indefensible because the actual, very specific situation is not spelled out in law, while common sense makes it clear that the act or acts are unacceptable?

How does one know what is right … and where does personal responsibility enter the discussion? How do individuals shape their lives so they make wise and good decisions?

These kinds of questions are easily lost in the fog and storms of a moral drift. At such times people can come adrift from their usual reference points. Lacking guidance, they may do what they would not normally do.

Some commentators look through rose-tinted glasses to an earlier age when everything seemed sensible and reasonable, and suggest society is falling apart—but I think the concept of drift makes more sense than decay. We still have a level of security and certainty, but in the midst of insecurity and uncertainty. And like the inflexion point of the sigmoid curve, where the maturing initial curve intersects with the new upswing, current conditions are made worse by not knowing how long they will continue.

Many people experience moral uncertainty and lack direction. In a fast-moving world they are unsure of how to live their lives in the best possible way. They yearn for a safe harbour. The traditional fixed points and authority figures found in business, government and society have largely lost their moral authority. At the very time we need to lift our moral capability, those who could have shone a light and shown the way have let the moral flame go out.

Much of society finds itself drifting on a wide, wide sea wondering if tomorrow will bring greater clarity … and wondering where leadership will come from. Because it's not coming from the leaders of some of our most respected institutions, who have squandered the trust placed in them. The leadership of tomorrow will come from people who understand people, who understand how to make choices that promote human wellbeing, who understand what it means to put people first.

And one of their great tests will be to defend the human person against impersonal algorithms.

CHAPTER 4

Shift 5: The convergence and crossover of 'man' and machine

'I'll be back.'

THE TERMINATOR (T-800 MODEL 101)

The last shift I want to examine is the convergence and crossover of 'man' and machine. I fear this shift is largely unseen, yet like the forest hidden in the trees it is there for all to see. You just need to look through a human lens, rather than an economic or technology lens.

This observation draws together two trends that, when combined, signify a game-changing shift. These trends are:

- the 'humanisation' of machines as a result of advances in artificial intelligence, from computational computing, to cognitional computing, to conscious computers

- the 'mechanisation' of humanity as a result of the evolution of *Homo economicus*, from the 'rational person who pursues wealth for their own self-interest'[1] to the view of people as units of economic production and the correlative slogan 'people are our greatest asset'. This could also be defined as the 'dehumanisation' of humanity.

Navigating this chapter

This last shift is a reflection on the rapid advances in artificial intelligence and the imminent arrival of conscious computing accompanied by an increasing tendency to view people as a means to an end, rather than as individuals. I refer to this as the 'humanisation' of machines and the 'mechanisation' of humanity and suggest that we are about to witness a crossover where one could dominate the other.

We are approaching the point where the (falling) trajectory of human development intersects the rising trajectory of machine development (see figure 4.1). While we expend vast amounts of time and money on facilitating the rise of machines, we remain largely oblivious to the slowing trajectory of human development, blinded by the prevailing view that people are merely units of economic production. Viewing humans as machines feeds into our ignorance of the need to upgrade our humanity and in particular our moral capability.

Figure 4.1: the crossover of 'man' and machine. Will artificial intelligence outstrip human intelligence? Do we face existential degeneration?

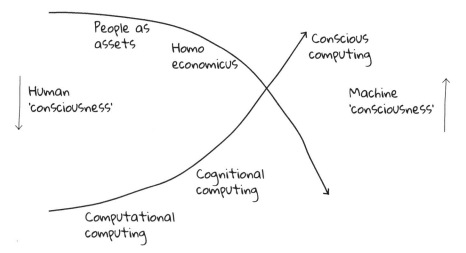

Conscious computers?

There is a scene in *Terminator 2: Judgement Day* where Arnold Schwarzenegger's robot character races a Harley-Davidson Fat Boy to save the teen-age John Connor, who is being pursued by a shape-shifting T-1000 terminator driving a huge truck. While I love the thumping sound of the Harley, I am particularly struck by both terminators' unblinking focus on their mission. The scene captures the whole idea that machines just get the job done. No emotion. No distraction. No morals. Just the mission. The first *Terminator* movie was set in 1984 and featured a cyborg sent back from 2029. It may yet prove to be prescient (the cognitive aspect... not the time travel).

It seems inevitable that machine processing power will one day achieve cognitive capability—the ability to 'think' in human-like ways. And conscious computing—the ability of the machine to learn about the world and itself—may not be far behind. Dr Ian Pearson of Futurizon, one of the world's leading futurists, believes that conscious computing will be with us before 2030, and perhaps as early as 2025.[2] We can scarcely imagine the disruption this will cause. Some people are convinced we risk a robot apocalypse.[3]

Watson, a child of IBM and a descendant of Big Blue, is one of the leaders in the field of artificial intelligence. It is already scanning the medical literature that overwhelmed us in chapter 2. This supercomputer and its relatives in other laboratories show cognitive computers approaching human thinking capability. Although they are perhaps Neanderthal versions of *Homo machina*, their grandchildren may well sit alongside our children in the classroom, and us at work. They could be largely indistinguishable from *Homo sapiens*. Their siblings are already driving trucks at remote mine sites, answering phones and responding to queries, writing newspaper articles and performing medical diagnoses. Their parents have been working on the assembly lines of factories and delivery lines in warehouses for a generation. Evidence of artificial intelligence is everywhere. Your job is at greater risk from an algorithm than an immigrant.

While fascinated by the concept of machines one day becoming human, we remain just a little anxious about the dystopian world that might result. This is the kind of world the *Terminator* franchise imagines, with its wars between humans and machines and global destruction.

The answer lies not in halting the march of technological progress but in accelerating *human* development. We have to upgrade human moral capacity to manage the moral complexity of tomorrow. When machines exceed our cognitive capability we need to be ahead of them in moral capability.

And at this point we are at risk. While we remain enthralled and fascinated by machines becoming human, we are oblivious to the danger of humans becoming machines, programmed to respond in particular ways rather than as free-thinking people. We have become the 'doers' who deliver outcomes for organisations, just as computers are becoming the 'thinkers' who process information and generate reports and recommendations.

The machines are becoming human and the humans are becoming machines. This is a dangerous inversion.

People are our greatest liability

People are measured, assessed and retained based on their contribution to the economic wellbeing of the organisation. The seeds of this error were planted a few hundred years ago when industrial-scale productivity emerged from the Industrial Revolution. Now everyone is assessed using a similar measure: how much do you contribute to productivity? Education systems are designed around preparing, not citizens, but workers, as curricula are determined by the needs of the workforce and the desire for the country to remain competitive.

People have become a factor in the productivity equation, whether for their muscles or their mind, and are often treated as just another line in the spreadsheet or number in the welfare queue. I'm not lamenting the benefits of development and change, and I acknowledge the progress that has been made on many fronts. I do deplore the gradual shift in our understanding of what it means to be human, of what it means to be a person.

This is captured in that modern claim of caring corporations: 'People are our greatest asset'. It is shouted in boardrooms and at conferences, expressed in annual reports and corporate values statements. It is presumed to indicate 'we care' and 'people matter' and 'people first'. The reality is a polar opposite.

'People are our greatest asset' is one of the most disingenuous claims of all time and should be permanently eradicated from our language. Because the way people are generally treated often bears no relationship to care or concern for them and their needs. We measure assets such as real estate by considering, for example, the return on investment, and sell when the return is insufficient. All too often organisations think of their people in exactly the same way. When the return on people is insufficient we outsource, outplace and dismiss.

Organisations, or more specifically the people who run them, can treat people in the most appalling manner, particularly when they are not delivering the necessary return on investment. Although explanations can be couched in terms of 'productivity', the reality is that human labour is viewed in transactional terms. The firm gives the employee a wage to perform a task, and expects them to generate income at multiples of what they have been paid in order to justify ongoing employment.

In pure financial terms people are considered not as an asset but as a liability, and successful firms want to manage and reduce their liabilities while increasing their assets. In this sense the reality is that people are our greatest liability in cash terms, which is why reducing headcount is usually the organisation's first response to slowing sales, changing market conditions or economic headwinds. Firms want to lower their costs, and the effect, for example, of reducing headcount by 10 per cent is more immediate than selling off real estate in a difficult market.

People: an asset or a liability?

Consider this for a moment. Where does a company show the value of its assets?

On the balance sheet, which lists a wide range of assets including machinery, buildings and equipment, patents, intellectual property and brand value—that is, both tangible and intangible assets. Each year assets are depreciated as their value decays (the building gets a bit older) or increased as their value improves (the brand is worth more).

Have you ever seen a balance sheet that includes human assets? Those people who are 'our greatest asset'? What would happen if we decided the lifetime value to the business of a worker is $1 million in terms of productivity (I suspect it's more), and so we want to maximise the life of that asset through training and development? If their lifetime value to the firm was conservatively valued at $1 million, reducing each year as they neared retirement, what would appear on the balance sheet of a firm with 45000 employees?

Unfortunately, people appear in the Profit and Loss Statement under salaries, alongside other costs associated with running the business. People are a cost in the same way that electricity or printing is a cost.

And firms keep costs down. Why spend money on increasing wages or training and development, since these drive costs up? And when revenue suffers firms reduce costs in order to maintain margins. It is much easier to reduce headcount costs by laying people off.

But if people were treated as real assets on the balance sheet we would be much more careful, because laying off 1000 people might reduce our costs by $100 million (at an average wage of, say, $100 000), but it would reduce our assets by $1 *billion*. How would shareholders view that impact on the value of the company?

And if people were listed as an asset on the balance sheet, what effect would that have on the share price and the value of the firm in the event of a possible takeover? How would that influence talent practices, as executives grasped that their failure to look after and improve their human assets could devalue the company?

Very few firms will employ two people when they believe one can do the job, even when that person is overworked and under-resourced. Most firms will quickly outsource jobs that can be done at a lower cost in another location. One friend mentioned a company that decided to move a 'category' of positions to areas where they could pay workers less. She explained that a Project Manager in San Francisco, for instance, draws a higher salary than one in Philadelphia ... so the company reduces salary overheads by slowly moving job openings for Project Managers to another city.

Alas, far from being 'our greatest asset', people are treated merely as units of economic production.

Homo economicus: the person as a unit of economic production

The prevailing view in modern companies and countries is that a person is a unit of economic production. Governments want full employment not primarily for social reasons—that is, for the good of the person and society—but to increase their taxation base so they can pay their bills and remain competitive with other countries. It's sensible to avoid a deficit and remain competitive. However, a failure to appreciate people's hopes, dreams and aspirations means society risks becoming harsher and less caring. People are expected to keep the wheel turning, like a frenetic mouse, but I fear that the mouse is not getting sufficient nourishment and is nearing collapse.

The push for more women in the workforce, for example, is often argued in terms of economics rather than human dignity.[4] Statistics are produced to demonstrate the impact on GDP of helping mothers return to the workforce. I find it extraordinary that women kept our economies running during World War II, then returned to their homes to have babies for the good of the economy when men returned from the war—and now women are being encouraged back to work for the good of the economy.

Does that strike you as not quite right? Is there more to being a woman (and a man, for that matter) than benefiting the economy? Could there be an alternative, human-centred perspective that encourages people to join the workforce for their own benefit, rather than primarily for the good of someone or something else?

The way we talk about the people who work in our organisations further dehumanises them. We speak of 'Full Time Equivalent' (FTE) workers and fractions of FTEs. Although I understand why a company may allocate, for example, 1237 FTEs to a division, the abstract, clinical language further demonstrates the emergence of contemporary *Homo economicus*. I have never had a coffee with an FTE, let alone a 0.75 FTE. I don't work with FTEs but with Paul and Jane and Janice…

Why do we value people and judge their worth according to their output, rather than their intrinsic humanity? In the world of *Homo economicus*, focusing on improving individual productivity, and hence a person's economic contribution, is what enables them to become the best (that is, the most productive) person they can be.

As a vision for my life I find this completely uninspiring.

It makes work—or a very narrow view of work as productive output—the central meaning of life. It explains why some think those who do not work are immoral, since they are 'unproductive'. Societies imbued with this ethos fail to appreciate the contribution of the retired, the elderly, the disabled and the unemployed, seeing them as a burden on the economy. Young people are (simplistically) those who are yet to work, and the best education is one that prepares people for their future economic contribution. The focus on STEM (Science Technology Education Mathematics) curricula is a current example. The objective is to prepare people for work and to make the country competitive. On the other hand, what about art and architecture, music, literature and language, geography and history? What about the subjects that expand the human heart as well as the human mind, that build a creative richness into our culture that goes far beyond balance sheets and GDP?

Work is an important aspect of being human as it gives us opportunities for creativity, growth and self-expression. We can make a meaningful contribution to society, but only when we are appreciated and respected and able to grow in our humanity—not when we are merely an economic asset.

* * *

Like the proverbial boiling frog, the mechanisation of humanity has been a slow, almost imperceptible process. By unwittingly allowing this mechanisation, we have lost sight of what it means to be human. It is time to turn the tide and refashion a person-centred world, marked by Human-Centred Leadership.

'People are our greatest asset' is the rallying cry of the mechanised world.

'Human capital' is the watchword of *Homo economicus*.

'People first' is the foundation stone of a humanised world.

Time for human-centred leaders

Part I opened with some observations about the leadership environment, and then discussed some shifts and transitions in the technological and moral domains. We are living through a moment of enormous change, and although the future is wide open, full of boundless possibility, we appear to lack the leaders with the vision, foresight and capability to build a fully human future.

While there have been any number of technological advances in the past 100, 200 or 2000 years, I have little confidence that the way we conduct ourselves and relate to one another has made much progress. Our growth in moral maturity or moral capability has not kept pace with our technological progress.

Institutions such as churches, which traditionally influenced the advance of moral competence to stay abreast of a changing world, have not held up their end. They have been embroiled in scandal, dogged by self-interest and short-sightedness, and slowly drifted away from much of society. They are now considered an anachronism and patronised in the same way one politely smiles at grandma while continuing to do as one pleases. In short, many institutions have lost their moral authority, their teaching authority, and any semblance of leadership.

Could this be the time when humanity makes a moral breakthrough? Not one imposed from above or beyond, but one that arises from within? Could it be an age when we break through in the way we relate to one another? Could we advance our relationships in a way that mirrors the massive advances in technology? Imagine if we still depended on the horse and cart, or on waterwheels and windmills? How grindingly slow and how unsustainable human life would be. Yet at a human level we stumble along in personal, political and commercial relationships in which distrust, exploitation and selfishness are not uncommon.

Imagine if human relationships — in every sphere — were marked by trust, care and compassion, service and generosity (among other things). What would that world be like?

The solution lies in human-centred leaders who put people first, and who integrate the technical with the moral aspects of life and leadership. These are men and women who are grounded in timeless human values, who choose wisely and well, setting an example for how to act by the way they act.

Human-centred leaders change the trajectory of history by responding to the pressing needs of the age in new and visionary ways, gazing as they do from a different plane.

And anyone can be a human-centred leader.

How do you become that sort of leader … a human-centred leader?

Firstly (and briefly) you need a map for the journey …

The Journey Map: a model for Parts II and III

The most destabilising aspect of transitions is that there are no established rules to follow, no role models to copy or learn from. Whether leading yourself or an organisation, you are operating in uncharted waters, without a reliable map.

To travel from one place to another you need clarity about where you are starting from and where you are going, and an understanding of how you will get from here to there. It also helps to recognise that the journey involves both doing and being—both outward activity and internal character. You will find it helpful to have a map for the journey that captures these key elements, and to which you can refer at any time. This can be depicted in a simple but powerful Journey Map (see figure A). This is a model that I use with clients to help them create a high-level map for their life and their leadership.

Figure A: Journey Map

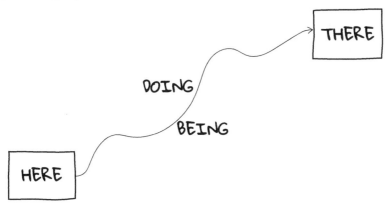

The Journey Map answers four key questions:

- *Here:* Where are you today?
- *There:* Where are you going?
- *Being:* Who are you going to be on the way?
- *Doing:* What are you going to do to get there?

Figure B shows what the map looks like when you add those questions.

Figure B: building the map

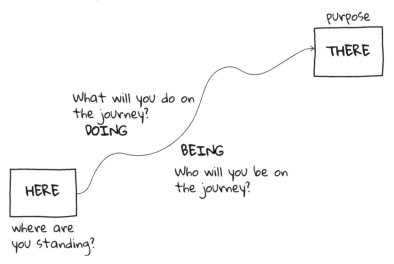

Once you have created this map and answered the big questions, you can scale it to any time frame or any context. For example, knowing your overall life's purpose, you can build the map on a 12-month time frame: Where are you today? Where do you want to be at the end of the year? What steps do you need to take to get there? What aspects of your character will you focus on this year? Or in an organisational context, once you are clear about the firm's purpose you can build a strategy (the *doing* component) and a culture (the *being* component) that align with this purpose.

Your Journey Map can be applied to any situation, beginning with your personal life, and can be scaled to assist your leadership of a company, community or country. In Part II you will build your own map. In Part III you will learn how to create a version to suit whatever leadership role you find yourself in. Then you will learn how to integrate the two maps at the place where your talents intersect with the needs of the world, and so to launch humanity onto a new trajectory.

PART II

Foundations for human-centred leaders

A map for your life

The aim of Part II is to provide you with a high-level map that you can use throughout your life, along with some tools to help you on your journey as a human-centred leader. It will offer a process for constructing the elements of your own map, and 'instructions' for living in accord with that map, creating the foundations for Human-Centred Leadership.

Chapter 5 challenges you to become the best version of yourself, recognising that you do this in relationship with other people. We will then address the four key questions:

Here: Where are you today?
Before you start out on a journey it's important to be clear where you are starting from, or where you are standing today. Lack of clarity about your starting point creates just as much aimlessness as lack of clarity about where you are going. Chapter 6 will help you reflect on and explore your current situation, and in particular answer the question 'Where are you standing?'

There: Where are you going?
Your destination answers the question 'Why are you on this planet?' or 'What is your unique contribution?' It is your purpose, your final goal, the place from which you will look back and see the impact of your life on the lives of others and on the world. Chapter 7 introduces the powerful

concepts of Beauty, Goodness and Truth, and explains how these lie beyond your destination. Chapter 8 shows you how to discover your life's purpose and orient your decisions and actions toward it.

Being: Who are you going to be on the way?

This most often overlooked question is the underlying thread that runs through this book. It is a question about your character, about the person people will encounter when they meet you. Who will that be? Will you be a human-centred leader? Following the path is the easy part. Forming yourself into the best version of yourself—that's the hard, although most inspiring, part. Once you are clear about who you want to be on the journey, however, you can be that person today. You don't have to wait for the future or until you arrive at your destination.

Chapter 9 explains how a life of virtue can give shape to the design of your life—to who you are and who you want to become. Chapter 10 provides an introduction to the virtues of humility, wisdom, courage, justice and self-control, and their application to leadership.

Doing: What are you going to do to get there?

The path from 'here' to 'there', from where you are to where you are going, is not a straight line. It involves twists and turns, and sometimes the sense that you are making little progress. Once you know your destination, however, you can constantly recalibrate every decision and action against that point, moving nearer and nearer to your goal over time. Chapter 11 offers you a framework for thinking well, and therefore making wise decisions. Chapter 12 adds to this framework by showing how you develop and use your conscience to choose well when making decisions.

Finally, chapter 13 will draw all these elements together to help you construct a compass to guide you on your journey. As you move through uncharted waters, this compass will guide you in the darkest night or thickest fog. Pointing unerringly toward your destination, it will demonstrate an uncanny ability to skirt the rocks and shoals that could sink your ship. There will still be storms, but using this combination of tools will give you increased resilience in the face of whatever tempests life throws at you.

Part II will show how you can navigate the shifts and transitions in the world. It proposes a foundation upon which you can stand, and from which you can develop a human-centred approach to leadership and life.

CHAPTER 5

Becoming the best version of yourself

'Knowing yourself is the beginning of all wisdom.'
ARISTOTLE

'I want to be a better person ...'

Andrew is a very successful senior executive, with responsibility for strategy across global markets in his firm. When we met to consider the next 12 months I asked what he would be focusing on during the coming year.

'I'll focus on the things that matter,' he replied, 'and not lose sight of these when under pressure'.

He then outlined three key initiatives that mattered, in addition to business as usual—one about people and talent, another about a multi-billion-dollar fund and the last involving commercialisation of a new market offer. After stress testing his thoughts, prodding and poking to confirm his thinking, I threw in a curve ball.

'What really matters to Andrew, to you?' I asked. 'Delivering organisational results without doing what matters to you would be a poor outcome.'

'At the end of this year I want to be a better person,' he said after a short reflection, and he proceeded to list a few areas in which he could grow and develop.

Andrew is fit and healthy, financially secure, and has a warm, loving relationship with his wife and children. Many people would say that he has it all, he has it made, which is true by most material measures. He has enough self-awareness, however, to recognise that becoming a better person is a lifelong journey toward a destination that, like the horizon, we never quite reach. As we grow and develop, with each step more opportunities for growth emerge.

As with many high achievers, Andrew's list of areas in which to improve was quite ambitious and could have caused dismay in the event that he fell short of such lofty targets. Then he revealed that he felt something of a fraud, imagining what others would think if they knew what he was really like.

He is not alone in that feeling. Most people I know are painfully aware of their shortcomings, and live with the anxiety that they may be found out one day. Frailty and weakness are part of the human condition. We all have times when we fall short of the standards to which we aspire. We all have areas of our life we are not proud of, weaknesses we struggle to overcome. Not necessarily addictions but flaws, demonstrated, for example, when we lose our temper too readily, disregard other people's feelings, have a few too many drinks on the weekend, hold onto a grudge too long, avoid helping colleagues because they don't help us ... the list, of course, is endless. None of us is perfect as we all struggle with our humanity.

I showed Andrew the Cherokee story of the two wolves and waited while he read it.

The two wolves

An old grandfather said to his grandson, who came to him with anger at a friend who had done him an injustice, 'Let me tell you a story ...

'I too, at times, have felt a great hate for those that have taken so much, with no sorrow for what they do. But hate wears you down, and does not hurt your enemy. It is like taking poison and wishing your enemy would die. I have struggled with these feelings many times.

'A fight is going on inside me. It is a terrible fight and it is between two wolves. One is evil—he is anger, envy, sorrow, regret, greed, arrogance, self-pity, guilt, resentment, inferiority, lies, false pride, superiority, and ego.

'The other is good—he is joy, peace, love, hope, serenity, humility, kindness, benevolence, empathy, generosity, truth, compassion, and faith. The same fight is going on inside you—and inside every other person, too.

'Sometimes, it is hard to live with these two wolves inside me, for both of them try to dominate my spirit.'

The boy looked intently into his grandfather's eyes and asked, 'Which one wins, Grandfather?'

The grandfather smiled and quietly said, 'The one I feed.'[1]

Andrew sat quietly after reading the story. I suspect he was wondering which wolf he fed. After a few moments of reflection he asked, 'How do I become a better person?' with a deeper appreciation of the challenge ahead.

Navigating this chapter

This chapter looks at the idea of becoming the best person you can be and notes that you do this in relationship with other people. It has three sections:

- 'A relational anthropology' discusses what it means to become your 'best' and to be a 'person' in relationship with other people.

- 'The four key relationships' identifies the relationships that matter, and provides a model for thinking about, and making the most of, these relationships.

- 'Relationships as the key to navigating systemic challenges' suggests that taking people and relationships as a starting point could be a better way to resolve complex problems.

The question 'How do I become a better person?' has been asked for thousands of years. The answer provides the starting point for building a life of greatness.

Making the effort to become a better person is a noble pursuit, a project worthy of your life. Becoming the best person you can be is the greatest quest you can embark upon. You will never be finished since you will continue to find new areas for learning, growth and development.

And in case you think this sounds self-centred or self-indulgent, I would like to suggest that this project will result in you giving more of yourself to society as you live out your purpose.

There is an important distinction to be made here between building a great life and doing great things. One is the precursor to the other. Building a great life enables you to do great things. Whatever greatness you possess today gives you the power to influence your immediate community. The greatness you build tomorrow, though, will give you the power to change the world.

A relational anthropology

The quest to become the best person you can be invites two questions about meaning: the first about the word *best* and the second about what it means to be a *person*. This is an 'anthropological' question, a question about humanity.

What does 'best' mean for you?

Best is not about high performance. (Is that a sigh of relief I hear?) Can I suggest that you are not on a lifelong journey to become a high-performing person, although you may take on roles that require high performance? High performance is an unfortunate term that springs from a modern (misplaced) desire to measure everything—and then 'lift the bar' ever higher. Imposing high performance standards on moderate performers (that is, most of us) can simply overwhelm people.

The search for high performance stretches the wire until just before it breaks, or leans the motorbike into corners at speed until immediately before it loses traction. High performance seeks to obtain the maximum outcome possible, which means living near the edge of failure. Measures of what constitutes high performance are usually derived from an elite group who exist at the right-hand end of the bell curve—which is generally unhelpful since most people live in the middle. Showing you where your acceptable performance falls short of someone else's exceptional performance, and pushing you to match them, can be demoralising, demotivating and damaging.

Trying to achieve your 'personal best' is a far more useful approach than striving for high performance. 'Best' in the context of becoming the best person you can be means your personal best (PB), a term well known to athletes who often focus on improving their PB.

You know where your personal best lies. You know when you have done or exceeded your best. Unlike an athlete who delivered their personal best in the Olympic stadium many years ago, you can continue to improve your personal best in the arena of life. You may not be able to run as fast as you once could, or lift extreme weights, but you can gain more insight. You can become more virtuous. You can become a better leader. You can become a better person. Learn from others, but don't compare yourself with them. You don't know what raw material and life processes have influenced who they are or where they are going, but you do know yourself, and you know whether or not you have achieved a PB.

What does it mean to be a 'person'?

All models of personal development, whether of work, family life, politics or society, contain underlying anthropological assumptions of what it means to be a person, even when these are not recognised or articulated.

To take an extreme example, people who engage in the slave trade demonstrate a low regard for human life and dignity. Their actions indicate an anthropological assumption that a person is an object that can be bought and sold and used for another's pleasure or enrichment. They show no regard to the humanity of the person being trafficked or traded. When we 'depersonalise' someone we can treat them as an 'it' or a 'thing' and so excuse the most appalling behaviour.

Or another example: businesses that focus on profit with scant regard for people demonstrate an anthropological assumption that a person is simply a unit of economic production. We considered this concept in chapter 4 without commenting on its philosophical framework.

These two examples illustrate how your underlying view of what it means to be human can have profound implications for the way you act toward yourself and others. Is a person someone you can buy and sell? Is a person someone who exists to make your life better? You cannot begin to be a human-centred leader unless you grasp what it means to be a human person.

'I think, therefore I am' ... Am I?

It's almost four hundred years since René Descartes, wrestling with the question of meaning and existence, reached the conclusion, 'I think, therefore I am'. This insight has provided a foundation for much of Western philosophy since that time.

In coffee shops and conversations in Paris and London, in Stockholm and Beijing, I wrestled with the same question, 'What does it mean to be human, to be a person?' I ruminated on this question over many years while Descartes drummed his fingers in the recesses of my mind. My eureka moment came when I suddenly grasped, 'I am in relationship ... therefore I am'. I realised that I become human in relationship with others, and by deepening and strengthening relationships I become more human. This is also true in the plural: 'We are in relationship ... therefore we are'.

Now this is not an original idea. I am not the first to suggest this, and almost certainly have been influenced by others, although I'm not sure who. It was a breakthrough for me, however, when I made the shift from dissatisfaction with the Cartesian 'thinking proves I exist' to 'relationships prove I exist'. I know myself not primarily by thinking, but by relating with you. This is not dissimilar to the Zulu concept of *ubuntu*: a person is a person through other people.

This led me to the view that *a person is a relational being*.

This means that I pursue beauty, goodness and truth with you, live out my purpose with you, grow in virtue with you, become the best person I can be with you. This *relational anthropology* is my starting point for thinking about humanity and all we can be. It underpins my thinking about morality and about leadership, about work and about life. It is a human-centred approach.

Relational in this context has particularly human dimensions, not simply awareness of another in the way that animals relate to one another. Are they 'people', according to my definition? The answer is no, since contained within my position is an integration of everything else I believe about humanity: our capacity to love and be loved, to know ourselves and others, to recognise Beauty, Goodness and Truth, to be guided by purpose and to practise virtue, to think and to choose ...

To say 'a person is a relational being' implies that you become more fully a person—or all that you can be—in relationship with other people. It also implies that if you are denied relationships, your humanity is diminished, and potentially can cease to exist. The impact on children in Romanian orphanages who were deprived of human contact demonstrates this point in a powerful way. These communist era children 'were so punished that they were depressed', according to Jane Aronson in an interview with *The Washington Post*. She says many demonstrated 'psychotic features, autistic-like behaviour...severe failure to thrive and were tiny'.[2]

They experienced only minimal attention or nurturing, both of which are foundational to future intellectual and emotional capability. In the absence of human interaction 'they suffered from attention deficit hyperactivity disorder, post-traumatic stress disorder, psychiatric illnesses...bipolar disorder, [and] the most severe reactive attachment disorder' Aronson has ever seen in any orphanage she has studied.[3]

A relational anthropology can help to explain why loneliness can be so painful, and why we seek friendship. Even the hermit in their lonely cave is seeking a relationship with a being beyond our space and time. Rather than being diminished by the absence of human relationships, they appear to grow in grace and wisdom and what might be called 'holiness'.

The four key relationships

While pondering this relational idea I realised that there are four key sets of relationships that need to be cultivated in order to live a human-centred life (see figure 5.1, overleaf). These include your relationship with:

1 your self
2 your circle of family, friends and colleagues
3 your society and the global community
4 the transcendent.

Figure 5.1: the four relationships

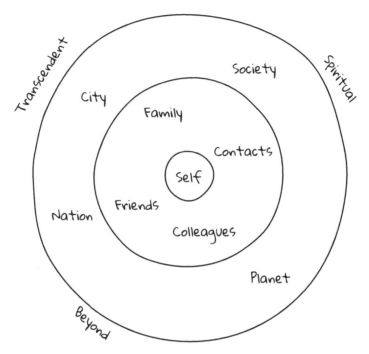

What do these relationships look like?

1   Plato's injunction to 'know yourself' has resonated through the centuries. Growing in self-awareness, learning who you are and becoming comfortable with that is an enormously rewarding endeavour. You learn about, and shape, your vision, values and purpose. You understand and appreciate your strengths and weaknesses and become more at ease with yourself. Self-awareness, along with self-acceptance, provides a sound foundation for relationships with other people.

2   Soon, however, the focus shifts from you to others in the second circle. At some point in your development you recognise that life is lived in community, and it's not all about you. The second circle includes your family and friends, your work colleagues and the community of which you are a part. These are the people you regularly engage with, regardless of where they may live and work. This is the 'network' that you put your energy into and that replenishes your energy.

3   The third circle of relationships is with the community that extends beyond your network. It includes all those who live in the same city, the same country and the same world. This breadth of humanity includes therefore a breadth of moral values and perspectives, the good and the bad, the rich and the poor. You are a part of the wider world, and it's worth taking the time to consider where and how your relationships extend into that world, and then to reflect on your impact. For instance, you purchase goods made by others, often in another country. You may well make goods or deliver services to people in another place whom you never meet. The way you use the world's resources may be limiting the access that others have to the same resources, either today or tomorrow.

4   The fourth set of relationships is not contained within a circle but includes what lies unbounded beyond the circle. It could include ultimate Beauty, Goodness and Truth. Some people say this space is the realm of spirituality. Some give it a name and call it God. I use the term *transcendent* to include all these views, but recognise and respect that this does not capture the depth and breadth of various religious perspectives. When I use the word transcendent in relational terms I am inviting you to consider that which transcends everything else, all time and all reality. Pursue this with openness to truth and draw your own conclusions.

Who is in your four circles?

In order to grow and develop as a relational human being, pay attention to who is included in these four key relationships. To become the best person you can be, it follows that you will want to cultivate the best possible relationships.

Search out relationships that expand your thinking and lead you to ever more Beauty, Goodness and Truth. Search out relationships with people who demonstrate virtue and model yourself on them. Search out people who live by principles, in alignment with their purpose, and learn from them.

Perhaps now is a good time to pause and reflect on your relationships.

- What is the current state of your relationships?

- Do your friends influence you toward becoming a better person, or do they undermine your efforts?

- Who encourages you to feed the 'good wolf' rather than the 'bad wolf'?

- Who are the people you most admire as wonderful examples of human beings?

- With what kind of people do you spend the most time?

- Who is in each of your circles?

- Are the circles well populated or sparse?

- Do you have close relationships with people you care about and who care for you?

- Do you have close relationships with people who encourage and support you on your journey?

- Do you have relationships with people who confront and challenge you when you fall short of your personal best?

- What is the nature of your relationships beyond the second circle—with the wider world and the transcendent?

Part I examined some of the challenges that confront the world now or that we are about to confront. The relationships you develop will be vital to navigating these challenges in the best possible shape and will be crucial to your effective leadership.

Relationships as the key to navigating systemic challenges

Searching for answers to a major challenge usually starts with the idea of 'solving a problem', which can result in arguments about the nature of the problem and the proposed solutions. Starting with what we have in common, our humanity, rather than the things that divide us can be much more helpful.

For instance, we can continue to argue about who or what caused climate change, the extent to which it is or is not occurring, and the advantages or disadvantages thereof. Although it can be very emotive, this debate happens at a logical level—arguing about whose version of the facts is correct and about the conclusions to be drawn from those facts.

What would happen if we shifted the conversation to a human level, starting with our shared humanity and our shared relationships? The immediate insight is that we are all on this planet together and have a responsibility to ourselves and those who come after us. The next insight is that focusing firstly on our relationships—a human-centred approach—encourages us to find points of agreement rather than disagreement, searching for understanding rather than error or dispute. People in relationships search for truth together. Can you imagine how much heat would be sucked out of the argument—and possibly the Earth—if we could first agree that we all want to live harmoniously and that none of us wants to damage our planet irredeemably, and start working from there? This is a human-centred approach to problem solving, with far greater potential for finding effective, sustainable solutions.

A commitment to maintaining relationships is fundamental to resolving differences. The relationship of marriage, for example, needs two people to initiate it but only one person to bring it to an end. Once a commitment to relationship is removed, differences become grounds for argument and reasons for division. Relationships based on mutual respect and shared humanity are the starting point for finding answers to many of the problems that beset us.

You are a person who can build and maintain deep and enduring relationships — with yourself, with others, with the world and with the transcendent. As a relational being you are a member, along with me, of one large human family, and you have much in common with even the most dispersed members of this family.

Since leadership involves people, it fundamentally involves relationships, and not just economic or strategic relationships but personal relationships. It is self-evident therefore that leadership, true leadership, is human centred.

* * *

Leading others starts with leading yourself. It starts with knowing who you are, where you are going and how you are going to get there. It starts with having a solid foundation. And that foundation is your answer to the question 'Where am I standing?'

CHAPTER 6

Foundations of leadership

'Give me a firm place on which to stand and I will move the world.'
ARCHIMEDES

The influence of upbringing

Imagine this for a moment.

You are enjoying your first board appointment, the first woman on the board, among a dozen men. You are keen to do the right thing in every sense: governance, strategy, financial... Your reputation for sound judgement and commercial insight precedes you and contributed to your appointment.

Before long it becomes apparent, however, that your probing questions are not welcome. The board gangs up on you a little, implying that your concerns about the power of the CEO and his relationship to the board are ill considered and demonstrate a lack of understanding about how things work. You can see that the board is failing to ask all the right and relevant questions. While the rest of the board settles back in its complacency you become more uncomfortable.

What will you do?

- Challenge the board and risk your position?

- Stay silent until you perhaps do understand things a bit better?

- Resign from the board because of a fundamental conflict of values?

- Speak out and expose yourself to an unwelcome gender conflict with the old boys' club?

Take a moment to think deeply about your answer. And while you are doing so, consider this situation.

Years later you are Chair of a bank's Remuneration Committee, responsible for signing off on executive bonuses and pay. The very well paid CEO is in line for a bonus of about fourteen million pounds as long-term incentives (LTI) fall due and an annual performance bonus in the order of £3 million. Although payment of the LTI is due as a result of previous decisions, payment of the annual bonus is open to debate. There is a sound argument for suggesting the CEO has not fully met the eligibility criteria and the bank has been embroiled in a damaging scandal. There is also a public perception that greedy bankers are enriching themselves at the expense of struggling families and businesses. On the other hand, the CEO has done a very good job in difficult circumstances, denied any prior knowledge of the scandal and forgone his bonus for the past couple of years.

There is overwhelming support on the board for paying the annual bonus. As Chair of the Remuneration Committee you will be the public face of any decision. What will you do?

- Reject the annual bonus and even try to unwind some of the long-term incentive bonuses?

- Agree with everyone else and pay the annual bonus?

- Be prepared to publicly defend that position at the AGM and to the media and the public?

- Resign from the board because of a values conflict?

Now, before you read on, is a good time to consider your answers to these questions.

Dame Alison Carnwath faced both these dilemmas. In the first she challenged the board, eventually instilling better practice and installing better leadership. In the second she was Chair of the Remuneration Committee at Barclays PLC in the UK. The board approved compensation to Bob Diamond, the CEO, of pay, shares and perks that totalled £17 million, including a £2.7 million annual bonus. They also paid a £5.7 million tax bill on his behalf.[1] During the same year shareholders received £700 million in dividends and Barclays staff received £2.1 billion in bonuses.[2]

Dame Alison defended the board's decision in the face of stiff opposition from the public and the press, and after the LIBOR scandal that surrounded the bank was well known.

'Whilst we believe in good faith that we got our decisions and judgments broadly right for 2011, it is clear that this view is not shared by all shareholders,' she said at the AGM, where she was publicly booed and almost a quarter of the shareholders would not endorse her re-election.[3]

At the subsequent Commission on Banking Standards[4] she was able to break her silence and reveal that she had been a lonely voice arguing for a zero bonus.

'Bob Diamond had not achieved [some particular] objectives, although he felt entitled to his bonus since he had forgone it in previous years,' Dame Alison tells me.[5]

Other directors 'were shirking their responsibilities, or wanted to compromise,' she continues.

'However, banks have a "societal brief". The "great British public" is concerned about the size of payout to senior bankers, and so they should be. The public believed some of these [bankers] should be fired or at least their bonuses reduced.'

Dame Alison explains that a 'dissatisfied public' can apply moral pressure, and that boards should recognise and take that into account.

'I was convinced I was right,' she says, with regard to understanding public reaction to such apparent corporate largesse, and was not surprised by the outcry.

'Effective leadership is fearless and courageous,' she declares as we talk in the offices of Land Securities PLC, the FTSE 100 company where she is Chairman of the Board.

'Moral courage' is required to withstand the intense pressure that directors find themselves under. 'It makes one different, calmer, more likely to be followed,' she says, emphasising how important this is in contemporary society where people are looking for more comfort and confidence, rather than more stress and anxiety.

When I ask about the source of her moral perspective she replies unhesitatingly: 'Upbringing.' Dame Alison recalls family dinner table conversations about right and wrong, and how her schooling and social environment fostered and supported doing the right thing.

'I withstood any pressures to engage in any sort of slippage [in order to] make money or to attain power,' she states, not with any sense of pride but as a matter of fact, in the same way one would not consider touching a hot iron. It's just not sensible.

I wonder out loud why she has not 'slipped'?

'Too frightened perhaps?' she asks self-reflectively, more of herself than of me, before going on to observe that fear of consequences can be quite helpful in deciding how to act. Although it's not just fear of consequences I detect. It's a desire not to let down those who trust her to do the right thing, from her close friends and family to the 'great British public'.

* * *

John had executive responsibility for a prominent sporting team playing on the national stage. As we spent time together working on their strategy, he inadvertently provided an insight into the influence of upbringing in forming and shaping people.

Over many years in the game he observed a progressive decline in the character of new players, in that deep internalisation of a moral framework against which actions were measured. He noted that many of his players were young men, often living far from home, being paid large sums of money, and living in a somewhat illusory world where it appeared they could fulfil any desire and have whatever they wanted. He noted how advances in technology and communication had exacerbated the challenges players faced. Any indiscretion could be broadcast globally within seconds.

The biggest shift he noticed was that a team could no longer presume new players had a sound family and community upbringing that instilled traditional values, manners, and a sense of right and wrong. In many cases young men joined the team from dysfunctional families and social environments, and were using sport as a stepping-stone to a better life.

There was also a high likelihood that their living arrangements lacked any stable, supportive structure.

John explained how each team could make choices about which players they bought subject to a prescribed salary cap, making decisions to build competence and capability that aligned with overall team strategy. Every team had access to advanced research on high performance, diet, teamwork and coaching. In this sense it was largely a level playing field.

So what makes a winning difference? While some factors—a good or bad draw, for example—are beyond a team's control, what might be that one per cent differentiator that could deliver great results?

John formed a view that character could make the defining difference in winning grand finals. He recognised that strength of character enabled a young man to resist his friends' suggestion of 'just one more drink' and instead to focus on a good night's sleep before training. Character gets someone out of bed and to training on time and ready to perform. Character says no to an opportunistic liaison, an illicit drug. Character does the right thing when no-one else is looking, even when it's unpleasant, uncomfortable or unpopular.

Contrast this with the player who has no character foundation and has built their life around exceptional natural ability. They have been praised, promoted and promised all things from a young age. Exceptional skill has kept them on the team, and exceptional managers have kept their off-field behaviour out of the media. They have been applauded for their prowess and excused for their excess, learning how to keep this hidden and contained, to make excuses and to manipulate others.

John understood that a team built on character would beat a team of characters, so he turned his attention to character.

Since then I have observed with some interest how unsavoury behaviour seems to correlate with defeat, and solid, scandal-free work effort with victory. Although my observations are hardly scientific, in years when John's club was dogged by misconduct, they failed to put together a winning effort. A recent (unexpected) Grand Final victory seemed to coincide with a year that contained little scandal.

Navigating this chapter

This chapter looks at the starting point of the Journey Map: *Here: Where are you today?* and how it can be applied to your personal life. It will help you reflect on and explore your current situation, and in particular answer the question 'Where are you standing?' It has two sections:

- 'Leadership starts with being and manifests in doing' makes the distinction between who you are and what you do, emphasising the importance of your character.

- 'Where are you standing?' observes that character provides a strong foundation for standing firm and invites reflection on where you are standing.

Leadership starts with being and manifests in doing

Leadership can be difficult and complex to define, and even harder to live. There are two simple aspects to leadership, however, that need to be understood and embraced. On the one hand is the aspect of activity, of what you *do* as a leader. On the other is the question of character, of what sort of person you *are*, of what lies within. This is the primary focus of human-centred leaders.

The distinction is between doing and being, between what you do on the journey and who you are on the journey. It is a distinction between the outer manifestation of leadership actions and the inner foundation of leadership character, which are intimately related and deeply integrated in outstanding leaders. Character underpins your actions, and actions shape your character.

This concept is quite profound and worth considering for a moment before you move on.

Do you notice that your response to particular situations is different now from when you were younger? You may become less angry, for example, or less stressed. At some time you made a decision to respond differently then practised that response until it became habitual. Now the thing that upset or destabilised you in the past washes over you. Each time you decided not to let something bother you it became easier the next time. Do you see how your actions shaped your character, and your character now informs your actions?

The opposite is also true. If you get angry over the smallest incident, and continue to let things rile you, you probably find it's getting easier to shout at other drivers on the freeway or become short tempered with staff who don't act fast enough. If that's the case, you may have a reputation as an angry, ill-tempered person — that is, people describe not what you do, but who you are.

The distinction between being and doing means you have a choice about the source of your leadership authority. It can be derived from what you do, as shown by your title or your business card, or from who you are — your character. One is fleeting while the other is enduring. Human-centred leaders lead from character, not from their title.

The quality, effectiveness and influence of your leadership flows from your vision, virtue and purpose. It flows from the meaning you discover for life and the contribution you are making to the world. It flows from your character, from who you are. And it flows from the place where you are standing.

Where are you standing?

Most people are familiar with the powerful, although perhaps apocryphal, image of Archimedes, the Greek philosopher, running naked through the streets crying 'Eureka!' when he grasped how to measure the gold content in the king's crown using the principle of displacement. 'Eureka' became part of the popular vernacular, and still often bursts forth spontaneously when we grasp how to solve a problem in our own breakthrough moments.

Archimedes is also credited with the invention of the lever — although it seems most unlikely that this breakthrough occurred only in the second century BC, when people had been building huge structures such as pyramids for thousands of years. I suspect he wrote the mathematical formula that explained how the lever works. Although you may not know the formula, you relied on it when you visited the playground and sat on the seesaw.

While Archimedes gave us 'Eureka' to accompany sudden insight, he also passed on a more profound observation when he invented the lever, one that can shape your life.

'Give me a firm place on which to stand and I will move the world,' he remarked, conjuring up a vision of Atlas, not with the world on his shoulders, but standing on the universe levering our tiny planet into position. With a little imagination one can picture the Greek patriarch shaking his head in awe, sensing the structural challenges he could now solve.

The big insight, however, that allowed Archimedes to contemplate his breakthrough with great satisfaction is not in the power of a wooden pole to lift a heavy weight, but in the power generated by the solid ground on which you choose to stand. Where you stand makes all the difference.

It is no small shift from here to an even deeper insight, one that shaped my life: *If I am standing in a firm place, I can change the world.* The moment that thought entered my mind I set out to find this firm place as a precursor to making a difference, as a foundation to changing the world. I searched in philosophy and religion, in business and books, in dialogue and debate. This book explains the place I found and shows how you can find where you stand.

I frequently meet people who want to change the world, to leave it a better place as a result of their passing through. They often wonder how to do that, looking for some great cause to which to devote their life, something that will consume their passion and time, something that will offer them the satisfaction of a life well lived.

Archimedes' insight was that if you want to move something, first you have to set your feet in a firm place. You cannot use a lever to shift a large rock if you are standing on an unstable surface. You can exert little force if your feet are slipping or sinking.

So too with changing the world: you start not by examining the challenge, but by examining where you are standing. You need a firm foundation. And this is found in your character, in what you stand for rather than what you fall for, in what you hold rather than what holds you, in who you are rather than what you do.

Your character is the place where you are standing. Just as the deep roots of an ancient tree extend far into the ground, are largely unseen and enable the tree to withstand the inevitable storms, character gives you a firm grounding and provides you with the strength to withstand the storms that life throws at you. Character doesn't remove the challenges you will face, but it provides you with the resilience to stand fast against the trials and tribulations of life. It gives you strength in adversity. It is a key foundation to Human-Centred Leadership.

Now could be a good time to ask yourself where you are standing.

- Do you have a firm foothold in life, or are you standing on shifting ground?

- Where are your roots? Where are you standing?

- What matters to you?

- What values do you bring to each moment?

- How would you describe your character?

- How would others describe your character?

- Are you able to stand firm when your values are tested, or do you swing in the breeze?

- Do you have the courage to speak out in front of your colleagues or your boss?

- Are you clear about the distinction between right and wrong, and where your limits lie?

- Is acceptance by others more important than being true to yourself?

- Does winning at any cost overshadow doing what matters?

- Have you even taken the time to answer these questions and others like them?

Perhaps also ask a close friend or colleague how they would answer these questions about you. By doing so you will discover two things: first, people are enormously generous and encouraging, and second, you can gain rich insights into yourself.

Having planted your feet on firm and solid ground you can now turn your gaze to the horizon. What do you see?

CHAPTER 7

In search of Beauty, Goodness and Truth

'Everything has beauty, but not everyone sees it.'

CONFUCIUS

The next question that needs to be answered concerns the direction in which you orient yourself. Imagine for a moment you are planting the seeds of an oak tree. Which direction will the sun and wind come from? Where does the water naturally flow? Your character is in those deep roots that grow beneath your feet, so you need to consider your surroundings.

As you embark on this journey, therefore, first look beyond yourself, far out over the horizon to what the ancient Greeks called 'transcendentals'. (This is not to be confused with Transcendental Meditation, or the transcendent—what some people call God.)

The Greeks suggested there are three transcendentals: Beauty, Goodness and Truth. They believed that these three realities transcend, or go beyond, this place and this moment. Plato and his companions also saw in them the foundations of reality. What this means is that when you perceive the fullness of Beauty or Goodness or Truth you know reality, you know without doubt what is. Please restrain your desire to ask the pressing question: 'How do you know when you know Truth?' I hope this will be answered as we continue the journey together. At this stage I am suggesting that the Greeks were onto something when they noted that Beauty, Goodness and Truth are the foundations of reality, and that it is possible to know these even when you cannot fully explain them.

Another fascinating thing about the transcendentals is that each is fully contained in the others. When you appreciate beauty, for example, you recognise the presence of goodness and truth. When you grasp the truth about something you experience a moment of beauty in, perhaps, the simplicity or power of the insight. When you observe goodness in the actions of another person you are seeing truth and beauty in operation.

You can never possess all Beauty, Goodness and Truth. They are akin to the horizon that you never reach, even while knowing you have gone beyond previous horizons. The moment you reach the horizon you see yet another vista before you. In the same way, discovering Beauty, Goodness or Truth in the briefest moment or at the smallest juncture encourages you to look further, in an ever deeper search for more beauty, greater goodness and more truth.

Navigating this chapter

The next two chapters shift your focus on the Journey Map to the finish line, to *There: Where are you going?* This chapter introduces the powerful concepts of Beauty, Goodness and Truth and explains how these lie beyond your destination, and how the search for them deepens your own humanity. There are four sections:

- 'The pursuit of Beauty, Goodness and Truth' looks at why they matter and the difference they can make in your life.

- 'What are Beauty, Goodness and Truth?' explains the meaning of these terms.

- 'Conversion and change' talks about intellectual and moral conversion: having a change of mind and a change of heart.

- 'Leadership and the search for Beauty, Goodness and Truth' looks at the relevance of these for the work and public arenas.

The pursuit of Beauty, Goodness and Truth

The pursuit of Beauty, Goodness and Truth is a noble endeavour. It can set your life on an entirely different trajectory from the narrow embrace of ignorance, short-term reward and instant gratification. Searching for the transcendentals constantly expands your life into unbounded possibility, whereas ignorance, instant reward and short-term gratification are never fulfilling and ultimately diminish you. Strangely enough, both paths can be attractive and once started down are easy to follow. The pleasure of insight fosters a search for more insight. Similarly, the pleasure derived from instant gratification prompts a desire for ever more immediate enjoyment.

Beauty, Goodness and Truth exist both within you and beyond you. The search for them involves deep introspection and broad global scanning, looking in and looking out. It requires a readiness to grow and develop in response to emerging insight. It requires openness to other people and other points of view. By trying to find what is beautiful, good or true in other people, you will become more human yourself. You will transcend or go beyond yourself to touch and be touched by other people. The beauty, goodness and truth you discover in their humanity will quicken your own growth.

The search will change your life and the lives of those you touch, because you will become a better person — wiser, more caring, nobler — even in the midst of great trauma and tragedy. Alice Herz-Sommer, the oldest known Holocaust survivor before she died in 2014, aged 110, was a renowned pianist who spent two years in a concentration camp, and lost her husband and many close friends during the Holocaust.

'I am looking for the nice things in life,' she is quoted as saying. 'I know about the bad things, but I look only for the good things. The world is wonderful, it's full of beauty and full of miracles.'[1]

You may wonder if this pursuit is better suited to the quiet monastic life, or to Plato's Academy, without the distractions of a frantic, always-on society. It is not.

The pursuit is fundamental for human-centred leaders because it lifts your vision to a higher plane, enabling you to see further and to avoid irrelevant distractions. The pursuit starts right now, wherever you are today. Although it involves hard work, it's easiest when you are where you belong. You shape yourself and the world from where you stand, not by going somewhere else to shape another person or another world. The challenge is how to pursue Beauty, Goodness and Truth in each moment in your environment. As you do you will discover who you are and see the path to becoming the best version of yourself.

What are Beauty, Goodness and Truth?

Although it is beyond the scope of this book to give a full philosophical explanation of what constitutes Beauty, Goodness and Truth, you may find it helpful to understand how I define them.

Beauty

As I write I am surrounded by natural beauty. In every direction lie hills and valleys, covered in blue forests of eucalypts and green carpets of grazing pasture. Distant, snow-covered mountains touch a radiant blue sky. The rays of morning sunlight cascade down the hills and chase away the shadow of night, while birds burst into song to welcome the new day. Immediately outside my window, not much more than an arm's length from my desk, tiny honeyeaters with needle-like beaks swing from the stems of flowers as they feed on the nectar.

The countryside never fails to captivate me with its beauty. I could devote a whole chapter to the delight that every day and every change in the weather brings. Every moment contains an opportunity for appreciation, and no two moments are the same.

That's what beauty is like. It can be found in nature and art, in people and places, in buildings and business. Yes, even in that daily activity we call work. However, you need to be awake and aware, sensitive to its presence, or it can quietly pass you by unnoticed.

Take a moment to think about those times when you have gazed on a beautiful sunrise, surrounded by stillness and quiet as the new day awakes, a faint glow slowly creeping over the land, followed by rays of light reaching through the clouds, and then the moment of sunburst dispelling the darkness, bringing warmth and light. It can be a magical moment of contemplation, replete with beauty and peace and goodness. And even in the midst of such wonder, you know there are still other sunrises more wonderful.

Beauty is that which is aesthetically pleasing, such as a sunrise or an artistic masterpiece, a virtuoso performance, a fine wine or the workings of a fine watch. What is aesthetically pleasing goes beyond pleasure or satisfaction, even though we derive pleasure and satisfaction from the beauty we perceive and enjoy.

The aesthetic aspect of beauty helps us understand and distinguish between what may seem beautiful and what is actually beautiful—in other words, to appreciate the distinction between reality and the illusion of reality. A reclining nude may be beautiful, for instance, yet can be depicted in a pornographic or artistic way. The former is erotic, portrayed to arouse lust, with the illusion of 'relationship', while the latter is aesthetic, designed to inspire wonder.

Spending a life in pursuit of the aesthetic is ultimately more fulfilling, despite the short-term gratification that may be derived from the erotic. This does not mean there is no place for the erotic in a mutually loving relationship. What it does mean is that a life lived in search of self-gratification can become disordered, as we search for, say, physical pleasure to the detriment of emotional and intellectual satisfaction.

Cultivating an appreciation of beauty, searching for it in art galleries and creative communities, in people and places, expands your senses and your horizons. You grow and develop as you search out beauty.

Goodness

Goodness is a sibling of Beauty that I will touch on only briefly here, as the next section on virtue explores the concept of goodness in considerable depth.

In our contemporary vernacular, though, goodness has been relegated to a weak adjective that does little heavy lifting. You can have a 'good look', a 'good boss' or a 'good game'. You can enjoy a 'good meal', a 'good ride' or a 'good argument'. Through overuse, *goodness* has become a weak word that adds little to human knowledge. Does it matter anyway, because tomorrow there is a good chance you will have a good day after a good sleep? How can we pursue goodness when it sounds like a euphemism for mediocrity?

Goodness is more than an all-encompassing word to capture the vanilla essence of our lives. In a far richer sense, *goodness is that which promotes human flourishing*; it helps us become the best person we can be. It is easy to think of good as the opposite of bad, with the judgemental notion that this person has been good and that person bad. Good, and what is morally good, is what helps you become all you can be. We are going to come back to this point repeatedly, as it is a fundamental concept for living an effective life.

There is something attractive about goodness. We observe it in great role models such as Gandhi and Mother Teresa, in people who respond to a human need by doing what are traditionally called 'good deeds'. Large-scale tragedies, such as the Japanese earthquake and tsunami of 2011, or the wildfires that periodically ravage rural Australian communities, bring out the best in people. They bring out the goodness that resides so close to the core of our being and is drawn to help other people.

Truth

Truth is the third sibling among the transcendentals. When you see beauty in Michelangelo's *Pietà* in St Peter's Basilica or *Nike, the Winged Victory of Samothrace*, which greets you as you ascend a staircase in the Louvre, you are grasping a truth that the sculptor wished to convey.

Truth has a symphonic quality about it, analogous to an orchestra in which each musician stays true to the composer, themselves and their instrument, while you hear the beauty of the whole symphony. Truth can be perceived through what is beautiful, and enters your mind as both distinct elements and the harmony of the whole.

We live in a relativist age in which people often argue about the meaning of truth as a way of avoiding actual truth, such as the theologians who choose to enter the door marked 'discussion about heaven' rather than the door marked 'heaven'. The distraction of the debate can deny us the opportunity to appreciate truth itself. Imagine sitting inside a dark room debating the meaning of a sunrise when you could throw open the curtains and let the light burst in. It would be easy to agree that we each have our own truth. Unfortunately, that's a fallacy, because there is such a thing as objective truth. We cannot each have our own truth about exactly the same matter. Truth is often somewhere between or beyond our opinions.

Truth is the conformity of the mind with reality. It is that which is so, independently of my believing it.

Just ponder that for a moment before reading on. Could you accept this definition of truth? Can you see that I am making a distinction between what I happen to believe internally, in my mind, and what is the case, external to me?

For example, gravity is real whether I believe it or not. Oxford is real; it was real before I visited it and is still real after my visit. Napoleon existed. These are verifiable facts. You don't have to be able to see or touch them. Beauty exists and is real, whether I choose to recognise it or not.

What is not truth is opinion, no matter how fervently held. It is only with the passage of time and further information that you can discover if your opinion is correct. Clarity about what constitutes truth is very helpful in debate, as many people confuse opinion with truth. If you spend just a few minutes listening to almost any parliament in the world you will immediately recognise the confusion between truth and opinion.

The distinction between truth and opinion is important because many people use the 'my truth' defence as a way to buttress their opinion. They argue that you are wrong simply because they believe they are right, failing to listen and learn from any insights you may have.

Furthermore, failure to recognise that it is possible to discover the truth manifests in failure to confront bad behaviour, to call out opinions as merely points of view, to confuse the volume of an argument with the strength of the argument, and to allow a large number of people who find agreement around a position to outweigh the often lone voice of expertise.

Lastly, failure to appreciate you can discover truth can curtail your transcendental journey. Can you stop today, and live comfortably with all the unanswered questions and unsatisfied longings?

Archimedes cried 'Eureka' when he grasped the resolution to a problem not because he suspected he was right but because he *knew* he was right. In sheer delight he leaped out of his bath and ran through the streets, eager to share his breakthrough with whoever would listen. When we arrive at the truth of something it can delight us like a sunrise illuminating a dark corner of doubt or uncertainty. When we grasp the truth we feel it deep within our being. It touches our soul.

You can find truth in the words of a book, the comments of a friend or the silence of your thoughts. You can cultivate an appreciation of truth in museums and the study of history, in the great books and the great conversations, by exposing your thoughts to the light and seeing if they withstand reflection and review. As you seek after truth, you grow, develop and advance toward becoming the best person you can be.

> When old age shall this generation waste,
> Thou shalt remain, in midst of other woe
> Than ours, a friend to man, to whom thou say'st,
> 'Beauty is truth, truth beauty, — that is all
> Ye know on earth, and all ye need to know.'

John Keats, 'Ode on a Grecian Urn'

Isn't beauty in the eye of the beholder?

I hear your contention that Beauty—and hence Goodness and Truth—resides in the eye of the beholder. I agree. You perceive beauty where I do not, and vice-versa. I hold something to be true or good, and you have cogent reasons for disagreement. You may have a highly refined understanding of art and see beauty where I see only a painting. These differences can be attributed to any number of reasons, ranging from taste and preference, inclination and education, to objective reality.

I would like to suggest that rather than argue over who is right or wrong, we find a way to learn from one another. I need to be honest enough to recognise when you raise valid questions about what I hold to be true. My inability to answer your questions does not prove me wrong or you right, but it does provide the grounds for further questioning on my part, and hopefully on yours.

And to learn from one another we need to be open to a change of mind and a change of heart, to what could be called 'conversion'.

Conversion and change

The very word *conversion* may cause a bit of a jolt, because it can conjure up images of religious ceremonies. That kind of conversion entails entering into a relationship with a transcendent being, of joining a particular community and adopting a particular set of values within a faith tradition.

However, there are two other types of conversion that matter for our purpose here: intellectual conversion and moral conversion. Both are important to your growth and development as a human being, to becoming more human.

In order to grow and develop, you are going to need to change. You are going to become someone different, so different that friends from 10 or 20 years ago may not recognise the person you become. You are going to expose yourself to new perspectives, new insights, new friendships, new approaches, new … everything.

Intellectual and moral conversion involves conversion *from* something and conversion *to* something, from the views you held to what you now believe. Conversion challenges your thoughts and beliefs and allows you to review and refine your thinking and values. In each case you wrestle with something new, whether intellectual concepts and ideas or moral questions and dilemmas.

Intellectual conversion

Intellectual conversion, for example, can involve a shift from a belief that the world is flat to grasping that it is round; from holding that only what is measured can be managed to realising you manage people, not machines; from 'knowing' that your way of doing things is the right way to appreciating the wisdom of another person's approach.

Deep intellectual conversion requires you to be always disposed to truth, no matter how uncomfortable. However, as human beings we are 'permanently vulnerable to bias:

Neurotics are biased against learning about their problem.

Egotists are biased against learning about what benefits other persons.

Loyalists are biased against learning what might benefit other groups.

And common sense itself tends to be biased against deep analysis [and] historical study'.[2]

Moral conversion

Moral conversion, for example, can involve a shift from a belief in paying excessive executive bonuses to one tempered by broader social concerns;

from outsourcing jobs to save money to paying a fair wage and keeping people on the payroll; from command and control leadership, which treats people as tools, to a caring, people-centred management approach.

Moral conversion starts with those principles by which you live your life and your perspective on what is morally acceptable. It requires a disposition to learning new values and new insights, and is demonstrated by a commitment to searching for objective values that are constant and reliable, as opposed to those things that appeal to your preferences or happen to be the flavour of the month.

Whereas bias limits intellectual conversion, moral conversion is 'permanently vulnerable to wilfulness—the irrational phenomenon by which we can deliberately act against our better judgment'.[3] In other words, despite your best of intentions, you can find yourself doing the very thing you don't want to do because of the pleasure and satisfaction you will derive in that moment. And I am no stranger to that experience.

Leadership and the search for Beauty, Goodness and Truth

The way to remain open to conversion—*from* who you are *to* who you can become—is to commit yourself to searching for the transcendentals, for Beauty, Goodness and Truth. To my enquiring mind there is little more exciting in life, for this quest encompasses everything.

I search for truth in new places and new relationships. I discover beauty in new days and old friends. I find goodness almost everywhere. Although I occasionally find lies, ugliness and wickedness, these pale in the light of the Beauty, Goodness and Truth that dispel darkness.

Searching for the transcendentals as a part of your everyday life will change your life, as you delight in discovering hidden beauty, recognising goodness and uncovering truth wherever they may be found. Alice Herz-Sommer was grateful for her experience of the Holocaust because it taught her what was truly important in life: relationships, music, beauty ... You too will find what is truly important when you look toward the transcendentals.

This search is not just something for your private life, though. It is crucial to your effectiveness as a human-centred leader in the public arena. It fosters and encourages questions:

- What is the truth of the matter? What are the facts? Have these been disclosed or discussed?

- What is there to appreciate/enjoy/celebrate in this situation or with this person?

- What is the right thing to do, the right way to act?

- Is this action fair for all involved?

- Are we being honest here, or is something being covered up?

- Are we asking all the questions, or are particular questions being avoided?

- Do we treat people as individuals with hopes and dreams, talents and skills, or as mere units of economic production?

- Are we doing anything that deprives people of freedom, including freedom of choice, and the opportunity to express opinions without fear?

Being able to distinguish between reality and concept, between fact and fiction, between correctness and conviction, will stand you in good stead as a leader. It is a panacea to pride, an antidote to apathy, and allows you to quickly spot the dubious and the doubtful. And when you don't find reality you can ask further questions on the journey of discovery.

When you listen with an ear attuned to the transcendentals you are less prone to accept the undemanding answer or take the easy way out. You are likely to ask deeper questions that align with your guiding principles, and more inclined to put in the effort to practise good habits. In essence, a commitment to Beauty, Goodness and Truth fosters an aspiration to be the best version of yourself, be the best leader you can be, build the best organisation you can and so contribute toward a better version of the world.

Hidden within that last sentence is the means of resolving the challenge about whose view should prevail. My truth? Your truth? When you find yourself in this kind of argument, ask a different question. Ask a question about possibility, about aspiration, about dreams. Ask a question about being your best. Ask whether you, or your companion, could possibly find a better version, a better story, more beauty, more goodness. Rather than arguing over what may be obvious, discover what is hidden.

Seeking Beauty, Goodness and Truth is not always easy. It's challenging, beset with uncertainty and unknowing. It involves intellectual, aesthetic and moral struggle. Occasionally you will glimpse them clearly, but in most cases you will feel as though you are looking through a foggy window. If they are unclear, then, how can you discover and capture them?

There is a powerful way of orienting yourself toward Beauty, Goodness and Truth. That is by finding your noble purpose. And you can find that purpose in its full extent only if you remain open to Beauty, Goodness and Truth.

CHAPTER 8

Discover your purpose

'Martin wanted to serve, and the best place to do that was in the South ... He could have stayed at the seminary [after completing his studies]. But he knew what he needed to do.'

Dr Cory (CT) Vivian, telling me about his friend
Dr Martin Luther King Jr

Navigating this chapter

This chapter continues to focus on the finish line of the Journey Map, to the point marked *There: Where are you going?* You will meet my friend Ileana and through her story learn how to discover your life's purpose and orient your decisions and actions toward it.

A conversation about purpose

Ileana mentioned in an email that she was in a time of transition and searching for the next steps in her life and career. She recognised that a tendency to say yes to too many good things could be a distraction.

'When you open the door to opportunity,' she wrote, 'you never know what is going to happen. I am looking for a specific opportunity, but other opportunities are showing up ... so what to do? Should I consider them? Ignore them? Every opportunity could be a good one ... or not'.

Ileana's words expressed what I frequently hear and observe. There are so many roads you can choose that it becomes hard to take the first step, and harder still to remain on the chosen path since there are just so many opportunities. How can you make a choice when all of them are full of promise?

I asked her the only question that can provide a solution.

'Big question: what is your purpose in life?' I wrote, and then expanded on it: 'Why are you on this planet? How will the world be different as a result of your contribution? Don't be afraid in your answer. Be powerful'.

Ileana did not have an immediate answer, although she understood the clarity that would come with knowing it.

In the ensuing conversation we worked together to discover her purpose. She generously gave permission to reproduce an edited version of our correspondence, since it may help you understand both what your purpose is and how to discover it. You will also hear the wisdom in her words as she reflects on what really matters. As you read, you may wish to pause after each concept or question to write down your own thoughts.

Dear Ileana,
Would you mind telling me a story — in as much detail as possible — about a time when you felt closely aligned to your purpose? What were you doing when you felt, 'This is what I was born to do'? What did you feel, where were you, who were you with, and so on? How do you feel now when you look back on this?

Anthony

Dear Anthony,
This is an example. (I have many ...)
   2007–08, US city, leadership role building and managing ...
   I was in my state of flow: happy, healthy, with a job I loved. I was enjoying my career in the US and I was still discovering this country and all the opportunities this world had for me. I had a clear mission and vision.
   I was supported by my manager, and had a great team with whom I had a fun working relationship. The company was sponsoring my green card, so I was feeling appreciated, taken care of. I was doing an

outstanding job where I could add my creativity and Italian touch. I had room for growth and had my entire career in front of me.

I was feeling empowered, responsible for something important, supported, trusted ... people and team members were investing in me. It was not always easy, there were a lot of challenges.

Personal life was also going very well. In a few words: things were in a good balance and my day to day was rewarding and inspiring.

Why was I feeling very aligned to my purpose? There are a few elements that are crucial: I had room for growth, I had room to build something from scratch (my job was also a blank page ... I had the freedom and authority to write it in the way I wanted it), I was working as a leader and making decisions every day on my own, but I was also supported and guided (when needed). I liked that balance very much.

I was learning so many new things. I was studying during the weekend to do a good and a better job, I was managing a small team and we had good working relationships.

I was living abroad and establishing my life in the US. I also bought my home, which I still adore.

I was born to explore, to be a go-getter, to put structure where there is no structure, I was born to be a great facilitator, I was born to learn and to transfer that knowledge (not teaching, but investing in new talent), I was born to support my manager(s) and consider 'my' customer(s) and help them to succeed. I was born to contribute and make things better often in a simple way.

It is very clear that it was not the 'power' or the 'money' I had that made me feel that way ... serenity is more important than happiness. I desire serenity in my day to day, I live and breathe harmony and good positive energy. I had serenity all around me and was an inspiration for myself and others.

When I look back on those days I am very proud of 'me'. I remember going to work singing and happy. I remember my day to day without worry and fear of the unknown and uncertainty.

... I think I am at that age where I need more depth and meaning in my life. So, where is it? Where do I find it? The people in our life is a key element. I am searching for a great manager, team, company, mentor ...

Ileana

Dear Ileana,

You say: 'I was born to explore, to be a go-getter, to put structure where there is no structure...to be a great facilitator...to learn and to transfer that knowledge...to support...'

Imagine you are able to do that in everything you do, while working in the state of flow you described.

Who would be the people/group you would most love to be serving/helping? What draws you to them?

These people would then be different as a result of your helping them. And they would then touch others in a similar way. In other words, your impact would extend like a ripple in a pond.

What would happen in the world as a result of this spreading out, this touching and passing on what you started?

Remember, you are limited here only by your imagination. So dream big and don't be afraid of anything, no matter how grand it sounds.

Anthony

Dear Anthony,

I am not sure I know who I love most to serve and help.

I enjoy business and the 'good side of business'. I would truly enjoy working with and helping some of the greatest Italian companies to become multinational and enter the US market. I would also enjoy teaching. I also enjoy consulting because it is a way of helping a client to succeed.

What would happen in the world as a result of this spreading out, this touching and passing on what you started? This would result in growth, education, opportunities and changes in mindsets.

Dreaming big: I often think that I could dedicate my life to helping Italy from abroad. I'm thinking about becoming the Giovanna D'Arco of Italy. In the 1800s Giuseppe Garibaldi 'saved' Italy by making it one country.

Why am I not doing this? Lack of confidence, worry about dealing with powerful people and systems...

This would become a mission in life...not just a project.

This is one example. I have other dreams...working with artistic and cultural institutions like opera, where I currently volunteer.

Ileana

Dear Ileana,

Thank you for your thoughts, which thrill me with your passion and insight. More questions … We are drawing near to the end.

Imagine that you dedicate your life to helping Italy, helping it become perhaps 'the greatest country on earth', recovering its rich history and culture, and in some way showing the world how to really live. (I am thinking for a moment of the Slow Movement, which started in Italy.) Ignore any obstacles and assume you overcome them.

What would the world and its people be like? What would be the ripple effect of Italy becoming all it could be?

Anthony

Dear Anthony,

People would be fulfilled, mature, responsible, reliable, educated, generous, able to appreciate life at the fullest, able to dedicate time and resources to do good things and not waste them to fight bad things, etc.

The world would be a better world with values and principles that are often ignored. The effect is that other people would want that happiness, state of equilibrium, serenity … Other countries would probably learn from it … People would want to live, work, invest in Italy, etc.

Ileana

Dear Ileana,

Very last question …

Have you been completely honest with me (and with yourself) in what you have written? For example, do you have a bigger dream but are fearful of admitting to it?

Anthony

Dear Anthony,

Yes, I have been very honest.

As far as dreaming big, I no longer dream to have a penthouse and 200 pairs of shoes. I mean that I am 'simple' at the core. I need and dream for serenity more than happiness. I dream that one day I will take a course at Harvard. I dream of becoming a global expert in whatever my career is or will be. I dream to have my own family. I dream of spending more time in Europe with my family. I dream to have a little house at the beach. I dream one day to go back to teach business at my alma mater. I dream of achieving and accomplishing something powerful and good.

Ileana

Dear Ileana,

Thank you for baring your thoughts and your soul to me over the last few days. I loved hearing of your dreams and aspirations. To be fully human is to appreciate beauty, goodness and truth wherever we find them, and work to integrate these into our lives. You appear to be doing this well.

Here are my reflections on what you have written. Please note these are my observations, and only become yours if you choose to own them. You can accept none or all. If something resonates with you, then sit with it. If not, leave it be.

Purpose: The really big question we wrestle with in life is 'why was I born?' or 'what is the purpose of my life?' The broad answer is 'to do big things'. But which big things? Why was Anthony born? Why was Ileana born? What are we on this planet to do? What footprints will we leave behind? What will remain standing when we die?

Most people focus on creating a vision for their life. A vision—this job, that relationship, this location, etc.—is limited only by our imagination. And then we put together plans to make it happen: build our skills, make new connections…All very good and very wise, and important to life, but requiring effort on our part. And sometimes grinding effort. And sometimes after all the effort we still fall short of our vision.

Can I suggest to you that this appears to describe what you are going through: putting in considerable effort to create your future and being overwhelmed by the complexity, ambiguity and opportunity, compounded by distance from your family and culture? That's OK, by the way, and quite normal. But it's hard, hard work. And there's a better way.

And that way is finding your purpose. Purpose is far bigger than vision for one's life. Purpose is what you were born to do.

And here's the absolutely amazing thing, which overwhelms me every time I think about it. Fulfilling your purpose requires no effort at all. It just requires accepting your purpose and surrendering to it, which is almost always scary at the start. The reason it requires no effort is because the power to fulfil our purpose is derived from the purpose rather than us. Hope that makes sense. If not, read it again until it does.

Do you remember those science fiction films where the spaceship flies out to the intergalactic docking station, which then 'draws' it in? Purpose is like that. It is a gravitational force that draws us in. Resistance is futile, although if we don't know what our purpose is we tend to fight the pull, which is very tiring.

And here's the second absolutely amazing thing about purpose. As we move toward our purpose we meet others who have a similar purpose and can help us along the way. Once we surrender to purpose we orient ourselves in a particular direction. We are being drawn to 'this' place, and find ourselves moving more and more toward it. And then we meet the right people at the right time who are being drawn in a similar direction. Again ponder this until it makes sense. Just as you meet opera lovers at the opera, you will also meet the people you need to meet to support you on your journey toward your purpose.

And here's the third absolutely amazing thing about purpose. We can live it now. It manifests and grows over time, but once we surrender to our purpose it starts to grow within us and around us.

That's the background. Here's my suggestion about your purpose, gleaned from your own words, stated from your point of view:

'I was born to foster a new renaissance.'

You are a renaissance woman (think about that) with a rich cultural heritage and deeply held values. Italy is close to your heart in all its commercial, cultural, social, historical dimensions, where the seeds of the first Renaissance were sown.

You are drawn not just to 'renew' Italy, but to advance Italian insights to the rest of the world. This does not arise from a sense of superiority but a sense of service and generosity of spirit. It arises as you observe what is happening in the world around you and appreciate the true value that an Italian perspective can bring. Not everyone sees what you see. No-one has your unique set of gifts, skills and talents.

Everything you have written is about bringing Italy to the world, which includes bringing Italy to itself. This is a renaissance movement.

And you can do this. You put structure where there is no structure. You learn and pass on what you have learned. You can organise things and facilitate people. Your heart enjoys serving and supporting. I suspect you practise the art of *sprezzatura*—in the sense of the art of effortless living—or have adopted it unconsciously. If that is the case can I suggest you make it a conscious habit?

Do those words resonate: 'I was born to foster a new renaissance?' Could you surrender your life to fostering a new renaissance? Could you devote your life to helping Italy become all it can be, to helping good Italian companies prosper overseas, to helping people discover the richness of Italian culture and the (true) Italian approach to life? Can you get up each day intent on fostering the values of creativity and enquiry, of art and learning, of science and music, among those you meet?

What could this mean for work? If fostering a new renaissance is your purpose, what 'job' do you do? This is a very different question, and one that is overwhelming you at the moment. The answer is simple, although the decision may be hard.

Once we know our purpose, we then make choices that align with that purpose. This helps us get more and more aligned with what we were born to do.

Therefore, consider every opportunity—whether work, relationships, where you spend your time, etc.—and ask whether it helps you fulfil your purpose. This can be answered in two ways. A particular job, for example, may not align closely with your purpose but it will enable you to acquire or hone the skills you need, build contacts...Or, secondly, the work may set you more clearly on the path toward your purpose.

Look at the opportunities in front of you right now. Eliminate any that don't help you move toward you purpose (although remain realistic: you do need a job and you do need to eat).

It can take many years for everything to come into alignment. But don't despair, the journey is rich, varied and wonderful. Your career choices start orienting you in a different direction and you add new skills. Your relationships start shifting or refining. You start spending your time in different ways, and you stop wasting time. Slowly but surely your life comes into alignment as you surrender to your purpose.

Regardless of which job you choose, or how you spend your time, focus on living your purpose in every moment. As you go about your work, your role with the opera, meeting new people...always approach it from the perspective of 'fostering a new renaissance'. In practical terms, you could frame this as a question to ask yourself at the end of each encounter with someone, or at the end of each day. You could ask yourself, for example, 'Did I help move this firm/this person to become a little more cultured, a little more mature, a little more generous...?' (you can come up with your own questions). The point is that you can find ways to live out your purpose immediately and every day.

And as you find yourself at the end of each day a little further advanced along the road toward your purpose, then each month you are closer, each year you are closer. And then suddenly you are living it in every dimension of your life. And that is tremendously rewarding and fulfilling.

One final observation: most people are already living their purpose in some sort of way but have not articulated it. Once they can name it, it comes to life and the power in your purpose is unleashed.

Anthony

Dear Anthony,

This is so beautiful and truthful ... I will need to read it again and again. This is like when we find a new song: you really understand it — deeply — after listening to it 10 times.

Everything resonates with me. [Here Ileana provided some relevant proof points from her life.] I never considered calling myself a 'renaissance woman' and it makes perfect sense. It speaks to me. Now all the books that I have surrounded myself with over the past year make sense as well.

... everything I do ... usually has Beauty in it.

Thank you,

Ileana

Ileana's story is comparable to many others: the search for meaning, being so near yet so far, not seeing in yourself what others see in you, the desire to do great things. You may have recognised parallels to your own life.

A little aside. You may have noticed that I dedicated this book to Giovanna, the Italian Joan of Arc. This dedication is to you and for you. This book is for everyone who has a Giovanna or Giovanni, a Joan or a John, inside them wanting to burst out and change the world. This is for everyone who may think they are irrelevant and inconsequential in the world's eyes, yet who has a passion and purpose burning within. This book is for you as you accept and live out your purpose and so change the world.

What will remain standing?

As I searched for my own purpose many years ago I stumbled across 'I am not I', a poem by the Spanish poet Juan Ramon Jimenez, winner of the 1956 Nobel Prize in Literature.

The poet wrestles with the question of identity, the perennial question of 'Who am I?', and concludes by inviting the reader to consider what will remain standing when they die.

This question was served up to me like an unexpected bowling ball, knocking over all my pins and urging me to answer the question: 'What will remain standing?'

While Archimedes encouraged me to find a firm place on which to stand, Jimenez asked what would remain standing when I no longer stood there. It's an existential question at my ultimate moment of Beauty, Goodness and Truth. What stands cannot be a monument or a monologue, a dissertation or a deal. Since friendship precedes commerce then the answer must lie in relationships, not results.

I realised that the most enduring legacy I can create is in the lives of those around me. Would people meet my family and friends and sense my presence, my values, my purpose and my principles? I sat down and wrote my own eulogy, contemplating what people would say at my funeral—and naturally imagining words of wisdom and wit, of graciousness and kindness.

Expressing this helped me grasp both the people who are important to me, and the gap between where I was and where I needed to be if they were indeed to speak as well as I might hope. This generated a set of actions I could initiate for ongoing development. This perspective provided the impetus to focus on the end game, reorienting myself toward what really mattered rather than what was merely interesting. It motivated me to discover my purpose and answer the questions I had asked Ileana.

Those answers have shaped my entire life around relationships and humanity, toward helping people to be all that they can be, become the best leaders they can be, and so build the best corporations, communities and countries for the good of all people.

What is your purpose?

You may wish to take the time to ponder these same questions and exercises, being honest and dreaming big, remaining open to Beauty, Goodness and Truth wherever they may be revealed:

- What will remain standing when you die?

- What will people say at your funeral?

  - Imagine your family, friends and colleagues as they articulate the wonderful impact you have had on their lives.

  - Write at length what they will say.

- Write a story—in as much detail as possible—about a time when you felt closely aligned to your purpose.

  - What were you doing when you felt, 'This is what I was born to do'?

  - What did you feel, where were you, who were you with, and so on?

  - How do you feel now when you look back on this?

- Imagine you are able to do that (operate in close alignment with your purpose) in everything you do.

  - Who would be the people/group you would most love to be serving/helping?

  - What draws you to them?

- These people change in some way as a result of your helping them, and they will then touch others in a new and different way. Your impact will extend from one person to the next like ripples in a pond.

  - What would happen in the world as a result of this spreading out, this touching and passing on that you started? Remember, you are limited here only by your imagination. So dream big and don't be afraid of anything, no matter how grand it sounds.

– What would the world and its people be like?

– What kind of world would we all experience?

Can I suggest to you that your purpose is to be found here, in this final reflection? As you touch people in your unique way, they then touch others. This fosters a different world in both small and large ways. In this way you shape today and tomorrow and leave your mark on the world. We all leave a legacy. Yours can be profound.

Although Gandhi, King, Mother Teresa and Mandela may not have performed such a self-conscious exercise, this is what underlies their actions. It is knowing where to align their time and energy with the needs of world, and to do it in a way that has maximum impact.

You can do the same.

What is your purpose in life? Why are you on this planet? How will the world be different as a result of your contribution? Don't be afraid in your answer. Be powerful.

* * *

Having established your destination, it is time to consider who you will be on the journey. How will you show up among family and friends, at work and at leisure? You can choose to be a wonderful human being with a rich set of personal relationships, and you can become that today.

The secret to becoming the best you can be was discovered by Plato and the ancient Greeks and by Confucius and the ancient Chinese at a very similar time in history. That secret is a life of virtue.

CHAPTER 9

A life of virtue

'Virtue is its own reward.'

MARCUS TULLIUS CICERO

'What is your vice?' asked Graeme as we lounged over the ship's railing, gazing out on the Sea of Japan.

'Wine, women or song?' he prompted. He was sure that everyone had a vice, and that knowing which vice was a good way of getting to know one another, although I suspect it was his way of finding co-conspirators in immorality and wrongdoing. I was a new recruit, having left home—and all my upbringing, culture and sheltered environment—just a week earlier. I was now in a foreign land, embarking on a new life, making choices about the way I acted, free from family constraints and the intrusiveness of a small country town.

How would I choose? How would I reply?

'Women,' I blurted out, provoking a satisfied smirk and a twinkle in Graeme's eyes. Realistically this was an easy choice. I did not drink alcohol, so wine came a distant third, and music didn't seem like much of a vice. If anything it was a delight. So women it was, and at 17 I thought that sounded very grown up.

Graeme nodded knowingly. 'I think we've all got that one,' he said knowingly. We continued to gaze out at the sea, as mariners have done for eons, sharing an illusory bond of deep brotherhood.

Do I have a vice? I wondered. *Do we all have one? Is that how we get to know one another?*

It seemed to me a strange question. 'What football team do you follow?' or 'Where are you from?' were surely more appropriate opening lines. I think I had a set of 'moral' values, although had never thought too deeply about them, largely accepting the values and practices of those around me.

A few days earlier I had sat in the front end of a Japanese Airlines jumbo flying into Tokyo. A week before that I had been camping in a remote forest in south-eastern Australia. And a week earlier still I had been a schoolboy finishing his final exams. Now my world had been tipped upside down. The security of family and friends was substituted by a ship's crew of 37 men. The waterfront world in which we worked attracted every nation on Earth, and every variation of violence and vice.

I remember thinking during the flight that I was at a moment of transition and choice, an abrupt shift from childhood to adulthood, when I left one life behind and started anew … my own game-changing moment. Graeme's question was the first of many opportunities to choose, to shape my life in one direction or another.

We all encounter moments when the choice we make will influence and shape the kind of person we become. Clearly good choices will move you in the direction of becoming a good person, and good choices are in the realm of what are called virtues.

Navigating this chapter

Having considered *Here* and *There*, the next two chapters examine the question of *Being: Who you are going to be on the way?*

This chapter reflects on a life of virtue, and how the virtues can shape the design of your life, of the person you are and the person you become. It has six sections:

- 'Good habits become virtues' explains what a virtue is and introduces the four cardinal virtues: Prudence (or wisdom), Justice, Self-control and Courage.

- 'Virtue: acquired through practice' discusses the very practical things that can be done to grow in virtue.

- 'Virtue as a "mean" ' explains that virtues are not binary, as in either black or white, but rather the safe path between two extremes.

- 'Do virtues matter today?' suggests that they are just as relevant now as when Plato and Aristotle grappled with them 2500 years ago.

- 'Virtues are the foundation for a life of excellence' proposes that the virtues are a basic building block of character and an outstanding life.

- 'Virtues and Human-Centred Leadership' argues that because virtues are an important aspect of character, they are a critical component in Human-Centred Leadership.

Good habits become virtues

You may recall being told, 'Patience is a virtue', as your parents rejected your nagging entreaties. If you are anything like me you would have wished they had simply consented to your request rather than resorting to a cryptic proverb.

So what are virtues, and are they relevant today? I believe they are perhaps more relevant now than when the philosophers wrote about them almost two and a half thousand years ago. The virtues 'humanise' you, helping you to become more of a person, a better person.

Plato and Aristotle held that *virtues are good habits acquired by repeated practice*. They noted four in particular that they called 'cardinal' virtues: prudence, justice, courage and self-control.[1]

When Plato used the word *cardinal* he was referring to a 'hinge' around which a door swings, a fulcrum point if you like. I prefer to think of the four cardinal points of a compass—north, south, east and west. Just as these showed me the way across the seas, the four cardinal virtues are sound guides on the journey of life. They provide direction for living a good life, for navigating in uncharted waters.

The cardinal virtues are discussed in more depth in the next chapter, so for the moment a brief description will suffice:

- *Prudence* can be thought of as 'practical wisdom'. As you pursue your goal of becoming the best person you can be, prudence helps you choose well between good alternatives, with regard to what you should or should not do. Practical wisdom draws on what is true and good and shines a light on the best path for you to walk on your particular journey to greatness, and it enables you to help others on their path.

- *Justice* helps you to appreciate that we are all members of the human community and to balance what is owed to you with what is owed to others, while pursuing what is good for the other person.

- *Courage,* or fortitude to the ancients, gives you the strength to endure or stand firm in the cause of what is right, and to confront and overcome fear when doing so, even at the risk of a mortal wound. In a relational context it is the pursuit of what is good for someone else when it is difficult or dangerous for you to do so.

- *Self-control* integrates your physical and emotional desires to help you choose and do what is truly good for yourself and others. It provides the restraint you use when you refuse to be overcome by destructive pleasures in people or in things. It was once called 'temperance', before the term came to be linked with temperance leagues and prohibition and fell out of favour.

Plato believed that cultivating the virtues was the key to living a good or 'flourishing' life.

How do you cultivate virtue to build that good life? You practise.

Virtue: acquired through practice

Do you remember when you set out to learn a new skill such as riding a bike, learning a language or taking up a musical instrument? Do you recall those times you were pushed beyond your ability and put in long hours to learn new concepts and new jargon, to build new relationships? You may have read all you could on the subject or sought advice from others, possibly looked for a role model, or even invested in lessons or coaching.

Do you remember the learning experience—how strange and uncomfortable it felt at the start, and the times you wondered if you would ever succeed?

When you repeatedly perform the same action, you develop a memory of how to do it, so it becomes a bit easier next time. You learn how to balance on a bike or form foreign sounds or select the right note, or where to focus your leadership attention. As your physical and intellectual muscles strengthen the task becomes easier, and then habitual. After much perseverance you find that what was once difficult has become routine, and then you practise to maintain and advance your skill level.

Elite athletes, military personnel and professional musicians all understand the value of developing good habits so they can do what is necessary when it is necessary. Just as you can train to run a race, fight a battle or play Beethoven, you can also train to do the right thing. However, you need to keep working on the basic skills that underpin good habits, in the same way athletes keep working on their basic skills. In this way you develop the 'moral muscles' that strengthen your ability to make better choices, act in better ways and so become the best possible version of yourself.

Practising patience, for example, when you feel harried and rushed helps develop patience. Then one day you realise you are a patient person. You have acquired the virtue of patience (or at least its foundations).

Similarly, practising the little things you find hard and where you feel exposed—such as politely speaking out when you hold a very different point of view, or not ignoring someone who needs help—builds the habit of courage. And then one day you will do something quite courageous. You have acquired the virtue of courage.

Growth in virtue and good human habits—growth, that is, in humanity—is a lifelong work made easier by repeated practice. Hence you become more courageous by adopting a courageous approach to life and trying to be courageous whenever the occasion presents itself. The same is true of wisdom, self-control or any other virtue. You become more patient by practising patience, wise by practising wisdom, humble by practising humility.

However, like the horizon you never reach, you never fully acquire a virtue. The moment you consider yourself wise or patient you will almost certainly encounter a situation that tests the limits of your wisdom or patience.

In this sense the virtues are both part of your journey and a destination. They exist along a continuum: you steadily become more virtuous, more patient or more wise, for example. Although you may be patient in some areas, you can be painfully aware of those times when you show impatience. Although others may consider you wise, you are well aware of your lack of insight.

Imagine for a moment that continuum as a highway from one place to another. The path of virtue is not as narrow and well defined as the white line down the middle of the road. It is as wide and broad as the road itself, giving you room to manoeuvre, to drive to the conditions and still stay on the road. It is when you drift off either side of the road that you risk an accident. Virtue is like that. Rather than a black or white choice between virtue and depravity, between morality and immorality, it is actually the middle way between too much and too little.

Virtue as a 'mean'

The Greeks described the virtues as a mean, or midpoint, between extremes—like our road that runs through the fields. Virtue does not exist in opposition to vice, such as patience versus impatience, or generosity versus greed, but in the midpoint between two vices. One of these constitutes a deficiency of virtue and the other an excess of virtue, where excess means 'too much' rather than 'excellence', such as overcooking the steak or driving too fast on the freeway. While courage is your road to heroism, the excess of recklessness and the deficiency of cowardice lie off to either side. Impatience is a deficiency of patience, while an overabundance of patience means procrastination.

This concept of virtue as a midpoint is a very important distinction. People insist, for example, on honesty from their business and political leaders, and rightly so. However, when we have a binary view of virtue and so believe that whatever is not honest is dishonest, we can be too quick to accuse people of lying. Honesty is not the opposite of dishonesty, but rather the middle ground between withholding truth—lying—and telling far too much. There are some matters that should not be disclosed, and withholding them is not lying or being dishonest. It is usually being prudent. This distinction does not excuse the person who intentionally withholds information that they have an obligation to reveal.

I know a man who holds 'transparency' as perhaps his most important value. He has genuinely tried to make a virtue of honesty. However, he has failed to appreciate the nuance of virtue being the middle ground, and not one side of a coin. The consequence of this is that he believes that failure to 'tell all' is being dishonest both to himself and to others. Hence within a few minutes of meeting you he will reveal intimate details about himself and his world that you would rather not know, and often should not know. He will disclose corporate information and details of current and former relationships in an unhealthy and untimely way.

He has drifted to the excess of telling far too much, because he thinks the only alternative is dishonesty, which he repudiates. His habitual practice of revealing excruciating details and his inability to appreciate discretion mean those around him are very circumspect about what they say. In short, he is untrustworthy. This is a classic example of how a virtue can become distorted.

Perhaps the next time you hear someone (and it could be you) talking about a virtue or value, ask yourself whether they are adopting a binary approach, or whether there are in fact two extremes—on the one hand too much and on the other too little.

Do virtues matter today?

James Madison, the fourth President of the United States, asked rhetorically whether virtue might be found among us. If not, he said, 'we are in a wretched situation. No theoretical checks—no form of Government can render us secure. To suppose that any form of Government will secure liberty or happiness without any form of virtue in the people, is a chimerical idea'.[2]

Madison recognised the link between personal virtue and social cohesion. Is it possible that human society is being undermined by a deficit of character? Is it possible that society lacks the depth of character needed to address the shifts and transitions before us? Are we looking to external authorities, such as governments, to protect freedom and harmony, when the answer could lie within us?

Do we (generally) lack virtue, or am I being a bit harsh on humanity? To be honest, I sometimes feel like I am watching a car crash in slow motion as society drifts from the road of virtue to the paddocks of vice on either side. In case that sounds like I am preaching or moralising that is not my intent. I do not want to suggest how you should act or live. I do, however, want to suggest that a world committed to the search for Beauty, Goodness and Truth, to fostering and supporting lives of virtue, would look and feel different from what we have today.

Warning signs of the car crash appear frequently in the media:

Chinese students 'sitting their university entrance exams erupted into siege warfare after invigilators tried to stop them from cheating'. The supervisors retreated to the safety of the school offices while 'an angry mob of more than 2000 people had gathered to vent its rage, smashing cars and chanting: "*We want fairness. There is no fairness if you do not let us cheat*"'.[3] Parents in the crowd argued cheating was endemic, and so the only way to be fair was to let their children cheat too.

And before we start pointing fingers at the Chinese, 'around 60 students at Harvard University have been suspended and others disciplined in a mass cheating scandal at the elite college…'[4]

Even some lawyers lack virtue:

'Hendrick Jan van Es was found to be "not a fit and proper person" to remain on the Supreme Court's local roll of lawyers because he had taken forbidden notes, tucked down his trousers, into an "ethics for barristers" examination'.[5]

What kind of society would we enjoy if these kinds of behaviour become normalised and acceptable? Will it become harder or easier to know how to act in good ways, and to find role models we can emulate? It is already getting difficult.

Virtues are the foundation for a life of excellence

Have you ever found yourself doing things you don't want to do? Perhaps you haven't smuggled notes into an exam or cheated in order to level the playing field. However, if you are anything like me, you are well aware of things you have done that you would prefer had never happened. I'm sure without much reflection you can recall times when you have behaved badly, when you have not lived up to your ideals. I know I can. And if my memory fails me there are enough people close to me who are more than able—and often willing—to remind me of my failings.

Sometimes we choose to do things we don't want to do because of a desire for immediate gratification. Sometimes we enjoy what is 'bad' and only later consider the negative consequences of our actions on ourselves and others. We all do things we later regret. These become a problem, though, when you resign yourself to such behaviour and it becomes habitual.

What these tendencies indicate is firstly that you are human, not perfect, and secondly that you need to cultivate good habits to build a good life. Despite the best of intentions to be a good person, a good friend, a good worker, manager or leader, you can fall short of the ideals to which you aspire, be distracted by the siren call of pleasure in its many and varied forms, or be undermined by your own selfishness and self-interest. Unless you actively cultivate good habits and a life of virtue, you risk being caught up in fads, feelings and infatuations.

Virtues are the foundation stone to building a good life, because they give you the power to choose wisely and well. They are a basic skill set of character, not dissimilar to the fundamental intellectual skills of reading, writing and 'rithmetic. In a sense they are the fourth 'r': right living. By cultivating right living, or virtue, it becomes easier to do what matters, to do what is right, to do what needs to be done when it needs to be done. This is a basic skill for the art of living, and living with some form of excellence—for building a flourishing human life.

In the same way you develop, say, technical expertise and commercial acumen for success in certain roles and tasks, you also need to equip yourself for success in living, for success in relationships. The virtues help you do this. They give you the wisdom, courage, self-control, patience, generosity and humility to live well with yourself and others. Among other things, they can prompt:

- patience to endure another's faults—and also give them patience to endure your failings

- courage to stand up for others, and to stand in opposition to others when necessary

- a sense of justice that prompts you to treat others fairly

- the self-control that refuses to treat another person as only a source of pleasure

- humility to recognise you are not the centre of the universe

- generosity to be well disposed toward others and not hurt them

- wisdom to recognise when work is crowding out relationships that matter

- a wiser, more prudent, approach that fosters good relationships between individuals, societies and nations.

What do you do, though, when you don't feel at all virtuous?

Act as if

'Act as if' is a very powerful technique for improving our habits and growing in virtue. Here's how you can do this.

Assume for a moment that you are starting to feel you could do more for others, and so decide to practise the virtue of generosity.

The first few times you are generous feel a bit clunky and unnatural, even embarrassing. As you practise generosity in many little ways it becomes easier and more natural. While you are trying to be generous you can struggle with 'how much' or 'how little', unsure of who deserves your help and who doesn't. You can fail to be generous when you are feeling a bit selfish. That's okay. It's normal to have these kinds of inner conflicts.

Then one day you start feeling there is no end to the people who ask for your help, and you suddenly don't feel generous at all.

What do you do if you remain committed to generosity and yet realise that you don't want to help someone, that you would rather not be generous? This conflict occurs because you are trying to become someone different, someone generous, and working out what that means for you.

There are two things you can do when you face these kinds of struggles: firstly, remind yourself of your commitment to growing in generosity and becoming a generous person; secondly, in the meantime when you don't feel generous, act generously—'act as if'.

Act as if you are generous. Ask yourself what a generous person would do in your situation. Would they help? Then help. Would they make a donation? Then donate.

You may not feel generous. You may not feel differently after being generous. However, you don't need to feel generous to be generous. Although I can guarantee you that if you act generously in moments that call for generosity, you will grow in the virtue of generosity. And then one day someone will describe you as a 'generous person'.

You can 'act as if' to acquire any habit or virtue.

Virtues are a foundation to character

Cultivating virtue is the starting point for building a life of character. The virtues give you insight into what is good, empathy to understand what is good for others and strength to do what is good.

Benjamin Franklin made it his life's work to acquire virtue, annotating a journal with his progress or regress with respect to the virtue he was working on developing at each moment. His list of 13 virtues included very practical virtues such as silence, order, frugality, sincerity, cleanliness and humility. You can find the full list with a quick web search.

I once tried to emulate Franklin, drawing up a monthly calendar with a virtue to focus on for that month. Ticks and crosses indicating success or failure steadily accumulated. Before long I had a messy exercise book full of inexplicable marks, and a messy head from my efforts to scrupulously examine the intricacies of every action. The process overwhelmed me and I probably became less virtuous. By micromanaging the minutes I lost sight of growing in virtue and instead grew in obsessiveness.

Although I found Franklin's approach a bit too meticulous I learned two valuable lessons:

1   Focus on one or two virtues at a time. Remember, it is impossible to perfect any of them, let alone all of them.
2   Do this in a mindful way, reflecting on your progress and paying attention to those times when you do well, and those areas where you can improve.

You may wish to try a similar exercise. Search online for a list of human virtues and perhaps adopt one or two for your life and one or two for each year. For example, you may wish to devote your life to acquiring wisdom—a noble pursuit—and also focus this year on becoming more patient or generous or caring.

However, let me forewarn you. Have you ever noticed that when you decide to give up chocolate or wine—say, for a month—you find yourself confronted by an abundance of tempting chocolate or particularly good vintage wines? It can seem as though the universe is having a laugh at your expense. Focusing on a virtue can be like that. If you decide to focus on patience, or humility, or generosity, you will find more challenges to being patient, humble or generous than you would have thought humanly possible. And when you do ... laugh along with the universe.

Virtues and Human-Centred Leadership

By consistently acting in a virtuous way you will become a more virtuous person. A virtuous person is a person of moral character, someone who makes wise decisions about how to act and then implements those decisions in a virtuous way—with patience, humility, generosity ... Virtuous men and women are attractive leaders, because people know virtuous leaders care, know they are trustworthy and rarely self-centred.

Growing in virtue and the exercise of virtue is a lifelong work, but an enormously rewarding one. It is never too late to start and yet always too early to stop. A life of virtue is the key to human flourishing, the foundation to becoming all you can be. By extension, therefore, it is a critical component in Human-Centred Leadership, building human-centred enterprises and nations, and creating a rich and flourishing culture.

Having introduced virtue and the virtuous life, in the next chapter I will briefly explore the five crucial leadership virtues: humility and the four cardinals of wisdom, courage, justice and self-control.

A relational virtue ethics for the 21st century?

Something kept troubling me about Plato's view of the good life and human flourishing, but I found it hard to put my finger on it. Then I realised that although the virtues centre on others, it becomes all too easy to focus on me and my enjoyment of a good life.

When I landed on the concept that a person is a 'relational being' it started to prod my moral reasoning. I began to wonder if integrating ancient virtues with a relational anthropology might offer a slightly new perspective. Might this provide a 21st century virtue ethics? These are the kinds of questions that idea raises for me:

- In a 21st century virtue ethics is the 'good', as in that which promotes a good life, not just what is in accord with my humanity but what is in accord with being in relationship?

- Could a 21st century virtue ethics ask not 'Is this wise for me?' but 'Is this wise for us and for you?'

- Could an act be considered courageous, for example, when it is done in the pursuit of good for another? Do acts of courage mostly include care for others?

- Could this be true of all actions—that they have some sort of link to a person, whether me or someone else?

- Is true self-control (temperance, that is) when I temper my actions out of respect for your human dignity, not merely mine?

- Is 21st century moral leadership a selfless service of others through which I become all that I can be—that is, fully human?

(continued)

A relational virtue ethics for the 21st century? *(cont'd)*

- Is our full humanity realised only when we place others at the centre of all our decisions and actions?

- Rather than making decisions using either rule- or results-based ethics, what might happen if I made decisions based on relational ethics?

- Is 'Do nothing to damage your relationships with yourself, your family and friends, your society and world, your god' a reasonable principle by which to live?

Values or virtues

I am often asked if there is any difference between values and virtues. This question usually arises in a corporate context, in which people are encouraged to abide by a set of company values. You would be familiar with many of them: courage, honesty, integrity, openness ...

It's essential for organisations to clarify their values, and to imbue every aspect of the firm with these.

It's also possible to have a personal set of values. For example, I value freedom, which manifests in my response to everything from slavery to workplace bullying to respect for other people's opinions. This value, however, is a manifestation (for me) of a lifelong concern for the virtue of justice and becoming a more just person.

Values are not virtues, even though the words used may be the same or very similar. The power to act is derived from an entirely different source. Many firms, for example, include honesty in their list of corporate values. They explain how they intend to be honest in their dealings with customers and staff. They sound like pillars of virtue when they talk about openness and honesty, and can crumble like pillars of sand under close examination.

A totally honest corporate environment is extremely rare, despite the best of intentions and statements. Dishonesty can permeate an organisation. Board members are sometimes not fully frank in their dealings with one another, perhaps because they lack courage or don't want to rock the boat or endanger their position. Executives may pursue two agendas, one serving the firm and the other serving themselves. Colleagues can say one thing and calmly do another.

This behaviour is rarely called out because we can't quite put our finger on what's wrong. And besides, the job is getting done, results delivered, and staff, customers and stakeholders seem satisfied.

So what is the difference between values and virtues? The difference is that we can do honest things, because that's what the firm values, without being (or becoming) an honest person. Espousing the value of honesty does not necessarily mean developing the virtue of honesty. Someone can, for example, be honest at work—to the degree expected—and be a scheming liar outside of work.

The power to abide by values arises from the external influence of the organisational, or social, culture. The power to live a life of virtue arises from within, from your character. Values are written on the corporate wall while virtues are written in the human heart.

Do you think it might make more sense, therefore, for organisations to foster the virtue of honesty, which will result in honest practices and an honest culture? I think ethics training would then get a whole lot easier.

CHAPTER 10

Five virtues for effective leadership

'You must cultivate humility…'

CONFUCIUS

'All true readiness to help starts with humility toward the one I want to help, and therefore I must understand that wanting to help is not to rule and reign, but a wish to serve the person. If I can't do that, then I can't help anybody either.'

SOEREN KIERKEGAARD

Humility: *the* leadership virtue

Major General Andy Salmon, former head of the British Royal Marines, surprised me when he named *humility* as an element of 'commando culture'.[1] Who would have thought humility had a place in what appears to be such a tough, unforgiving world?

He explained that personal 'Commando Spirit'—determination, courage, cheerfulness in the face of adversity, and unselfishness—combines with collective values such as excellence and integrity to create the overall Commando ethos. Humility is one of the Commando group values.

'Commandos need humility so they can learn from their mistakes,' said General Salmon. 'Ego and prima donnas don't belong. As a part of our culture we practise "Team first, buddy second and self last". In order to be humble and lose your ego, you have to lose yourself.'

This sounds obvious in a military environment, since failure to learn from mistakes could have tragic consequences in combat. But it seems to me that everyone, not just soldiers, needs a little humility in order to learn, grow and develop.

Navigating this chapter

This chapter continues to discuss the question of *Being: Who are you going to be on the way?* Having introduced the concept of virtue in the previous chapter, this chapter provides an overview of the virtues of humility, wisdom, courage, justice and self-control, and their application to leadership. These virtues can accelerate your progress toward becoming a human-centred leader.

Humility enables learning

I sometimes provide fairly direct feedback to powerful CEOs, often confronting them on how they see themselves. This comes about because they acknowledge they can have blind spots, biases and behavioural issues that limit their leadership effectiveness.

The process involves talking to people who know them well, obtaining a sufficient range of perspectives to get a fairly balanced view. Although extreme surprises are rare, there are almost always profound insights. It requires humility for the CEO to take on board the feedback.

Not all feedback is as structured as this. Sometimes leaders get it without asking.

One day I was with a client at the regional headquarters of his firm, which overlooked the business centre and across to a bustling port. We discussed his board strategy presentation and the decision he intended to recommend. As we examined various options it became clear that he could not support an alternative decision, and would (graciously) resign if that was the outcome.

One month later he updated me on a number of initiatives and the challenges he was facing, and he casually mentioned that the board had adopted the decision he opposed and proceeded to talk about the implementation process. My mind was drawn back to our earlier conversation.

'You said you would resign if the board didn't accept your recommendation,' I responded (politely) in surprise, with perhaps a little hint of a challenge.

Everything went still…and quiet.

I sensed the turmoil in his emotions, as he frowned at me, and perhaps at himself, searching for a response to someone who had just confronted his thinking and his position. The feeling passed quickly as he gathered his thoughts and settled back into his chair with a thoughtful look.

'You're right,' he said. 'I'd forgotten about that. I wonder what that means?'

That moment of possible weakness—admitting he had done a complete about-face on something that mattered considerably—provided the foundation for a powerful conversation about his values and what *really* mattered. He remained with the firm, but with a far deeper insight about himself. His newfound commitment enhanced his leadership focus.

Over many meetings and many years I have seen how his humility keeps him grounded in reality.

What is humility?

Humility starts with genuine self-acceptance of who you are, recognising and accepting your strengths and weaknesses, your humanity, personality and capability. In this sense humility is crucial to embracing Plato's injunction to 'First know yourself'. The humble person recognises their own talents and abilities and has no need to tell others of them. They celebrate the success of others, and are not bothered when their own role or contribution is overlooked. Humility recognises that there is always someone better than you at a given task or activity, and that there is always someone not as good as you at that task or activity.

The extreme of humility (self-abasement) falsely says, 'I am the worst', while the deficiency (self-aggrandisement) proudly says, 'I am the best'.

The self-centred, egotistical CEO is a well-known manifestation of that deficiency of humility we call hubris or pride. These destructive leaders enhance their standing by standing on others. You may have worked for a CEO who makes themselves the centre of attention, takes credit for every success and absorbs all the emotional energy whenever they enter a room. Contrast this with the impact of Mandela entering a room and merely by his presence inspiring everyone to be the best they could be.

High-profile or excessively well paid leadership roles can boost pride in anyone with this self-interested tendency. They become disconnected from reality and seduced into assuming their high profile or pay proves their superiority, as happened at Barclays, where 'pay contributed significantly to a sense among a few that they were somehow unaffected by the ordinary rules ... [They] seemed to lose a sense of proportion and humility ... the reputational problems [of the bank] stem in part from the perception that ... some bankers have appeared oblivious to reality'.[2]

False humility, at the other extreme, takes pride in being humble. It can be observed in the person who ungraciously dismisses the praise of others for a job well done or suggests that 'this time I was lucky' or 'it's not my best work'. While it's rare in CEOs it can be a showstopper for becoming a CEO. You know when you are observing false humility. You may see it as being inauthentic, or perhaps aloofness. While those who do not appreciate others make bad leaders, those who do not appreciate themselves are unlikely to become leaders since they appear weak and disingenuous.

True humility finds a balance between these extremes and provides a foundation to great leadership.

Humility makes you easier to follow

I think humility might be *the* leadership virtue because more than any other it makes it easy for people to follow you. It makes you 'followable' because your leadership is primarily about others rather than about you. It is a service virtue that places others first.

If you want people to follow you, to get behind you ... then get behind them.

Your fundamental responsibility as a leader — whether as President, Prime Minister or CEO — is to create an environment in which your people can flourish. This is Human-Centred Leadership, which revolves around those you serve, rather than around you.

Industrial models of leadership were built around the leader, with directives cascading through the organisation in a hierarchical structure of command and control. Proud, self-centred leaders can flourish in this structure, sometimes at the expense of their staff and customers.

Human-Centred Leadership inverts the pyramid by placing the CEO at the bottom, supporting and serving those above. Proud, self-centred leaders fail in this environment, and rarely know why, so they blame the markets, the managers or the moment. Humility becomes a source of strength in Human-Centred Leadership models (see figure 10.1).

Figure 10.1: the 21st century leader as servant

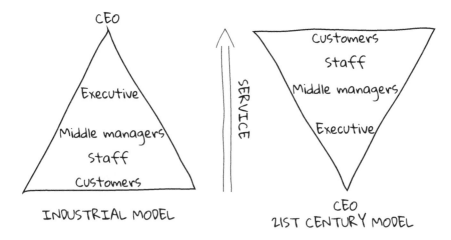

The impact of humility

Jim Collins and his team set out to find what makes companies great, as opposed to merely good, and described their findings in his landmark work, *Good to Great*. He considered specific measures of long-term financial health and sustainability as the hallmark of 'great' and extensively analysed similar companies operating in the same markets with the same opportunities, searching for those who met the criteria. He then compared those who, at an inflexion point, underwent some form of transformation to post long-term gains and stellar results with those who continued on their same trajectory and/or possibly fizzled out (see figure 10.2, overleaf).

Figure 10.2: from Good to Great

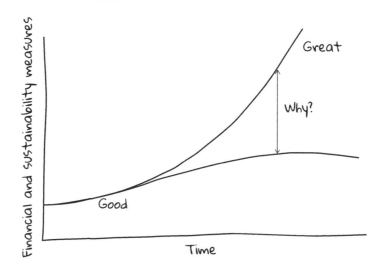

In *Good to Great* Collins explains the research process and suggests a number of factors that contribute to the success of the great. You will not be surprised to learn that quality of leadership has a significant impact. Firms that make the leap from mediocrity to superiority, he finds, are led by a 'Level 5 Executive: [who] builds enduring greatness through a paradoxical blend of personal humility and professional will'.[3] Collins suggests that when things go well these leaders point out the window to success factors beyond themselves, but when things go poorly they point at the mirror.

You may have heard the old saying, 'People join organisations and leave bosses'. While it is difficult to continue working for who puts themself first, it is much more difficult to leave a firm and leader who puts you first. Human-centred leaders who understand their responsibility to serve put people and their wellbeing first and so engender higher employee engagement and lower turnover.[4]

Humility allows you to be a servant rather than a master, to seek the wise counsel of others and listen carefully to their suggestions. It recognises and accepts the truth about yourself and others with regard to strengths and weaknesses, allowing people to 'be themselves' with no need to live up to an artificial or unrealistic ideal.

Humility is *the* leadership virtue, and hence at the heart of Human-Centred Leadership.

Practical wisdom

A wise old owl sat in an oak
The more he heard the less he spoke;
The less he spoke the more he heard.
Why can't we be like that old bird?

English nursery rhyme

The wisdom of a whistleblower

In 2004 Paul Moore, the head of Group Regulatory Risk at HBOS, a bank created in 2001 although with a heritage running back to the 17th century, courageously warned the board that the bank risked total collapse. He expressed concern that an unhealthy focus on profit was distracting the board and executives from systemic risk.

'We were providing low-doc loans, often in excess of the value of the property, in a booming property market, to people with little security other than the property. If the property market slowed, or the economy dipped, or there was any kind of a credit crunch, the size of our exposure to this market meant the bank was at risk,' he told me.[5]

He believed that the bank's strategy lacked prudence and that he had an obligation to speak out. His advice that the firm 'needed to review sales strategy to avoid risks' was ignored and not properly minuted by the board, enabling them to subsequently deny Moore had provided that advice.

'Risk managers predicted a crisis, but hubris prevented people from listening,' he said.

To Moore's great surprise he found himself in 'a battle of wits' with colleagues he had assumed would share a desire to do the right thing by the firm. As he continued to insist the organisation faced an existential threat he was progressively marginalised, until his legislated position was made redundant. In effect, he lost his job for providing wise advice in an environment where people were deaf to his concerns. His judgement was validated when Lloyds TSB acquired HBOS in January 2009 as it neared failure.

'It just never occurred to me that it would be less risky to be quiet . . . that I would be fired,' he said. 'I was acting out of love for the organisation. I did what I did because I cared. It never occurred to me that it would be misinterpreted as subversion.'

In my conversation with Moore I did not feel that I was sitting with a reclusive oracle as he delivered sage aphorisms, but rather with a dedicated worker who had tried valiantly to apply wisdom to the difficult and complex world of business and boardrooms.

'What would you do differently now?' I asked, both for my own insight and to discover if he had learned from his experience (one of the essential elements in acquiring wisdom).

'I would do the same thing,' he said without a moment's hesitation. 'But I would do it more slowly. I needed stronger relationships,' he reflected.

He continued to demonstrate the courage of his convictions and the wisdom of his insight. This is what Plato means by prudence: it is applied wisdom informed by courage and justice exercised in self-control.

I asked Moore the inevitable question: 'What influenced your moral formation?'

'This is what I was brought up with,' he said. 'My family taught me right from wrong, and it was in my nature to want to do the right thing. I always wanted truth, fairness and compassion.'

Prudence and practical wisdom

Ah, prudence . . . the queen of the virtues. I find her so alluring and have spent my life in search of her. Yet she continues to elude me, offering gossamer glimpses, fleeting touches and the occasional warmth of her radiance.

Only poetry can describe the attraction of wisdom. But just what is it?

Plato spoke of 'prudence' where we might speak of 'wisdom', so I will use these words interchangeably, although in both cases the meaning is very practical. Along with Plato, we are interested here in applied wisdom — practical rather than existential wisdom.

Prudence helps you integrate the virtues so you can 'figure out' how to act in a specific situation, by casting light on various good options and helping you discern which is best in your current circumstances. It is a powerful aid to decision making, enabling you not to avoid risk, but to take sensible risks. In that sense prudence guides your actions as the Venetian gondolier guides his craft, with a gentle sweep of his oar this way and that.

Think about that for a moment.

Do you want to know how to make better decisions and act in better ways? If you do, then commit yourself to growing in virtue, and wisdom in particular. (If you answered no, then you may wish to leave this book on a chair for someone else to pick up.)

Let me put it another way. Learning how to make better decisions and act in the best possible way will help you get promoted in business, recognised in government and respected in society. And in order to do that … grow in virtue.

You may not be leading a business, governing a country or influencing society, but you can prepare for that now by growing in wisdom. This is within your control.

The complexity, connectivity and convergence of the shifts discussed in Part I of this book require wisdom to navigate effectively. And wisdom requires deep thinking and reflection, which in turn require time and effort. This is one of the reasons why wisdom is often associated with age, although it can be acquired by anyone who wants to do the hard inner work on themselves — confronting biases and prejudices, rejecting the easy answers, becoming comfortable with discomfort.

Wisdom cannot be hurried. It needs time to think and reflect, to bubble to the surface.

How can you help that bubbling process?

Acquiring wisdom

Just as you can become more patient, or generous, or courageous, you can become wiser or more prudent. The foundation is a life of learning, seeking wisdom through the insights of others. Learn how to read for insight, not just information, study the Great Books, which provide a foundation to literature and thought; read widely across disciplines; read biographies of those who have influenced history and learn how they think and act; meet and interview people who demonstrate wisdom.

Another powerful way of growing in wisdom is to institute the practice of reviewing your decisions, both individually and collectively as a leadership team or board. Follow Peter Drucker's advice and write down why you make each decision, which options you have rejected, how you feel about the decision, what you will do to implement that decision, and specifically what the consequences of that decision will be in a given time frame.

This is a fundamental requirement for growing in wisdom. Most people think they make sound decisions, although they rarely subject these to rigorous scrutiny. Develop the habit of 'debriefing' your decisions and actions after the event when you can see the consequences in order to improve next time. As you learn to make better decisions, you acquire wisdom.

Robert Swannell, Chairman of Marks and Spencer, mentioned a very practical model for acquiring wisdom.[6] He recalled that when Citi acquired the investment banking business of the UK merchant bank Schroders, it instituted a 'wise elders' committee' consisting of a group of people who were not line managers and who could bring insight and perspective to a situation. Staff at all levels could approach this group at any time to hold an informal discussion and seek guidance on difficult reputational or risk issues.

'This practice replicated—in an unbureaucratic way—the practice of partners in smaller firms wandering into each other's rooms to discuss difficult issues,' he said. 'Convening the group was encouraged and equally failing to use it regarded as a failure. The reason for this is that failures and mistakes in investment banks are often the result of lonely or frightened people who feel unable or unwilling to seek help.'

Could your firm or organisation benefit from a similar practice? Nick Leeson, who brought Barings to its untimely demise when his £827 million loss (twice the bank's trading capital) was ultimately uncovered, told me he was too afraid to ask for help when he knew he was out of his depth.[7] A wise elder's committee could have saved both him and the firm from destruction.

Applying wisdom

When you are trying to decide on a course of action, you are applying wisdom to the problem at hand.

- Is Kirsten ready for increased responsibility?

- Should we grow organically or by acquisition?

- Is it time I moved on in my career to another role or another firm?

You have all the relevant reports and advice. You have the recommendations and suggestions. And now you must make a decision. You sense an element of risk.

You know there are no simple answers to these kinds of decisions. You are also aware that the choices made can have profound implications for you and others. Hence you require an element of wisdom, grounded in a questioning process, to choose wisely.

- What are Kirsten's skills and capabilities, how do these align to the new role and what development can we offer?

- Where are the opportunities for growth, what are the market trends, what are our competitors doing and what management capability do we have?

- Why am I considering leaving my current role, what opportunities exist and where will they lead?

Of course there are many more questions. The point is that you need wisdom not just to arrive at the answer but to know which questions to ask, from which disciplines and from which advisers. Practical wisdom enables you not to avoid risk, but to take sensible risks.

Then other virtues come into play. Wisdom may indicate a course of action, and courage may be required to promote Kirsten in the face of opposition, to approach another firm for a friendly merger or to back yourself for another role. Self-control may be required to wait until the time is right rather than acting in haste. Justice may insist on Kirsten's promotion.

Wisdom in isolation from other virtues sits on a mountaintop, sagely waiting for seekers to pose lofty questions. Wisdom informed by the moral virtues acts, and does so in the best possible manner. While wisdom may suggest a course of action, the other virtues provide the energy or power to act.

Courage

'I learned that courage was not the absence of fear, but the triumph over it... The brave man is not he who does not feel afraid, but he who conquers that fear.'

NELSON MANDELA

Courage does what's right

Mike walked casually toward the girls' tent and joined the conversation. It was one of the bravest acts I had ever seen, because he wasn't going to talk to the girls. He was going to distract troublemakers from the Mongrel Mob who were beginning to congregate.

We had met the two German tourists the night before, fellow travellers backpacking around New Zealand, sharing the camaraderie of life on the road. As we talked, the roar of cars and voices indicated the arrival of members of the Mongrel Mob, one of New Zealand's feared street gangs. Their brutality and violence was legendary, and grew with every telling. One gang member proudly recounted in some detail his initiation, including being thrown under a moving car after enduring several beatings and not showing weakness by going to hospital. Whether true or not, it was enough to put the frighteners on me.

The girls had quietly slipped away when the gang members arrived, hoping the thin fabric of their tent would act as a protective shield, despite our gentlemanly offer of greater safety in our cabin.

As we packed in the morning sunlight, early risers from the Mob noticed the girls and went across to introduce themselves. Mike and I kept a discreet watch as the tension built, with the girls becoming more anxious and the men looking more predatory. We agreed that the wisest course of action was to get us all out of there and back on the road before any others from the Mob were roused from their sleep. Hand signals toward the girls went unseen or ignored. I felt helpless, with no idea what to do.

And then suddenly Mike was walking toward them, telling the girls it was time we were all on the road, as though we were all travelling together. The Mob retreated slightly. The girls hastened their packing. The conversation tempo picked up as the gang members sensed a window of opportunity closing... and they were the sort of people who broke windows and kicked down doors. Mike continued calmly helping the girls get their gear together, while engaging in friendly banter with the threatening bullies.

Then the four of us slung our backpacks and walked determinedly out to the road, hoping we would pick up a ride before the Mob spotted our outstretched thumbs.

It worked out well, and Mike's example of courage stayed with me to this day. Unlike me, he refused to be a bystander, never betrayed fear or anxiety, and acted with confidence and courage in a potentially dangerous and highly volatile situation.

That's what the courageous do: they act for what is good even though their own wellbeing, and in some cases their life, could be in danger.

That's what Paul Moore did when he persisted in giving sound if unwelcome advice to protect the bank. That's what so many other whistleblowers do when they have the courage to speak out. They risk their reputation and career, and quite often their financial, emotional and physical health.

What is courage?

Courage is best known as a military virtue. We know and admire the heroism of soldiers in battle who are prepared to pay the ultimate price.

Courage also matters in business, government and society, and yet sometimes it seems to be in short supply. Where the soldier risks a mortal wound, the board director risks the loss of power, prestige, income and possibly friends by speaking out for what is right. The executive who confronts a board or questions company policy can require even greater courage, suddenly cast as an outsider against the inner circle. It takes courage for a CEO to advocate for the long term rather than the short term, for a President to promote peace in the face of conflict, for anyone anywhere to stand up as a lonely voice for what is right.

Courage is informed by truth and justice, and balanced by wisdom and self-control. Wisdom provides the insight to judge between alternatives: Should I say something or not? Considering all the options, what is the wiser course of action? What is the truth, or how close can I get to the truth amid a wide range of opinions? Courage then provides the impetus to act.

Where do you find the courage to challenge accepted policy or procedure? It usually starts as a moral sensitivity that detects something unacceptable, often in the way people or individuals are being treated. It arises from your sense of humanity and your concern for other human beings.

Human-Centred Leadership is courageous

Gandhi, King, Mandela, Aung San Suu Kyi and so many other inspirational leaders demonstrate courage in the face of overwhelming odds, often born of a sense of injustice.

It can be easy to decide from a distance how their character and destiny were forged in the heat of battle or through years of imprisonment. What we forget, however, is that the battle arose because they embraced their destiny, because they were true to their character. They had the courage to respond in the first instance.

When you say, 'I could never be a Mandela because I never spent time in jail for a cause', you are letting yourself off the hook, because Mandela didn't set out to go to jail. Gandhi was not the first Indian in South Africa to be thrown off a train. King was not the first African American menaced by the Klan.

But they were the ones who had the courage to say, '*It stops with me*'. In their words and actions they, and their ilk, say, '*No more*'. They refuse to accept the status quo. This response takes courage. This is the response you can make when you encounter injustice, inequality, corruption, intransigence, workplace bullying, board dishonesty, Cabinet disharmony or immorality.

If it's not right, it does not have to stay not right. And if you don't act ... who will?

This is what is different about great leaders. Not that they changed the world, but that they had the courage to stand up and go out into the world. This is why you can change the world, because in having the courage to stand and say, 'No more. It stops with me', you create the conditions for a new and different future. You have no idea where it will lead.

Justice

'*Let there be justice for all. Let there be peace for all. Let there be work, bread, water and salt for all. Let each know that for each the body, the mind and the soul have been freed to fulfil themselves.*'

NELSON MANDELA

Holding the moral ground

Major General Andy Salmon told me his father was a publican who ran, and cleaned-up, hotels in rough neighbourhoods, making them safe havens for the local community.

He described an instance when the police had been asked to help, but didn't because they wanted his father to receive stolen goods and inform on criminals. His father refused and was told by the local police that he was on his own, which gave thugs the opportunity to attack. Andy was 11 years old when violent men burst into their house, to be driven off by his father.

'After that incident,' he says, 'I was outraged, angry, disappointed and felt that justice had to prevail. Ever since then, I've wanted justice'.

This commitment to justice influenced Andy's decision to join the Royal Marines and informed his subsequent actions. To demonstrate this he recounted a story about a time he was on operations and received complaints from local people regarding activities some members of his unit were engaged in. He was initially defensive because he had commanded some of them during the Falklands War and had trusted them with his life. Nevertheless, he investigated the complaints to find them true and was shocked to find men he had trusted breaking the law. Reluctantly, and without hesitation, he charged some and sent the rest back to the UK.

As he recounted this story years later I could sense his enduring indignation at their offence against everything he believed in. They had let down their unit and had failed a fundamental test of virtue.

'I hate corruption in figureheads,' he continued, providing another example of how justice informs his thinking. 'It's just not on. So when I became the figurehead (in command of British forces in Iraq) I had a strong sense that I must stand for what is right, that I must occupy the moral ground.'

One CEO of a major firm was acutely aware of his responsibility to be more than a strategic leader. He wanted to exercise 'moral leadership' and wondered what this could mean with respect to his clients. The whiteboard before us was covered in words and ideas as he pushed his thinking and pondered on his and the firm's obligations toward various stakeholders.

He was committed to fairness and justice, and wanted to articulate this in a way that lifted the moral bar and that was readily understandable by colleagues and clients.

'I think we treat others fairly,' he said with reference to their clients. 'But I wonder if they feel the same way?' he added before I could get the question out.

'How about you ask them?' I suggested.

That seemed risky. What if they felt an inequality in the relationship, that they were not being treated fairly in some way? What could be the ramifications of that?

And then suddenly he had it, a new mantra that aligned with his own deeply held values: 'We don't take advantage of others for our own gain'.

This phrase is now driving a different conversation with clients of the firm, and puts fairness and justice front and centre in their dealings.

Justice responds to inequality

The need for justice arises when there is some form of inequality in relationships.

Hewlett-Packard was fined A$3 million for denying purchasers their rights to repairs under warranty, having instructed call centre staff to tell customers they had to pay for repairs and that replacements could be offered only after multiple repair attempts.[8] This is an astounding case of unconscionable corporate behaviour. It demonstrates a complete failure to treat people justly, taking advantage of the inequality in the relationship.

I cannot help wondering if any HP staff spoke out against this practice. Did anyone think it was wrong? Did anyone put themselves in the shoes of their customers?

A call for justice is heard when you are able to put yourself in another person's shoes and feel their pain and frustration. It builds on the simple idea of treating people as we would want to be treated in similar circumstances. Managers who deny liability to their customers would doubtless have no qualms about insisting on warranty repairs if their car broke down.

Justice gives to the other what is rightfully theirs—and this can be interpreted in surprising ways.

Sam Eisho fled Iraq to Greece with his wife in 1996 and was eventually sponsored by an uncle to come to Australia.[9] Arriving with nothing and struggling to make ends meet, the family relied on social welfare and government support. Sam eventually launched a construction business, which enjoyed modest success, employing a number of people and enabling him to put aside some money.

Then one day Sam walked into a government office with a cheque for more than A$18 000 to repay the welfare money he had received. A system set up to dispense money was unable to process a 'refund' so staff suggested Sam make a charitable donation, which he did in addition to other donations he has made.

His story demonstrates the virtues of hard work, of thrift, of generosity, of care and kindness (both given to him and received from him), of tolerance, of wisdom, and of justice with respect to the creation and distribution of wealth.

Justice starts now — with you

If we all had equal opportunity in every sense there would be no need for justice. The reality is, however, that some have more than others so have a special responsibility to treat them fairly and reasonably. Justice is other-centred rather than self-centred, and as such is an essential virtue for human-centred leaders.

Human-centred leaders appreciate that they are stewards of the business or community on behalf of others, including subsequent generations. They understand that justice dictates the need for fairness of distribution and equality of access to what is required for living. They understand that the privilege of leadership includes the responsibility not to take advantage of others.

A commitment to justice does not start when you become the CEO, however. It starts now, with your colleagues and companions, in your community and country. There are countless examples of injustice, whether because of the gender pay gap or the divide between rich and poor, or unequal access to fresh food and water, energy, medicine, education, fair pay for a fair day's work, a minimum wage that supports a reasonable standard of living...

I have suggested that humility might be *the* leadership virtue, because it is a service virtue that makes leadership about others rather than about you. Justice runs a very close second, since it is about how you treat others, about constantly trying to put yourself in someone else's shoes. Where the virtue of self-control is primarily about how you treat yourself, justice thinks first — and always — of others. It's a crucial leadership virtue.

- Do you give others, or help them obtain, what is rightfully theirs?

- Do you speak out for your female colleague who is underpaid? And if you are her manager, what have you done to ensure equity?

- What are you doing to help those who lack access to fresh food and clean water, to safe medicines and reliable sources of energy?

- What can you do for those who cannot afford legal justice or who lack educational opportunities?

- Do you see those around you, who you pass in the lift and on the street, who have so little while you have so much?

These are not questions to refer to the government, as if *they* should do something. These are questions for you, and they are questions for me. Justice dictates that we must find a way to respond that is sometimes outside our comfort zone. You cannot be a bystander and hope *they* do something about it, because there is no *they*. There is only you.

Self-control

'Lord, give me chastity and self-control, but not just yet.'
AUGUSTINE OF HIPPO

The attraction of distraction

'Just a quick scroll through the headlines,' I told myself, as I checked the overnight news online. Writing time merged into browsing time and my focus faded.

'Hmm, there's an interesting scandal about expenses in public office ... better read that, it could be a reference point ...

'And here's an article about character and bipartisanship in politics ... always looking for those ...

'There's a sports update ... just a quick look.'

When I was a child, a visit to the town library required permission from my parents and a 10-minute bike ride. I could then spend hours browsing the shelves. Now I can visit almost any library in the world with a couple of clicks—and then spend hours browsing wherever my fancy takes me. Sometimes the temptation to wander the web overwhelms me.

You may be familiar with this experience. Time enters another dimension ... and evaporates into a black hole. For someone like me who is fascinated by people, ideas and events, the internet is a treasure trove of trinkets, with an occasional gold nugget. I can easily convince myself that I am Indiana Jones on the trail of the Grail. The truth, however, is I am wasting time, completely distracted, and often filling my mind with pointless drivel. I become intoxicated by the search, and have an insatiable curiosity to know what lies beyond. *Click…click…click…*

I wish I could retrieve the hours I have wasted online.

This represents a failure in self-control. I have not effectively managed my behaviour so as to be satisfied with 'just enough' and am easily seduced into wanting, and giving myself, 'too much'.

It's normal to struggle

You are probably aware of aspects of your life where you are strong, others where you struggle and others where you experience minor temptations that distract you from time to time. There appears to be little rhyme or reason to who struggles with what, although *everyone struggles with something*. Your struggle can help you understand another's struggle, rather than judge them because they fail in an area where you happen to be strong. Recognising the universality of struggle should also help you be patient with yourself, accepting that you will never be perfect.

You may recall my earlier description of the natural beauty that surrounds our farm. If you turn your gaze for a moment to the land itself you will see weeds infesting the pasture. It's a never-ending battle to get rid of them, and when we think they are gone we find the roots lying dormant for next season, or seeds blowing in on the wind. It's a part of rural life.

You can never completely eradicate the weeds from your life. You can, however, manage them and substantially limit their impact. This is what the virtue of self-control does. It gives you the power to control the weeds.

I know when I am not managing the weeds. I know when I am rationalising something away, making excuses for what is, in reality, surrender to excess in one form or another. I can find any number of reasons to justify an extra piece of pie, or a block of chocolate rather than a couple of squares.

Self-control is critical for self-mastery

Self-control, or temperance to the Greeks, is the virtue that helps you resist self-indulgence and to moderate your desire for pleasure. Note the word is 'moderate', not 'stop'. Self-control helps me recognise when I have had sufficient pie and helps me manage the desire for more.

Self-control is the 'count to 10' virtue, the one that enables you to control your response to pleasure or pain, that gives you the power to resist temptation, to delay gratification. You strengthen self-control by practising the habit of saying no to yourself when necessary.

The foundations of this virtue are laid when your parents refuse to relent in the face of your wheedling demands. You learn that you cannot have whatever you feel like, that sometimes you need to wait even for what could be good for you. Learning during the earlier stages of life that you are not the centre of the universe, and that you cannot have what you want whenever you want, is a crucial building block for the virtue of self-control.

You may have heard of 'the Stanford marshmallow test', where a child was placed in a room with a tempting desert right in front of them ... and then told that if they don't eat it they will be given two a short time later. Videos of this experiment depict the children's mental anguish as they fight temptation and try to decide whether to eat it or not. Some devour it immediately with barely a moment's thought, others struggle momentarily, while others demonstrate iron will as they wrestle with their desire.

Exactly the same thing happens in your adult life. Circumstances place something attractive in front of you that you either should not have or for some reason cannot have now. This can be as simple as 'one more drink for the road' or as challenging as being offered a bribe. In those moments your self-control is tested, and if you have not practised the art of saying no to yourself you can find yourself in a terrible battle. The marshmallow test researchers found a relationship between the ability to exercise self-restraint as a child and as an adult. In other words, if you don't learn it early, you may find it hard later in life to say no to what you should avoid.

If you want to achieve mastery in life, you must first achieve self-mastery over your desires. The virtue of self-control is the key, since life will provide many opportunities to be self-indulgent.

'After many years of marriage I showed extremely poor judgement by engaging in an extramarital affair.'

This quote from a well-known public figure expresses a sentiment commonly avowed by those forced to admit to an affair. They recognise a failure of judgement after the event, yet they often demonstrate very sound judgement in every other area.

The affair, however, did not start with a lapse of judgement. It most likely started with a failure of self-control, in quite minor ways, until lust probably overcame logic. I believe most people who engage in affairs are aware of the dangers and the mistake they are making. They rationalise and find ways to excuse their actions, claiming, for example, a lack of intimacy in their marriage. While their judgement is working fine, the ability to control their passions in this area falters. This suggests a breakdown in virtue before a breakdown in thinking.

The time to resist one last drink, or a little flutter or fling, is not when you are at the bar or in the bedroom. The moment to resist is when you first become aware of the desire, when you feel yourself being drawn toward what you do not want to do.

Let me make a couple of important points about that sentence. Firstly, 'desire' is not immoral or wrong. It's okay and normal to feel desire, and sometimes powerful desire. It can lead you astray, however, if you do not keep it in check. Secondly, note the importance of the phrase 'what you do not want to do'. It is not 'what you should not do' or 'what others tell you not to do', but 'what *you* do not want to do'.

The picture you have created of the best version of yourself includes your particular image of physical, intellectual, spiritual and emotional wellbeing, and almost certainly aspects of relational joy and harmony. This picture informs your approach to food, drink, sex and love, since you want that picture to become real. Hence overeating, getting drunk or having an affair become wrong not because someone else said so but because you said so, because you decided these are incompatible with your view of excellence.

What you do not want to do is anything that leads you away from the good life, from a life of human flourishing.

* * *

This is the life you are designing for yourself by the choices you make in the pursuit of Beauty, Goodness and Truth, empowered by the virtues of humility, wisdom, courage, justice and self-control. They are essential aspects of becoming, and being, a human-centred leader.

CHAPTER 11

Making wise decisions: thinking well

'The great enemy of truth is very often not the lie—deliberate, contrived and dishonest—but the myth—persistent, persuasive and unrealistic. Too often we hold fast to the clichés of our forebears. We subject all facts to a prefabricated set of interpretations. We enjoy the comfort of opinion without the discomfort of thought.'

JOHN F KENNEDY, COMMENCEMENT ADDRESS AT YALE UNIVERSITY, 11 JUNE, 1962

When Plato and Aristotle considered a moral life, they thought in terms of a virtuous life, a well-lived life of human flourishing. This is quite different from our modern tendency to think in terms of right and wrong.

I find this idea quite attractive. I appreciate the idea of 'flourishing', with its suggestion of fully rounded growth and development, of success, wellbeing and thriving. Setting our goal on human flourishing, and a life well lived, invites us to make moral choices.

Moral choice is not primarily selecting what is right over what is wrong, but choosing to do what will help you become all you can be—to 'flourish' as a human being. If you make choices, for example, that involve violence toward yourself or others, even in small things such as clutching at anger, those choices limit your growth. They hold you back. They prevent you from flourishing in that area of your life.

Navigating this chapter

Having considered where you are, where you are going and who you are going to be on the journey, the next two chapters turn your attention to *Doing: What are you going to do to get there?* Both focus on a critical aspect of leadership—decision making, and in particular making wise decisions. This chapter provides a framework for thinking well. It starts with a story and then has four sections:

- 'Think better to lead better' argues that robust thinking is necessary for sound judgement, and hence for effective leadership.

- 'A model for thinking' offers an easily learnable model for thinking that can be used in any circumstance.

- 'The thinking model in practice' explains how to use this model by formulating questions that are relevant to the situation.

- 'Thinking and leadership' shows how sound thinking offsets biases, drives innovation and brings a critical mindset.

Think better to lead better

We had been pursued by a cyclone for days, buffeted by strong winds and heavy seas, never seeming to break free of its grip.

'Howard,' called the Captain when there was a lull in the storm. 'Get down to the hold and make sure everything's secure and there's no damage.'

I set off along the slippery deck for hold number 3, unscrewed the heavy bolts on the waterproof door to the access shaft, hoisted myself onto the ladder and closed the door behind me. The torch beam picked out the first few steps. Beyond that, inky blackness extended in every direction.

The groans, shudders and creaking of the ship and its cargo added to my unease as I carefully descended the ladder. Standing a few steps from the bottom, a quick scan with the torch indicated nothing adrift. Everything looked secure. Vehicles, industrial machinery and various goods pallets covered the floor of the hold. It seemed safe to continue.

Moving as fast as the shadows allowed I quickly checked bolts and shackles to ensure everything held fast, temporarily forgetting my surroundings while absorbed in the job at hand. A small van sat to one side. As the torch played over the sides and through the windows I leaned over to glance into the back.

A body lay there in the darkness, spreadeagled on the floor.

I scarcely touched the deck or the ladder during my frightened retreat.

'Get back down there and check it out,' replied the Captain to my wild-eyed story, as he handed me the keys to the truck. We had recently left a port rife with rumours of waterfront wars and unexplained disappearances, so a corpse in the hold was not implausible.

'Not me,' I said.

'Yes, you,' he insisted. 'Take someone with you.'

Reluctantly I retraced my steps with a sceptical although apprehensive crewmate. Tentatively we approached the truck.

'You open it,' I said.

'No, you,' he replied.

Marshalling our combined courage we opened the doors and approached the body, our torches picking out darkened limbs. I prodded a leg and it gave way.

'It's a wetsuit!' we both exclaimed in relief, drawing our first breath since entering the hold.

Someone had laid out a full dive suit to make it look like a body, and no doubt derived considerable pleasure from the thought of the consternation it might cause.

Although this story is a little dramatic, I tell it to demonstrate a very important point. It is very easy to draw false conclusions from what we see and hear, and so conclusions need to be tested in a way that allows us to prove their soundness.

This means you need a process for thinking. It's a key component in your leadership toolkit, and a prerequisite to choosing well.

The process of thinking, and how to do it well, has interested me since I was introduced to the philosophical work of Bernard Lonergan many years ago. When Lonergan died in 1984, *Time* magazine described him as 'one of the most influential thinkers of the twentieth century'.

Lonergan had an overwhelming interest in knowledge and knowing, framed by questions such as 'How do we know that we know?' and 'What is it we are doing when we are knowing?' He explored these and related questions in his opus *Insight*, which invites the reader to accompany him on a voyage of discovery about knowledge. It's not an easy journey.

I remember driving home from lectures asking myself if it was really me driving the car, paying little attention to the road. Dense questions filled my mind: 'Am I really here?', 'How do I know I am here?, 'How do I know I know?' and 'How do I know where to go?' Other drivers facing less philosophical challenges would occasionally offer their own answers to this last question, although their suggestions often seemed somewhat impractical.

The best action among a variety of options is based on a wise choice. The wisest choice is based on sound judgement. Sound judgement is based on robust thinking. And robust thinking is based on having a solid, repeatable process for thinking. It's a crucial skill to have in your toolkit as you search after Beauty, Goodness and Truth, and as you make decisions that impact on the wellbeing of your company, community and country.

A model for thinking

Lonergan developed a straightforward method for thinking that can be applied in any situation.[1] To begin with, he noted that a number of different kinds of operations occur when you are thinking. These include 'seeing, hearing, touching, tasting, smelling, inquiring, imagining, understanding, conceiving, formulating, reflecting, marshalling the evidence, judging, deliberating, evaluating, deciding'.[2] It is apparent from this list that while hearing is similar to seeing it is quite different from deliberating.

This leads to Lonergan's observation that there are four quite distinct dimensions or levels of thinking:

1   *The level of data, of experience and the empirical.* These are the operations of seeing, hearing, touching, tasting and smelling.
2   *The level of intellect, and the effort to understand experience.* These are the operations of inquiring, imagining, understanding, conceiving, formulating, reflecting and marshalling the evidence.
3   *The level of judgement, when we endeavour to decide the correctness of our understanding.* These are the operations of judging, deliberating and evaluating.
4   *The level of deciding how to act based on our judgement.* This decision then manifests itself in action.

This thinking process (see figure 11.1) is both repeatable and reversible. This means you can use this method to help you make and review decisions. It can aid decision making in any situation *and* you can work backwards to unpack your decisions by questioning your judgement, the understanding that led to that judgement and the data you relied upon to form your understanding.

Figure 11.1: the thinking process

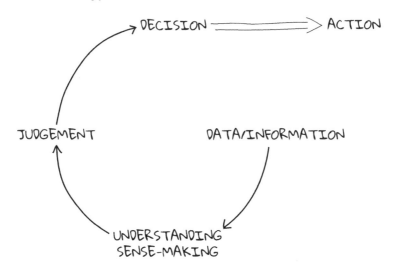

Only when you have been around this loop can you have confidence in your decision. My judgement that there was a body in the van was wrong because I jumped from what I saw (data) to convincing myself it was the case (decision), without taking the time to gather more data and test some options about what I was seeing. (And I'm sure you noticed that fear hijacked any potential for clear thinking.) Even if it had been a real body, I would 'know' this for certain only when I had asked all the relevant questions.

Before you say you 'know' something, you need to be confident you have considered all the relevant data and asked all the relevant questions. If you have ignored, overlooked or missed some data or questions, then you really only have an opinion. And opinions are fine, as long as you recognise they are opinions and remain open to other opinions.

Different questions for different levels

You can use different kinds of questions at each level to help you, and others, appreciate what is happening.

At the *first level* you ask questions such as 'What is it?', 'Where is it?', 'Who is it?' or 'What does it say?' The answers to those questions were 'It's a van', 'It's in the hold', 'There's something in the back' and so forth. The answers are like labels. You can quickly recognise when doing this if you are missing information, and you should also be aware if you are ignoring information.

At the *second level* you are looking for an explanation, an understanding: 'What does all this mean?' You float ideas and test hypotheses: 'It looks like a body.' Or you jump to conclusions, as I did when fear hijacked my thinking, only to be proved wrong.

The *third level* seeks an answer to the question 'Is it so?' This requires a yes or no answer. And this can drive you back to the earlier levels of questioning.

'Is it a body?' ... Well, I actually don't know for sure. I need more information. I need to get up close. Having done so I can then make a judgement on my hypothesis: 'No, it's not a body'.

At the *fourth level* you answer the question about what you will do, you make a decision about the action that follows from your judgement.

The scenario I described required no further action, other than enduring the ridicule of my crewmates. If, however, the answer had been 'Yes, it is a body', that would have launched quite a different set of actions.

The thinking model in practice

I'll let you in on a little secret: sometimes I have no idea what clients are talking about. They say things that are very familiar in their world yet sound foreign to me. You may find yourself in a similar situation, whether around a boardroom table or in a community consultation.

The only way out of this is to ask questions. This does three things: it shows you are interested, keeps you listening intently and leads to further questions.

The key is knowing which kind of question to ask. You can tell which kind of question to ask based on what people say. Listen carefully when people speak. The language they use indicates the mental process they are employing.

Here are some examples that show people operating at different levels, and the kinds of questions that can be asked to 'unpack' what is going on.

The decision level

Do you remember the story in chapter 10 about the client who did not resign when the board made a decision he had previously opposed? His action implied a *decision* (not to resign) so I challenged his *judgement*: 'You said you would resign if the board didn't accept your resignation'.

He then remembered the earlier conversation and moved to the level of *understanding*: 'You're right,' he said. 'I'd forgotten about that. I wonder what that means?'

His invitation to ask further questions enabled us to move to the *information* he had used to form his understanding, where it became evident that family stability was paramount at that time and hence job security mattered. Without thinking through the process — when the decision not to resign was made—he had subconsciously introduced this factor. This process of reviewing the decision, however, unearthed and reinforced his commitment to his family, and he then became more conscious about the way his decisions impacted on his family.

The judgement level

'I plan to do this,' said Angela, explaining in a short sentence a key point she would make in a presentation the following week. 'What do you think?'

This is a question about *judgement*. Although Angela had not made a decision, she had formed a view based on her understanding. Her request to me invited questions about the options she canvassed, how she understood each of those, and then the information she relied upon to form that understanding. It became evident very quickly that she had overlooked an option, so my question became, 'What about this option?' As I write I don't yet know what she decided to do.

The understanding level

'How do I make sense of all of this?' is a common question, often accompanied by a feeling of being overwhelmed by information. Clients who express this are operating at the understanding level. They are trying to understand and make sense of their world. Questions at this level revolve around *meaning*. They require an ability to screen data, look for what is hidden in the gaps, set aside what is irrelevant, 'join the dots' and detect patterns. By the way, 'sense-making' capability will be a defining leadership skill in the 21st century, and hence something you should actively cultivate.

The data level

Finally, sometimes people are operating at the data level. This is very obvious, as they present slide after slide, data point after data point, facts and figures. Questions at this level revolve around *what is missing from the data*—where are last year's figures, for example, or the competitive report, or the product review?—and then ask what it all means, as you move up to the understanding level.

Thinking and leadership

Does all this matter for you and for being a human-centred leader? It certainly does, for three reasons.

First, sound thinking processes offset the influence of biases and mental models. Have you noticed a tendency among people not only to ask questions within their field of expertise, but to give added weight to data from their world? Finance directors can overemphasise financial data, and marketing directors can overemphasise brand information. At the same time each can overlook or discount what is contained in the other's reports. The lens through which you look can inadvertently and unintentionally filter out vital data from another source.

Great leaders understand the limits of their own knowledge, remain open to diverse opinions and perspectives, and work with other people to generate new insights and deeper understanding from a wide range of sources. This aids sound judgement and fosters better decision making.

Second, sound thinking processes provide an engine for innovation. You have an abundance of raw material (data) and the opportunity to turn it into something of greater value (insight and understanding) via effective questioning. Inquiry adds value to data. Questions provide the power, or energy, to do this, so you become more efficient as you learn to ask better questions. Better questions are the precursor to better answers, and the key to creativity and innovation. Hence anything or anyone, including a domineering, opinionated leader or artificial time pressure, that shuts down questions will curtail insight and innovation.

Third, a solid thinking model helps you critique thinking, both your own and that of those around you. When you are listening to, or preparing to give, a presentation consider asking questions at each of these levels:

- Are you hearing raw data, with no real analysis, presented as fact?

- Is there sufficient data for reaching a proper understanding or are there gaps?

- Does the presenter presume a shared understanding that is not borne out by the data?

- Have they asked all the relevant questions and tested their understanding with the reflective question 'Is it so?'
- Have they jumped from data to decision without demonstrating the intervening insight and judgement?

Leaders act. Courage can help you make a decision and act on it. A robust thinking process will give you confidence in that decision, and a framework for reviewing and refining it as necessary. As you work to become a better person, work also to become a better thinker, because better thinking processes foster wiser decisions.

A decision also invites another question: Is it good? What can you do to test whether the decisions you make are good decisions in the moral sense, in the sense of fostering that flourishing human life? Not just good strategically or economically sound, but morally acceptable.

Human-centred leaders make their decisions with an ear tuned to an inner voice, or what in the past may have been called 'conscience'.

CHAPTER 12

Making wise decisions: choosing well

'There is a higher court than courts of justice and that is the court of conscience. It supercedes all other courts.'

MAHATMA GANDHI

The subtlety of a gift

A waterfront enforcer, who I would not want to meet on a dark night, approached as I kept watch by the gangplank. Striking up a conversation he suddenly, unexpectedly, handed me a brown envelope.

'What's this?' I said, accepting it reflexively.

'We've just passed the hat around. It's a little bit of help for you,' he replied.

'Thanks,' I said, returning the envelope as if it was on fire, 'but I don't need it. I'm okay'.

'Don't worry,' he said, quietly and insistently pressing the envelope back into my hand. 'We know you don't earn much money, and we always take up a collection for the apprentices.'

After only three months at sea I was surprised he was even aware of me.

'Thanks for thinking of me,' I replied, playing another round of pass the parcel, while desperately trying to think of a way out of the physical and moral danger. This was a man I did not want to offend.

'You're right,' I said. 'I don't earn much money, but I don't spend much either. I live on the ship, so all my food and accommodation is free, and all my pay just goes straight in the bank.'

He held my gaze for a long moment and then slid the envelope into his jacket with a shrug. We never spoke of it again, although our paths often crossed. I had little doubt, however, that acceptance would have made that envelope the first of many, and we would still be speaking of it today.

I tell the story not to suggest I was an especially upstanding individual, but to observe how in moments of moral challenge something within comes to our aid to help us choose wisely. What is that? How can you strengthen it? How can you work out what is right or wrong and choose wisely between them?

In the past you could often rely on authority figures, perhaps in the church, business or government, to provide moral guidance. Unfortunately leaders of these institutions have largely squandered our trust through their corruption, cover-ups and failure to abide by the values they espouse. Furthermore, in the morally complex world in which you live and work, you almost certainly face dilemmas and challenges with which they cannot help and into which they cannot intrude.

So who do you turn to? Where can you look for guidance that fits with who you are and where you are going? This is a very important question to answer.

One CEO told me that when working in a foreign country he refused to pay when regularly asked for cash to help business run more smoothly. When I asked what informed his thinking he pointed to the Ten Commandments. However, he said, the real challenge was in working out how these applied to his daily life, where he faced regular moral dilemmas. His attempts to 'personalise' moral thinking showed an awareness of the very real difficulty of knowing what to do in specific situations.

Leaders make moral decisions every day. You make decisions that have good and/or bad consequences for you and all your stakeholders. To make the best possible decisions you need a sound internal moral framework to guide you, particularly when you are operating in an ambiguous or corrupt environment. Without some sort of framework you risk operating in ignorance, with a finger in the air to test the wind, hoping everything turns out okay.

For many people that framework is usually formed by their upbringing and influenced by their environment. Very few people, however, are able to articulate a sound process to guide and enhance their moral decision making.

That's what I have attempted here — to unpack a moral decision-making process and provide a model that can quickly become second nature, based on developing your conscience, or what you could think of as your 'moral muscle'. You will be able to use it yourself and use it with others.

It's a crucial skill for human-centred leaders, and will become ever more important in an increasingly morally ambiguous world.

Navigating this chapter

This is the second chapter to discuss *Doing: What are you going to do to get there?* My interest is in the decision-making aspect of getting to your destination, and having laid out a model for thinking well in the previous chapter, this chapter explains the role of conscience in choosing well. It has six sections:

- 'Conscience: an inner voice' explains what conscience is (and is not).

- 'Formation of conscience' talks about how to develop and improve your conscience, and the remaining sections explain what happens when you turn to your conscience:

- 'Conscience: certain or doubtful' makes a distinction between the times when you are sure and those when you are unsure.

- 'Conscience: correct or incorrect' explains how you can get it right and sometimes get it wrong, yet in both cases think you are doing the right thing, and discusses how to deal with that.

- 'Conscience and principles' highlights the need to base your decisions on sound principles, and offers some you can use.

- 'Conscience and relationships' builds on the concept of the person as a relational being and proposes that your actions can be judged by the impact they have on others.

Conscience: an inner voice

Like the just-mentioned CEO refusing a facilitation payment, how can you figure out right and wrong in any moment? What do you do when the law or the circumstances are unclear? How do you make the best possible choice, one that fosters rather than diminishes the wellbeing of yourself and others?

That's where conscience comes in. It's the inner voice, or sense, that prompts you toward what is good and away from what is bad, and in particular to do what is truly good for other people. Since we are relational beings, our conscience can assist us to make choices that improve, rather than damage, those relationships. It helps us answer the question 'Will what I am about to do enhance or diminish my relationship with others?'

I sometimes find that people confuse conscience with being conscious, or with intuition, which is a misunderstanding. *Conscious* refers to a state of awareness. When you don't have it you've either passed out or passed away. *Conscience* is an inner conviction about how to act. You hear it used, for instance, when elected representatives seek a 'conscience vote' in government or a pacifist registers as a 'conscientious objector' to war. Both of these indicate the high regard our society has for individual conscience and hence how important it is to develop a sound conscience.

Nor is conscience the same as intuition. *Intuition* is that feeling I get that prompts me to ring my sister or follow up with a client. As I get older I have learned to trust these promptings and have ceased to be amazed when someone says 'I was just thinking about you', or expresses a need that can be met in that call. Conscience, on the other hand, is the prompting of an inner voice that alerts me to the fact I am letting down my sister. Whereas intuition in some strange way prompts me to call her, conscience can foster guilt that I have delayed calling her, encouraging me to do something about it.

When you take time to listen to your conscience it can propose a course of action:

- Have you ever wanted to do something, and found 'a voice within' trying to get your attention to tell you to stop, to avoid this, to do that instead ...?

- Have you noticed that when you do something you would prefer not to have done, something that conflicts with your values, a voice within prompts you to make things right again?

- Have you noticed those times when you are genuinely unsure how to act, and a tiny flame lighting a path can be detected in your moments of quiet reflection?

This is your conscience, the inner voice of reason that redirects you gently — or, if necessary, vigorously — toward what is right and away from what is wrong. As you practise listening to and responding to this voice, you will make better choices and grow in wisdom.

How can you improve that capability?

Formation of conscience

You can shape your conscience in the same way you shape a sculpture, your body or your thoughts. Just as there are tools and practices that bring out the beauty in the stone, or enhance your health and wellbeing, or expand your mind, there are practices and habits that can shape your conscience. This is called the 'formation' of conscience.

Four practices help you form your conscience, making it easier to choose what is good as distinct from what is bad, to choose what is beautiful and true.

1 *Recognise that your conscience is strengthened by regular use,* in the same way that virtue grows through repeated practice. Ignore your conscience and it will grow silent. Develop the habit of listening and it will become a trusted friend, rather than a voice of judgement.

2   *Your conscience is formed by what you feed it, by which wolf you listen to.* A steady diet of hard-core pornography and violent video games, to take extreme although not uncommon examples, can diminish empathy and allow some (I think most) users to see other people as objects for their own gratification. They can then lose sight of how to treat others with honour and respect, and lack insight about their own self-centred behaviour. When, on the other hand, you choose to fill your life with culture and classics, with learning and loving, your conscience becomes more finely attuned both to yourself and to others, helping you steer a path through the subtleties and nuances of human life.

3   *Your conscience is formed by the decisions you make.* Each decision either reinforces or reshapes a previous decision. When your conscience prompts you to stop putting other people down, for example, the choice you make creates a little stepping stone toward the next choice. Deciding not to make self-aggrandising jokes that belittle others makes it just a bit easier to remain silent when the next opportunity presents. In fact, you might choose to publicly praise others.

4   *The guides you choose to follow form your conscience.* You can choose wise guides or you can choose someone who may lead you astray. Wise guides can be found in the past — in great literature and oral traditions — and in the present. They are women and they are men. They don't necessarily occupy positions of leadership. If you meet such people, ask how they have faced and resolved life's dilemmas. How have they wrestled complex problems to the ground?

As you form your conscience your ability to make good choices improves. This accelerates your progress on the road to becoming the best person you can be. Making poor choices, on the other hand, slows your progress.

You can form your conscience diligently, with the best of your endeavours, or carelessly, with very little effort and ignoring whatever you find a bit challenging. The four practices above describe the diligent approach to reasonably and sensibly forming your conscience. If you follow this approach, you can be confident that as you reflect on your decisions, watch your moral diet and choose guides wisely, you will make better choices that more closely align with Beauty, Goodness and Truth. You can, that is, confidently follow the promptings of your conscience.

On the other hand, you can be careless and dismissive of conscience, choosing to remain wilfully ignorant. This happens when, for example, you ignore information or insights from educated sources because they challenge your views, or when you refuse to listen to good friends who politely explain the damage your actions are causing to you, them and others. The man who is sure that gender wage disparity is acceptable, while summarily dismissing research, reports and any sense of fairness and justice, is choosing to remain wilfully ignorant. Blocking yourself from sound learning stunts your conscience, so it becomes an unreliable guide and not one you should sensibly follow. Classical philosophy calls this a conscience formed 'in bad faith'. This behaviour enables a person to say, 'I am following my conscience', when they have not given their conscience the opportunity to become a sound guide.

In short, take active steps to form your conscience. Follow a well-formed conscience, and be wary of listening to one that has been poorly formed. As you pay attention to your conscience, you will notice that sometimes you are quite sure about how to act, while at other times you lack clarity.

What you are observing is that conscience can be certain or doubtful.

Conscience: certain or doubtful

This distinction, although perhaps obvious, is very important. It matters to a human-centred leader because it helps you understand the way people make choices and why at times they vacillate and (as discussed in the next section) why at times they do the wrong thing while believing it is right.

When you find yourself facing a choice about how to act, you give the situation very careful thought and consideration. You possibly talk to friends and colleagues. Then one of two things happens. Either you form a view and say, 'This is what I am going to do', because you feel 'certain' about what to do. Or you remain in doubt, saying, 'I just don't know what to do'.

Certain

When you are certain about how to act, you can reliably follow your conscience. This is the situation that arises, for example, when a political party allows a conscience vote. Each politician considers, reflects, deliberates, decides and then confidently votes for or against the motion. Your choice reinforces what you consider to be right or wrong, so you have an obligation to follow your conscience.

When you are certain about what to do, and your conscience is well formed, then you can reliably assume it is prompting you toward what is good, and often what is noble. This is the voice heard by Oskar Schindler, who saved 1200 Jews from the Nazi death camps. Can you imagine what courage that took?

Many people express great certainty about how they should act although they have formed their conscience 'in bad faith' and seem quite comfortable in their ignorance. This happens, for instance, when your boss intentionally ignores your well-researched report on the negative impact of his HR policies, implying he knows better. In this case he is deluding himself about what is right, trusting to luck to make it all work out, but really he should not follow his own advice. Perhaps with a moment's reflection you can think of people who claim to know it all while ignoring opinions that oppose their own.

Doubtful

When you remain in doubt about what to do, having what is called a 'doubtful conscience', it is unwise to act. With a doubtful conscience you really cannot make up your mind—so you abstain from voting, for example. When in doubt it is better to wait until things become clearer, otherwise you risk supporting an action with consequences that could diminish goodness and allow what is bad to increase. It's okay in many instances to admit you just don't know and need more time, particularly on issues of honesty and integrity, of justice and fairness. It's right to want to get these things right.

As you read this you are probably thinking about those times when you really don't know what to do yet you have to make a choice. Perhaps you are operating in a foreign country with a very different view on what might be considered acceptable behaviour. Circumstances don't provide the luxury of time for further reflection, and your advisers cannot agree. This is the pointy end of leadership. This is what it's like in the prow of the ship where, like Ulysses choosing between a rock and a hard place, you have to make a call.

You have raised the question about how to resolve moral dilemmas. The short answer is to back your judgement and be guided by your moral compass, constantly reviewing your actions in an evolving situation. I will address this at more length in Part III, where we consider the application of your leadership foundation to the reality of Human-Centred Leadership.

You may also be wondering about those people who are certain they are right, while in fact they are wrong. This happens because a 'certain conscience' can be correct or incorrect.

Conscience: correct or incorrect

Despite our confidence, we can be right or wrong about our conclusions. You can be certain and correct or certain yet incorrect. Figure 12.1 may help show what all this looks like.

Figure 12.1: conscience

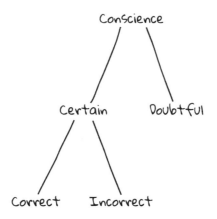

Remember our earlier story about Paul Moore warning the board of HBOS that their strategy was fraught with danger? He was certain he was right, and was proven to be correct. The board, however, were certain they were right, and were proven wrong. Subsequent events showed how they had ignored key data—they had acted, it could be said, 'in bad faith'.[1]

How is it possible to do your best to form your conscience in good faith, and be certain about the correct way to act—and yet still be wrong? Sometimes people do the wrong thing, believing wholeheartedly that it is the right way to act.

Let's imagine for a moment that Dave has recently started his first job as a labourer on a building site. One day he finds he runs out of bricks—too few have been delivered. The schedule will be thrown into disarray if they have to wait for a new order.

'Just grab some from the site around the corner,' says Dave's boss. 'I noticed when I drove by earlier they had too many. One day they'll run short and will take some from one of our sites. That's the way it works in this game.'

So Dave fills his truck with hot bricks, trusting his boss and confident ('certain', although incorrectly) that he is doing the right thing. Any niggling doubts are removed when it happens a few more times and he notices others doing it.

Did Dave do the right thing? No, he didn't. Relying on assumptions about 'the way things are done here' has brought many people unstuck, and poor Dave is unlikely to be the last. Although, to be fair, his honest ignorance somewhat mitigates his responsibility. There is a difference between someone who knowingly breaks the law and someone who does so unwittingly.

What this story shows is that Dave—or anyone else, for that matter—is not the final arbiter of what is right or wrong. He may believe that what he did was morally correct, but that does not make it so. Does this make sense?

The 'correctness' of an act is established by some external, objective entity or force. Sometimes this is the law, which spells out legal boundaries. However, sometimes the law is unclear, or has not dealt with your particular issue, or it's not a legal but a moral challenge you face.

In the discussion about self-control I referred to a man whose lapse of judgement led him into an affair. This is an example of a moral problem. No laws were broken. Both people probably justified their actions at the time, confident that at that moment, for them, they were doing the right thing. There may have been any number of extenuating circumstances that supported such a view. In other words, they could have agreed in good faith that an affair was acceptable. If this view was correct then no subsequent apology would have been necessary.

Can you see that an individual—or even a couple working together—cannot be the final moral arbiter of what is correct? Only by looking through the lens of an external principle can you determine the correctness of an act.

Where can you find a reliable source of moral truth? To argue, 'We each have our own truth', is a bit of a cop-out, because it's often plainly obvious that what some people hold to be true or good is not the case at all.

You can find truth, and reality, in the transcendentals. I mentioned earlier Plato's view that when you know Beauty, Goodness and Truth in their fullness you know reality. I also suggested the transcendentals lie out there 'over the horizon'. But although you cannot see them fully, you can head in the right direction—toward what is beautiful, good and true—by living in accord with timeless human principles. Where can you find those principles in a world that generally distrusts traditional moral authorities? You start with 'first principles'.

Conscience and principles

Most laws and beliefs arise out of some other law or belief. Robbing a bank, for example, is illegal because of the underlying principles around respecting property and opposing theft.

The foundations on which other arguments rest are called 'first principles', starting points that are self-evident and do not rely on another underlying principle. For example, in mathematics: $x + y = y + x$. Or in logic, a thing cannot be and not be at the same time (the principle of non-contradiction).

People who fail to grasp or appreciate first principles are virtually impossible to reason with.

There are also first principles of morality—that is, self-evident principles that require no further proof. In other words, if you unpack a moral teaching—such as 'Don't take what doesn't belong to you' or 'Treat others with respect' or 'Don't cheat'—by asking 'Why?' repeatedly, you will ultimately arrive at a first principle: a self-evident truth that stands in its own right.

Perhaps the best known first principle of morality is: *Act in a way that actively promotes good and avoids what is evil.* You may recognise the influence of this in Google's 'Don't be evil' slogan.

From this principle it is a small step to the golden rule: *Do unto others as you would have them do unto you.* Although I much prefer this variation: *What is hateful to yourself, do not do to others.*[2]

I suggest that you adopt one of these principles—or a variation thereof—and begin to use it to filter your decisions and actions. How would you feel if someone arbitrarily varied your bonus downwards? How would you feel if the government rezoned the park behind your home for a freeway?

Conscience and relationships

Since to be a person is to be in relationship with others, another way of determining the 'rightness' or 'wrongness' of what you do is to reflect on the impact it will have on your relationship with others. It is self-evident that killing someone, or carrying out an act of violence toward them, damages your relationship, so this would be the wrong way to act.

'Will what I am about to do enhance or diminish my relationship with others [whether they are near or far]?' is a very reasonable test. You don't need to be present to be affected by the actions of others. The impact of Bernie Madoff's Ponzi scheme extended way beyond New York City and those in his immediate circle. People affected by your actions can live in another place, or perhaps are not yet born.

A key aspect of moral decision making, therefore, is to identify the people who will be impacted by your decision.

Where the Greeks determined the appropriateness of an action by whether it promoted human flourishing (that is, 'In doing this do I become more of a person?'), I am suggesting that appropriateness of an action can also be determined by whether it promotes human relationships.

* * *

If you have made a commitment to cultivate harmonious relationships, to search for Beauty, Goodness and Truth, to practise the virtues and follow your conscience, it is likely that you will choose well rather than poorly.

You are looking more and more like a human-centred leader and now have all the tools you need to construct your own moral compass and answer the question: *Where are you standing?* And it is to that question we now turn.

CHAPTER 13

Navigating life with a moral compass

'But we do not have to think that human nature is perfect for us to still believe that the human condition can be perfected. We do not have to live in an idealized world to still reach for those ideals that will make it a better place. The non-violence practiced by men like Gandhi and King may not have been practical or possible in every circumstance, but the love that they preached—their faith in human progress—must always be the North Star that guides us on our journey.
'For if we lose that faith—if we dismiss it as silly or naïve; if we divorce it from the decisions that we make on issues of war and peace—then we lose what is best about humanity. We lose our sense of possibility. We lose our moral compass.'

BARACK OBAMA

A moral compass

'I was given a moral compass second to none,' said Marty Holleran, former President and CEO of Electrolux Home Care and Thomson Consumer Electronics (RCA).[1] He attributed this to the example of his parents and the strong community environment in which he was raised.

Just as the ship's compass pointed to magnetic north and so enabled me to take a bearing and follow a course with confidence, you can rely on your moral compass to point toward 'north' and guide your journey. When you find yourself in a fog of uncertainty, when you have no map for the voyage and the path is unclear, your compass will provide a reliable bearing that you can follow with confidence.

A moral compass (see figure 13.1) aligns itself with Beauty, Goodness and Truth via your purpose and in accord with timeless human principles and virtues. You follow it by choosing wisely according to the promptings of a well-formed conscience. A sound moral compass provides the best means of emerging safely on the other side of the chaos and confusion that happens during major shifts and transitions. It can guide you today, tomorrow and throughout your life.

Navigating this chapter

This chapter draws together all the preceding elements to help you construct a compass that can guide you on the journey. As you operate in uncharted waters, this compass will guide you in the darkest night or the thickest fog, because it will point unerringly toward your destination, and provide you with an uncanny ability to skirt the rocks and shoals that could sink your ship. It will not stop the storms, but the combination of these tools will give you increased resilience in the face of whatever tempest life throws at you. The compass is the key tool of a human-centred leader.

Figure 13.1: your moral compass points through purpose toward Beauty, Goodness and Truth

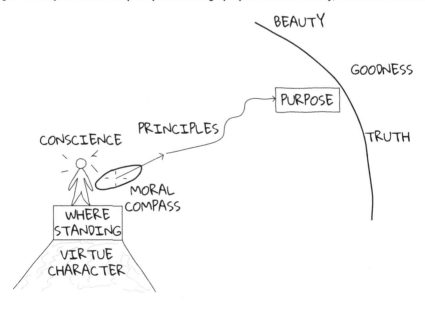

A moral compass provides a sound guide in a world that lacks guides. It gives you the footing for a good life, for a full and flourishing life. However, like any compass, you need to keep it in working order.

'Swinging' the compass

Here's an interesting thing about the magnetic compass on a ship: it is subject to two significant impediments. If you fail to understand them you will get into serious trouble and risk running aground or not reaching your destination.

First, the compass aligns itself to the Earth's magnetic field and so points to magnetic north. This means that if you head north according to the direction your magnetic compass is pointing you will never reach the North Pole. Navigators correct this error by using tables that indicate the correction to apply in order to steer toward true north.

Second, the accuracy of the ship's compass deteriorates over time because of the operating environment, such as the metal of the surrounding ship. With this problem you never know exactly the size of the error. The solution is to 'swing the compass'. This exercise is undertaken in open water by an expert who patiently aligns the ship on a number of known bearings. For example, the professional knows that when the ship is in a particular position, which she ascertains via radar, the nearby lighthouse should be exactly due north. After allowing for magnetic variation she knows that the metal in the ship is the cause of any remaining error in the compass. By patiently 'swinging' through a number of positions the error can be calculated with some precision. She then recalibrates the compass by placing small compensating metal spheres nearby. The navigator can now proceed with the confidence that the only compass deviation is that caused by the Earth's magnetic field, which is readily knowable. A diligent mariner swings the compass on a regular basis.

Your moral compass suffers from two similar flaws.

First, it operates in a 'moral field'—a global environment that pulls it in the direction of the prevailing forces. The overall culture in which you live and work can subtly influence you to think and act in ways that don't quite fulfil your highest ideals. This should be immediately evident by checking in against your purpose and the ideals of Beauty, Goodness and Truth—your true north.

Second, and much more insidiously, your immediate environment of friends, colleagues, and the places—both physical and virtual—where you choose to spend your time and energy, can erode your sense of what is good or what is right. You can find yourself rationalising away actions that you know are unacceptable to the person you aspire to be, the highest version of yourself.

A classic and well-known example of moral decay is the 'what goes on tour stays on tour' argument. (I cannot help wondering who thought that was acceptable, other than the tourists themselves.) This argument encourages the notion that different standards apply in different environments, particularly those where you are away from your normal, stable environment. The longer you remain in a corrosive environment, the more your senses become dulled and excessive or deficient behaviour becomes normalised.

Any change in environment can present a challenge, as our friend Dave discovered when he began loading bricks for a living. Every environment has its own set of rules and behaviours. These are not what is written in the company manual. They are what is demonstrated by your staff and peers, your colleagues and friends—so take care and choose your relationships wisely.

Maintaining your moral compass

Human-centred leaders keep their moral compass in the best possible condition, in full working order.

The first task for ensuring the accuracy of your compass in the prevailing moral field is to ensure you have a sound moral framework that underpins your thinking and acting. This framework includes knowing your purpose, focusing on Beauty, Goodness and Truth, living a life of virtue and following a well-formed conscience—the practices we have described in detail in this part of the book.

The second challenge is presented by your immediate operating environment and is much more insidious, since it can operate like a hidden cancer, slowly eating away at your moral compass. Just as daily exercise keeps you in shape and maintains your health and wellbeing, there are simple daily practices that can maintain your compass. At first these may feel a bit 'clunky'; however, with time and practice you will be surprised how easy they are and how powerfully they can shape your life and leadership. *Ten to fifteen minutes on these each day will radically transform your life.*

There are three practices for keeping your compass pointing toward 'true north' on a human-centred path:

1   setting your intent
2   knowing where you are standing
3   daily reflection.

Setting your intent

This practice answers the question, 'Who is going into the world today?' Or, put in a slightly different way, 'Who will people encounter when they meet me today?'

Meryl Streep is one of my favourite actresses. I admire her ability to take on a wide range of roles and totally project each character into my lounge room. She has a wonderful ability to understand every aspect of the character she is playing, and to fully and completely 'put herself in their shoes'. I assume that when she is acting as Margaret Thatcher or Julia Child she intends to be them, not to be Meryl playing them. I doubt she is thinking about her shopping list while playing the daughter of a grocer who became the British Prime Minister.

Why do I think that? In simple terms, because I only see the PM ... I only see the character Meryl intends me to see.

This is the power of intent. It determines who shows up and who others encounter. However, there is one significant difference between you and Meryl. At the end of the day, she is still Meryl Streep, while you are still the Prime Minister or President, Chairman or CEO, the leader or the luminary. She is playing a role — you are living a life.

Who do you intend people to see? Who turns up and sits in your seat at meetings? Please don't assume I want you to be someone you are not. What I want is for you to take charge of who you are and not allow anything to intrude upon that, not allow any doubts or anxieties, distractions or disturbances, to undermine your being the very best version of yourself.

This is the Renaissance man or woman, the person who is doing good in the world, the person you have shaped and are shaping. If you don't yet feel fully like that person, then 'act as if'. Act as if you are a leader so the leader in you can emerge. Act as if you are courageous so you perform acts of courage. Act as if you understand in order to ask questions to develop understanding.

Think about each encounter you will have with people today. Take a quick look at your diary and remind yourself who you will be meeting. Then ask yourself who they will be meeting when they sit across from you. How do you want them to be at the end of the conversation as a result of spending time with you? Do you want them ready to step down or step up, discouraged or encouraged, disempowered or empowered?

Your presence will have an impact, for better or worse. When you align your intent with your purpose, and allow the person you are to show up for others, they will reaffirm that in you. This accelerates your path toward becoming all you can be.

For the sake of this exercise, imagine for a moment that you set your intent to be 'a wise listener who asks good questions'. Your intention, therefore, is that those you meet will encounter someone who listens deeply, asks good questions and demonstrates wisdom by the insight they bring. You will quickly see by their response whether that is the case. If it isn't, do what Meryl does, and practise over and over.

Knowing where you are standing

This practice answers the question, 'Where are you standing today?' If you have worked through the kinds of questions posed in this book, you have an overall answer for your life. The question now is more immediate — about where you are standing *today*. Here is a powerful exercise to help you answer that question.

Take a moment now and feel your feet on the floor. Press them into the floor wherever you are, whether standing or sitting, whether wearing shoes or barefoot. Feel your feet on the floor. Press hard.

This is the place where you are standing right now.

1 Is this a place from which you could move the world?
2 How do you measure up against your aspirations for Beauty, Goodness and Truth, for a purpose-driven life guided by principles and empowered by virtue?
3 Are you standing on solid ground, on a firm foundation?
4 Where do you need to improve your footing?

You will discover the answers to these questions by taking a moment now to listen to yourself.

Next, you can also leverage the power of this question by blending it with your intent.

When you get out of bed each morning, feel your feet on the floor. Remind yourself where you are standing — in a place that aligns with your purpose, for Beauty, Goodness and Truth, and so forth. As you look in the mirror, feel the floor under your feet and declare your intent out loud:

'Today I am a wise listener who asks good questions. People will be in a better place after they meet me than at the start of our meeting'.

The first time I did an exercise like this I burst out laughing and could barely convince myself. And if I didn't believe myself then why would others? It felt strange and a little self-important. However, I persevered, convinced of how I wanted to project myself in the day ahead.

I pressed my feet into the floor and repeated to myself, 'I am a wise listener who asks good questions. People will be in a better place after they meet me than at the start of our meeting'. I repeated it until I believed it . . . until I 'owned' it.

And then promptly forgot as the pressures of a busy diary took over.

So I repeated the exercise every day until I became more conscious, more aware, more mindful. And then I noticed myself trying to listen to others yet being completely distracted by random thoughts of the next meeting, the last meeting, my inbox . . .

When that happens to you, quickly and quietly press your feet into the floor. No-one will notice except you. This has the powerful effect of reminding you of your intent—where you are standing today—and brings you straight back into focus. I have felt my facial expression relax and change when I do this, and then observed a positive response in the other person. You can apply this same technique in situations you find challenging and difficult, whether presenting to a board or to an audience of thousands, giving a colleague bad news or engaging in a difficult negotiation.

Set your intent in advance, stand in that place and return to it by pressing your feet into the floor.

Daily reflection

This practice answers the question, 'How did I do today?' It asks, in effect, whether you have done your personal best.

This is the most powerful practice you can ever discover for rapid advancement on the path of human flourishing.

If you read that sentence carefully you may have been surprised and even sceptical. 'The most powerful practice...'? There's a very simple reason.

When a ship sets out on a voyage the navigator draws lines on the chart between one port and the next, noting a series of waypoints determined by factors such as weather and obstacles. Setting the destination and mapping the course is the easy part. Staying the course is the hard part, as unexpected events get in your way. A hurricane needs to be avoided, sending you off course for days. Your navigational equipment breaks down and the weather closes in, making the use of a sextant impossible.

Throughout the voyage the navigator continues to plot the ship's position, sometimes with precision, sometimes with an educated guess.

Self-examination is like this. It involves plotting your position against your course, and then recalibrating toward your destination. It is the only way to advance safely and with confidence toward becoming the best person you can be. Failure to reflect on where you are, to have some level of self-awareness about your situation, means you are drifting through life, hoping the wind and the tide will carry you to a land of fruit and honey. But in my experience of drifting, you end up nowhere—aimless, disappointed and frustrated.

Take a few minutes at the end of the day and simply ask yourself, 'How did I do today?'

Then say nothing ... be quiet ... spend a few minutes in silence.

In one of the wonders of what it is to be human, your conscience will gently and quietly remind you of those moments when you did well and when you could change course a little. Naturally if you have done something grievously wrong, such as defrauding the company or lying to Parliament, your conscience was probably ringing alarm bells much earlier (and if it wasn't then it's time to 'swing the compass').

Your daily reflection involves holding up a mirror to your life and actions, and comparing those with the aspirations and intent you set for yourself. You are not checking if your clothes match; rather, you are seeing if your thoughts and actions align with the best version of yourself:

- Were you as honest and truthful as you could have been?

- Were there moments when you fell short of being as good as you would have liked?

- Could you have been kinder and more generous to the colleague who asked for help, rather than dismissing their concerns?

Having established your destination you need to check in frequently to see if you are still standing in the right place relative to that. Are you still standing on the wide highway of virtue or have you ventured off onto the rocky verge? Did the wise, thoughtful listener turn up at work today—and then stay there, to be replaced by the selfish boor at home?

The daily reflection creates the time and space you need to notice the subtleties and nuances of life, to grow in self-awareness, to check your compass and set yourself more precisely on course.

Where are you standing?

It matters not how strait the gate,
How charged with punishments the scroll.
I am the master of my fate:
I am the captain of my soul.

***Invictus*, William Ernest Henley**

Nick had just been selected to join one of the nation's leading football teams and was off to a training camp with 25 of the best athletes in the competition. Men who were household names. Men whom others looked up to, admired and emulated. Men who were role models to the younger generation.

He quietly took his seat at the back of the bus, watching as the legends of the game boarded, and then settled in for the two-hour trip to the training camp.

As the bus got underway the driver started a pornographic film on the entertainment system. Nick was shocked and taken aback. He shifted uncomfortably in his seat, wondering what to do.

'I tried closing my eyes,' he said, 'but the sounds still penetrated. I didn't want that stuff in my head. I thought it was wrong to just play a film like that as if everyone wanted to watch it. And I certainly didn't want to watch it for the whole trip'.

Although he felt compelled to act, he was unsure what to do. He was painfully aware of being the 'new boy' on the block and not wanting to get offside with the team.

Suddenly Nick found himself out of his seat, walking toward the front of the bus ... with no idea what to do when he got there. He felt every eye on his back as he desperately searched for something reasonable to say.

As Nick neared the front of the bus he noticed a younger player, also on his first trip with the team, sitting behind the driver.

'I think we could be breaking the law with that film,' he said in a moment of insight. 'There's a 17-year-old on the bus.'

Without a word the driver flicked a switch and all went quiet ... and Nick began the long walk to the back of the bus, now with every eye upon him. Nobody said a word. Not that day. Not ever.

In that moment Nick set an example of leadership, of being true to yourself, of having the courage to do what is right, acting in a straightforward way to deal with a difficult situation.

Many years later Nick received an invitation to a function attended by members of the championship team who had been on the bus.

'Do you remember that day when you stood up and turned the video off?' asked an old team-mate. The memories came rushing back.

'We all talked about it,' he said. 'Other people admitted they weren't happy with the video but didn't say anything. We thought what you did was one of the most courageous acts we had seen.'

Nick knew where he was standing before he stood up and walked down the bus. He knew where Beauty, Goodness and Truth lay in his life and the principles he wanted to adhere to. He had cultivated a life of virtue—of good habits—and learned to listen to the promptings of an inner voice. It didn't mean he had the answer to what to do, but it did give him the courage to step up and believe it would work out.

Where are you standing?

Have you taken the time to reflect on and consider these foundational elements? If you have then you will know more clearly where you stand, and have a map for moving forward.

When people ask, 'Where is the new Mandela?', or the next Gandhi Mother Teresa or Martin Luther King Jr, I suspect they are looking for people who are committed to Beauty, Goodness and Truth, who are guided by a sense of purpose and a life of virtue, who think clearly and make wise choices that align with timeless human principles. I believe these are the foundations to a great life and outstanding leadership, to what I would call moral leadership, to Human-Centred Leadership.

These foundations will help you navigate the most difficult, complex and challenging times ahead and so are a key to success in the 21st century. They provide the unshakeable place upon which you stand. Now it is time to consider your leadership foundation, the place to stand to be a human-centred leader at your point of contribution to business, government or society—or all three.

PART III

Human-Centred Leadership in action

A map for your leadership journey

Part II introduced the concept of the Journey Map for your life, building the elements that move you from where you are to where you are going, emphasising who you are on the journey before focusing on what you do along the way (figure C).

Figure C: life Journey Map

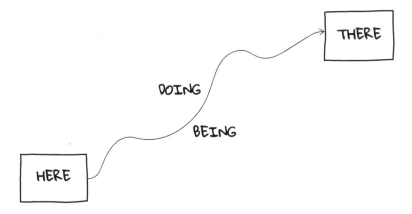

The Journey Map gives a framework for answering four key questions:

- *Here:* Where are you today?
- *There:* Where are you going?
- *Being:* Who are you going to be on the way?
- *Doing:* What are you going to do to get there?

The map can also be applied in your role as a leader of a company, country or community, asking the same questions albeit in an organisational context.

Figure D shows what the map looks like when you add organisational questions.

Figure D: organisational Journey Map

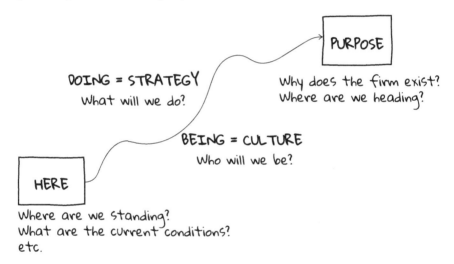

Although this map does not capture the complexity of running a vast enterprise, it does enable you to look out toward your Purpose while maintaining an overview of Strategy—how you are going to fulfil that Purpose—and Culture, or the kind of organisation you want to lead.

Like your own Journey Map, once you have created this map, and answered the big questions, you can scale it to any time frame. When you know why your organisation exists, you can reduce the map to a 12-month time frame: Where are you today? Where do you want to be at the end of the year? What aspects of culture will you focus on this year? What steps do you need to take?

A considerable amount has been written on all of these aspects, much of which is very good, and you need to be familiar with it. My aim is to put a human overlay on this map, and look at it from the perspective of a human-centred leader, with the Journey Map firmly in mind.

Chapter 14 explains two defining aspects of Human-Centred Leadership: it puts people first and it integrates the technical and moral dimensions of leadership. The chapter notes that Human-Centred Leadership operates at the nexus of business, government and society, and so can unite all three toward a common purpose.

Here: Where are you today?

Chapter 15 points out that you can lead from where you are today, regardless of your role, and attests to the impact of leading via influence rather than title.

There: Where are you going?

Chapter 16 considers the question, 'Why do we exist?' in an organisational context, and discusses how the answer liberates people, lifts engagement and profit, and provides long-term direction. It also touches on how to clarify or discover your purpose.

Being: Who are you going to be on the way?

In chapter 17 we go below the line on the Journey Map to examine the relational aspect of leadership and the four key relationships that matter for success. Chapter 18 builds on those relationships and considers your responsibility as a leader to build character and moral capability in your employees.

Doing: What are you going to do to get there?

Chapter 19 goes above the line, and discusses stages of moral development as a way of understanding the different moral reasoning processes people use. Understanding this gives you greater insight into people, helping you become a more human-centred leader. Chapter 20 provides some tools for helping you navigate your greatest strategic risk: moral risk. It offers a framework for decision making in the midst of moral ambiguity and complexity — for resolving moral dilemmas.

The organisational Journey Map will help you captain the ship of state or commerce through the challenges ahead. It provides a foundation upon which you can stand in the enterprise, and from where you operate as a human-centred leader.

An important proviso

While Part III is relevant to everyone in leadership roles, wherever you find yourself, the focus is on Human-Centred Leadership in action at the apex of organisations, since it is there that the shifts and transitions, the complexity and ambiguity, the technical and moral, come together in the lives of the people in and beyond your organisation. Therefore, most examples and questions relate to the challenges facing Directors, Presidents and CEOs as you apply the principles of Human-Centred Leadership at your level. This book is written to help you if you are there or to prepare you for when you get there.

CHAPTER 14

Human-Centred Leadership

'A leader … is like a shepherd. He stays behind the flock, letting the most nimble go on ahead, whereupon the others follow, not realizing that all along they are being directed from behind.'

NELSON MANDELA, *LONG WALK TO FREEDOM*

Puts people first

Human-centred leaders start by putting people first. Although this may seem like an easy thing to do, it requires a single-minded focus and an enduring commitment.

Paul O'Neill, Alcoa

When Paul O'Neill became CEO of Alcoa in 1987 he asked to be judged by one measure: reduction in time lost to injuries. He understood that business is about people, and that when you look after your people, the profit will follow.

Charles Duhigg, writing in *The Power of Habit*, quotes O'Neill's presentation to analysts upon his appointment: 'I want to talk to you about worker safety,' said O'Neill. 'Every year, numerous Alcoa workers are injured so badly that they miss a day of work. Our safety record is better than the general American workforce, especially considering that our employees work with metals that are 1500 degrees and machines that can rip a man's arm off. But it's not good enough. I intend to make Alcoa the safest company in America. I intend to go for zero injuries.'[1]

O'Neill's failure to address profits and margins, capital ratios and inventories, confused analysts and led some to advise clients to exit the stock. Twelve months later Alcoa posted a record profit. After 13 years of O'Neill's leadership, days lost to injury per 100 workers had fallen from 1.86 to 0.2, and net income had increased by a multiple of five. His legacy continued and by 2012 days lost dropped to 0.125.[2]

Paul Polman, Unilever

Paul Polman, the global CEO of Unilever, has repeatedly expressed the view that 'business cannot survive in a community that fails'. He understands it's all about the people: those who make your products, those who use your products and those who work together to bring products to market. When he became CEO in early 2009 he imported this fundamental belief into a business strategy that combined targets for both ambitious growth — doubling the size of the business — and aggressively lower dependence on resources. At the same time he rejected shareholders and analysts who favoured short-term profit over long-term sustainability and purpose.

Rather than asking how to maximise profits and minimise costs, he wondered how Unilever could help society be better — socially, economically and environmentally. Asking this question at Unilever he created three significant 10-year objectives: 'To help more than one billion people take action to improve their health and well-being; to halve the environmental footprint of the making and use of our products; and, to source 100% of our agricultural raw materials sustainably'.[3]

This compelling vision is delivering outcomes for the traditional stakeholders of the firm, for the communities of which Unilever is a part and for future generations. Sixty-five per cent of employees felt engaged in 2008, rising to 73 per cent in 2010 — after Polman's aspirational and visionary targets — and 83 per cent in 2012.[4] Employee engagement has translated into financial wellbeing: since Polman arrived in 2009 revenue has increased by about twenty-five per cent, operating profit is up 50 per cent and earnings per share up 41 per cent.

Peter Scott, Perpetual

Peter Scott, Chairman of Perpetual Ltd, one of Australia's Top 100 listed companies, believes that healthy, sustainable relationships are one of the keys to success—or more precisely that success in relationships matters more than success in business. I once hosted a group of human resource professionals in a conversation with Peter over lunch. When he talked about a former CEO role he explained the expectations he had for his executive team: what they needed to deliver, the numbers that mattered, the outcome that mattered.

'But at the same time,' he told them, 'what *really* matters is that if you are married now, then you are still married in 12 months' time'.

He expanded on this by explaining that success at work could never replace success as a spouse, partner or parent, and that he expected people to tell him if work pressures were creating family pressures. This did not mean that he did not expect performance or results, or recognise that there are sacrifices to be made, but that it was important to be clear about what really mattered. For Peter, relationships trump results.

Some years later one of my clients was promoted to an executive role requiring even longer hours and more extensive travel. We discussed the 'end game'—where he wanted to be after three to five years in the new role. After listing some strategic objectives he looked at me and said, 'What really matters is that I am still in a loving relationship with my wife'. I was touched by this spontaneous recognition of the importance of his family, his deep sincerity, and the clarity he had about the relationship between work and family.

I tell that story because I subsequently discovered that he had once reported to Peter Scott and had been influenced by Peter's commitment. Peter, in turn, was heavily influenced by Dick Dusseldorp, the founder of Civil and Civic, which later became Lend Lease Corporation. Dusseldorp believed that if you focused first on people—growing and developing staff, looking after the customer—then the numbers would take care of themselves.

Paul O'Neill at Alcoa, Paul Polman at Unilever and Peter Scott at Perpetual are outstanding leaders with proven track records of success on any commercial measure. What is clear from their stories, however, is that the key to their success is putting people first, whether family, staff, customers or community. They don't put people first in order to succeed, though. They put people first because it's the right thing to do.

These people find the balance between results and people, between technical and moral leadership. They are human-centred leaders.

Navigating this chapter

This chapter highlights the two key aspects of human-centred leaders. First, they put people first, and second, they integrate the technical and moral dimensions of leadership. It then explains how Human-Centred Leadership exists at the nexus of business, government and society, and why it can be a force for unifying all three.

Integrates the technical and moral

Leadership has both a moral and a technical dimension.

The technical dimension is more closely associated with management, with marshalling resources in an effective manner to deliver results. It includes strategy, operations and stakeholder management, commercial acumen and financial insight, compliance and governance.

People who focus almost exclusively on the technical aspect of leadership are results-centred leaders. They can be successful leaders, with tremendous ability to take the firm to new heights and overcome new challenges. However, those who work with and for them find something is lacking — and that is almost always something to do with people.

Although results-centred leaders do all the right technical things, they don't quite engage with the people — they don't care for people to the extent that is necessary. Stories emerge about 'casualties' around them, as a result of their style.

Results-centred leaders lack an appreciation of the moral dimension of leadership.

Leadership is fundamentally a moral undertaking because it involves people, and their hopes, dreams and aspirations. Remember my earlier comments about the Greek philosophers' concept of the good life? They talked about morality in terms of those actions which promoted human flourishing and wellbeing, those choices which help you become all you can be. This is very different from thinking of morality merely as a question of right and wrong. In this full 'Greek' sense, therefore, moral leadership involves leading people in the right way, to do what is good, to become the best version of themselves — and in particular creating the environment in which that can happen.

Moral leaders can also lack technical leadership skills. Virtuous people with highly attractive character and vision can demonstrate leadership capability. They can be elected to government, appointed to CEO roles... and then do nothing, as they lack the strategic capability, or operational prowess, or understanding of influence and teams, that is required to deliver results. They can be a greater disaster than a good technical leader.

What is needed is a more rounded vision of leadership that strikes a balance between moral and technical leadership.

I propose that true leadership is Human-Centred Leadership, and that Human-Centred Leadership integrates the moral and technical dimensions of leadership. Results-centred leaders are technically capable, but often obtain results by using people as a means to an end. Human-centred leaders have technical *and* moral competence, and obtain results by helping people grow and flourish, so they can freely choose to deliver exceptional results. Results-centred leaders need command and control models of leadership to keep everything and everyone moving in the right direction. Human-centred leaders create environments in which people can flourish, and trust them to head in the right direction in accord with purpose and principles.

Human-centred leaders build a technical edifice on a moral foundation, and so become great leaders in business, government and society.

Dictators and tyrants are not leaders

Dictators and tyrants do not display true leadership. These people present a distorted vision of what is beautiful, good or true, manipulating the doubts and anxieties of others, and exercising power by bullying and fear. They can have outstanding technical capability — they may be great strategic thinkers, for example — but lack the moral dimension. And they are not restricted to the political sphere. Artificial leadership can be found in the boardroom and battlefield, the Congress and the convent.

At the nexus of business, government and society

When business, government and society are driven by results, outcomes and self-interest they focus on profit, power and privilege, creating a fundamental tension between all three (see figure 14.1). Success is measured in terms of making money, winning elections, attaining status. That's understandable, since if a business doesn't make a profit it fails, if governments don't gain power they are unable to implement their policies, and if society doesn't increase prestige for some then others have little sense of aspiration or hope.

Figure 14.1: the tension between business, government and society

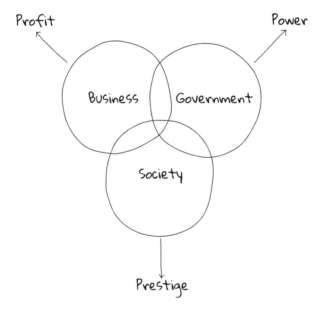

You can probably see the weaknesses and risks inherent in this approach, as the extremes become normal. Not satisfied with sufficient profit, owners demand maximum profit at the expense of people and society. A relentless focus on power fosters destructive displays of partisanship at the expense of people and society. Prestige becomes associated with possessions and displays of wealth, alienating those who lack status and standing. Individuals can be consumed by ego and greed and want ever bigger bonuses, more power and more prestige. Principles and values can be lost.

Human-Centred Leadership, on the other hand, focuses on people, people and people. It is the only form of leadership that effectively unites business, government and society around the human person, who is central to all (see figure 14.2). Human-Centred Leadership recognises that business, government and society are communities of people and that leadership is fundamentally about those people and their hopes, dreams and aspirations. Leadership is about what it means to be human, and what it means to live and work together with others. It is about how you can become the best possible version of yourself, and how you can support others in a similar quest. And lastly it is about how, in the midst of change and transition, we build more human governments, businesses and communities: a more human world. Not an unattainable utopia or Shangri-La perhaps, but at least a better place for successive generations.

Figure 14.2: the person at the nexus of business, government and society

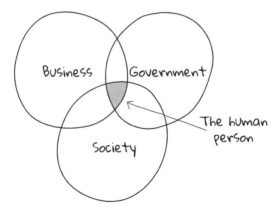

While the respective focus on profit, power and prestige feeds an unhealthy tension between business, government and society, shifting the focus to the human person—which is as simple as consistently putting people first—unites business, government and society. The human person is the starting point for constructing a human society, human business and human government. The human person sits in the sweet spot between the three, and the key to the best possible future for business, government and society is to keep the human person front and centre in every decision and action. The future depends on Human-Centred Leadership exercised by human-centred leaders.

And it starts with you today...wherever you find yourself.

CHAPTER 15

Lead from where you are

'There go my people, and I must follow them, for I am their leader.'
MAHATMA GANDHI

James lamented the fact that he was not a 'leader' and so felt unable to influence the direction of the firm or engage with clients in the way he wanted. Like many others he looked forward to the day when he would 'become' a leader by promotion to a role with a 'leadership' title.

He was making the mistake of equating leadership with a role or a title. This view implies that titles such as President or Chief Executive contain within them a subtext that says to the world, 'Made it. I am a *leader*'. Sometimes people who have the title fall short of what a leader can or should be.

A change of title on your profile or business card does not transform you from a follower into a leader. You don't finish work on Friday as a follower and arrive at work on Monday as a leader merely because your title changed or last week's peers are now your direct reports.

If you were a follower on Friday, you will still be a follower on Monday, because you are thinking like a follower, because you see yourself as a follower. You are yet to grasp that leadership flows from who you are to those around you, wherever you are, regardless of your title. However, if you see yourself as a leader now, you almost certainly will consider yourself a leader tomorrow, and act accordingly.

I pointed out to James the many ways in which he was being a leader. People looked to him for insight and advice. He influenced outcomes. His input and guidance were transforming the manner in which the partners of the firm engaged with clients. His current title, with its emphasis on business development, bore little relation to the power he wielded or the people he touched.

'You lead from where you are,' I told James. 'If you cannot lead from there, if people don't see you as a leader now, you will not be a leader tomorrow. Don't confuse the number of people who report to you with the number of people who follow you.'

Leadership starts with an attitude and intent, not with a title. Leadership flows from your personal authority, from your gravitas ... from who you are. It flows from where you are standing, not from where you are pointing.

Navigating this chapter

This chapter considers the place where you stand today as a leader and the influence you can have, regardless of your role. It is the starting point of your journey as a leader, and has two sections:

- 'Lead by influence' highlights that people respond to you, not your title, and that you are a leader whenever you have a follower—which is most of the time.

- 'Lead from where you are' invites you to let your leadership light shine in such a way that others can see it.

Lead by influence

Leadership by definition implies 'followership', since if no-one is following you then you are not yet exercising leadership. However, it is not always clear who your followers are. You almost certainly have followers now, whether you know it or not.

Pause for a moment and think about the times when someone sought out your opinion or advice. Or the times when someone noticed — confirmed by a compliment — the work you had done or the contribution you had made. Or the times when someone copied your manner of thinking or acting, and perhaps you felt offended because you expected them to think for themselves.

In all these situations you are being a leader, because you have a follower. And that follower is almost certainly looking for your guidance in some way. They observe the way you act and speak, and try to emulate you. For whatever reason they have formed a view that they want to be like you, or some aspect of you, and also believe you can help get them to a different place. They are putting their trust in you. Hence you need to remain aware at all times of the example you are setting. What you say — and even more what you do — tells other people what you consider acceptable. Your actions give them permission to do the same thing. I'm sure you appreciate the power of a bad example. Imagine, however, the power of a great example. Imagine the courage, or the wisdom, you could impart to others.

Although leadership can be highly structured and defined, such as when you are leading a team, it is often unstructured and ill-defined. At those times you are leading by influence: the best and most powerful form of leadership. Influencers lift followers to want to be different. Influence generates internal motivation in others — they decide for themselves how to act. Leadership by telling almost always involves more telling. And then more telling. It's hard work.

You are a leader now. Today. In this moment. Don't think about your title or role, but think about your influence.

1   Where do you influence others?

2   Where do you set an example for others?

The very simple secret to leadership is to lead from where you are, to show up and act like a leader in every moment in every situation. And the very simple secret to Human-Centred Leadership is to put the good of the other person first when you act. By putting them first you will find they want to follow, because you care for them before yourself.

Once you have grasped, and are living, this simple secret—leading from where you are—other people will start treating you like a leader. Showing up and acting like a leader in every moment and every situation will further reinforce your leadership standing. People will look to you for insight and advice. People will look to you for judgement and decisions. While your official role may not change immediately, you are now firmly on the leadership journey.

You don't need to wait for your name to go up in lights. Let your leadership star shine today.

Lead from where you are

There is a compelling scene in *The Life and Death of Peter Sellers* that illustrates this point. When the radio celebrity auditions for a movie role the casting agent reminds Sellers that the script calls for a war veteran. She points out that while he may be 'quite big' on radio, film is 'a visual medium...a very unforgiving visual medium...', with an ill-disguised reference to Sellers' lack of film-star looks. Sellers is quickly rebuffed and the interview is over before it starts.

'Send in Mr Cobblers,' says the casting agent in a later scene, as she continues to audition potential actors for the key role. The broken-down old soldier, struggling with the pain of a shrapnel wound, explains to the agent that although he has no acting CV his deeds in battle speak for themselves.

'You're nearly perfect for the part,' she declares, as Cobblers' authentic emotion draws her in—before, to her brief annoyance, the character straightens up to reveal...Peter Sellers.

People see you the way you present yourself in dress, language, style, attitude and so forth. It is crucial that you fully grasp this powerful point.

People look across their desk and see you in the way you present yourself today, not what you believe you can do or who you aspire to become. They think of you in the context of your current role—as, for instance, the CFO rather than the CEO, the candidate rather than the President.

They don't see your creativity or leadership unless you choose to let it shine. Doing so involves risk. You could get knocked back or knocked down. You could be rejected or refused. But unless and until you take that risk you will never become all you can be. Until you step out of your comfort zone, and start looking and sounding like a leader, you will never get the opportunities and promotions through which your full leadership capability can be unleashed. The old saying, 'Dress for your next role', contains a deep insight.

In this sense, life is an act. I have met many people who consider this a 'game' and so refuse to play, thinking that it is either beneath them or manipulative. They want to be chosen on their merits, selected on their capability, chosen in a fair and objective manner. However, it's not a game, it's reality: we quickly form impressions of one another, and those impressions can be very hard to shift. As the Sellers story illustrates, people can develop opinions about you before you even meet them, so the way you present yourself is critical for influencing and potentially changing those impressions.

Show up and act as the person you know you are, as the person you want others to meet. Set your intent and be the leader of tomorrow ... today.

Take your moral compass out, and be a human-centred leader, because people are looking to you to help them navigate the challenges they face.

CHAPTER 16

Your organisational purpose

Why does your business exist?

Human-centred leaders understand implicitly that business has a moral purpose, not just a technical purpose. What is that purpose? Why *does* your business exist?

Although this sounds like a straightforward question, very few people can answer it quickly and easily, in a way that attracts others to their enterprise. Very few organisations articulate this on their website or in their marketing materials. Many, it seems, just don't know why they exist, or they assume you already know.

Take a moment to write down your answer in one short sentence:

This organisation exists to ...

Navigating this chapter

This chapter shifts your focus to *There: Where are you going?* It asks the question about Purpose—'Why does the firm exist?'—and discusses how the answer liberates people, lifts engagement and profit, and provides long-term direction. It also touches on how to clarify or discover your purpose.

Just as your purpose gives meaning and direction to your life, an organisation needs a purpose to give it meaning and direction. The way that is articulated may change, but the purpose is relatively fixed and unchanging through time and generations. You are appointed to lead the firm toward this purpose, not to change it.

What if you are not *the* leader at the top?

Try to uncover the firm's purpose, or at a minimum the purpose of your division, department or unit. Think perhaps in terms of service: who do you serve, perhaps by delivering something that enables people in another part of the business to succeed? Similar questions can be asked in subsequent chapters. Although you may not yet have the responsibility or authority to implement the practices I describe, you can affect your sphere of the enterprise, and in so doing develop your influence — and almost certainly draw attention as a future leader of the firm.

The organisation is a group of people who work with and for you — and they need to know the answer to the question, 'Why does the firm exist?' They need to be able to come to work each day believing they are making a difference to something that matters. If you want to liberate initiative, particularly during times of great change or confusion, you have to provide a compelling answer to the question, 'Why does the firm exist?'

The most common answer is 'to make money'. What an appalling, unattractive purpose. Can anyone explain how making money for executives and shareholders is meant to give staff a sense of meaning and purpose? All it does is reinforce a sense of bonded labour. A friend who recently completed an MBA said he was the only one in his class who disagreed with this statement. This does not augur well for the future of business and its people, and by extension society.

Imagine your dentist is in business to make money. She has developed a system that ensures fast consultations, frequent patient visits, and high-cost, high-margin procedures, while working in low-cost facilities. She uses your teeth to take a bite out of your wallet. Or does the aged-care facility that looks after your elderly relatives rely on low staffing ratios, poor-quality food and high-cost medical interventions that attract large government rebates in order to maximise profit? Grandma's poor health is contributing to management's good financial health. What happens when your political leaders are in government to make money, and so promote legislation that allows coal leases on land they own, or siphon aid funds into their own bank accounts, or purchase land knowing it will be rezoned and revalued? Their good fortune in getting elected translates into a personal fortune at the country's expense.

When any enterprise exists *for the purpose of making money* it exposes itself to the corrosive power of self-interest. When you believe the firm exists to make money, you will prioritise this end above all else. You will almost immediately lose sight of people—your colleagues and customers, and those who live in the wider communities touched by your firm. This is because people become a means of making money—units of economic production or consumption—not men and women with hopes and dreams and aspirations.

If you believe your business exists to make money, then it's time for a reality check.

Purpose drives profit

Making money is a benefit that flows from delivering against purpose, from putting people first in the attainment of that purpose. A noble purpose without sufficient profit is nothing more than a feel-good statement. Even 'not-for-profit' organisations need to generate a profit—the difference is they recycle it into the cause rather than into dividends. The blind pursuit of a noble purpose with scant regard for commercial realities is just as reckless as the blind pursuit of profit that undermines the social standing of the organisation. Profit without purpose is little more than greed.

Human-centred leaders, who integrate the moral and technical dimensions of leadership, recognise that purpose *or* profit is a false dichotomy. They recognise the balance that must be obtained, that noble purpose drives sufficient profit, and that sufficient profit maximises social harmony.

Jim Stengel, the former Global Marketing Officer at Procter & Gamble, writes in *Grow: How Ideals Power Growth and Profit at the World's Greatest*

Companies that maximum growth and high ideals are 'inseparable'.[1] His research confirms that an ideal- or purpose-driven organisation is considerably more profitable than one that is not.

Stengel studied 50 000 brands over 10 years and found that 'companies with ideals of improving people's lives at the centre of all they do outperform the market by a huge margin'. Investing in what he calls his top 50 over those 10 years would have delivered a 393 per cent return, against a loss of 8 per cent in the S&P 500 in the same period.

After P&G lost $85 billion in market capitalisation in six months, AG Lafley, its legendary CEO, asked Stengel to help transform the culture into one that was customer centred, human centred.

'To hit these big targets,' Stengel writes, 'we needed an even bigger goal: identifying and activating a distinctive ideal [or purpose, as P&G dubbed it] of improving people's lives inside every business in the P&G portfolio. We could then establish each business's true reason for being as the basis for new growth, and we could link them all into a strong foundation for P&G's recovery by building each business's culture around its ideal'. Every business in the group then developed a purpose that aligned with P&G's purpose of improving people's lives.

I asked earlier if you know why your organisation exists. What did you write? Did you describe it in human terms ... in terms of the good it does for people? If not, please take the time to develop a people-centred purpose that can inspire the people you touch.

What could be the impact if you now focus on delivering that purpose and asking your people how they will deliver that purpose? The outcome could amaze you.

Purpose provides long-term direction

Remember the dip that occurs during an inflexion point on the sigmoid curve, or the break brought on by a game-changer? The transition from one cycle to the next starts with an initial dip, which can feel like a loss of direction and be financially and emotionally draining. Living in and through the chaos and confusion of inflexion points and disruption is hard work—and as pointed out earlier, there are many happening in the world now, or that can be expected in the immediate future.

Sometimes the inflexion point is forced on you by an event such as a global financial crisis. Suddenly what was clear becomes murky, what was straightforward becomes confused. Strategic plans are binned before they can gather dust. Employees are not sure how to act or what to do. The firm is facing a crisis, and you are the leader at the helm. What do you do?

Only one strategy works in times of chaos and confusion: Lead by purpose. Ensure people know the reason why. You have no idea how long it will take to work through the inflexion point, nor any great clarity about how things will look on the other side. In times of clear weather and steady-as-she-goes navigation you can make three- and five-year plans. In times of confusion and chaos you can focus only on longer-term purpose, since only it remains clear. Purpose stands like the North Star, or a distant lighthouse, toward which you can steer through the storm.

In the same way your own purpose orients you toward the horizon of Beauty, Goodness and Truth—toward something noble and worthwhile—organisational purpose orients a firm toward a noble horizon. And since that horizon is never reached, the firm can ensure long-run success—that is, sustainability—by continuing to aim for that horizon, with its strategy firmly directed toward fulfilling a grand, people-centred purpose.

When you are working in uncertainty, unsure of what to do or how to act, the purpose provides direction. You need only answer a simple question: 'Does this action move us in the direction of our purpose?' If the answer is yes—even if in a slightly tangential way, like a yacht tacking into the wind—and you are acting in accord with the principles and values of the firm, then you can act with confidence. Having the freedom to make decisions that fulfil purpose liberates initiative among your employees.

What could the purpose be?

Like an individual's purpose, organisational purpose expresses some form of positive impact on people. This does not mean the firm is a charity, or needs to have a charitable-sounding cause, or cannot make a reasonable profit. But it does mean it has a social impact.

- The Academy for Global Citizenship, for example, wants to 'develop mindful leaders who take action both now and in the future to positively impact their communities and the world beyond'.[2]

- American Financial Group says, 'Our purpose is to enable individuals and businesses to manage financial risk'.[3]

- GE has a purpose to make 'a world that works better'.[4]

If you are unsure what your purpose is, or are able to articulate it only in technical or financial terms, can I suggest you take the time to discover a more noble purpose? Although there are a number of ways you could do this, you could begin by finding answers to the following questions:

- Why did the founder/s start the firm?
    - Was it in response to a social need?
    - Has this been lost over time?
- Who do we serve?
- Why do we serve them?
- What difference do we make in their lives when we serve them in the best possible way?
- What impact do they then have on people they touch?
- What difference does this then make in the world?

As the leader, you 'own' the purpose of the organisation. During your tenure you are the 'guardian of the flame' or the 'keeper of the light'. In the midst of almost constant distraction and in the depths of fog, uncertainty, ambiguity and complexity, you keep the firm focused in the right direction.

This generates a very important question for your direct reports: 'How do you deliver the purpose?' The answer to this question shapes strategy, translates into measurable deliverables for the period ahead (12 months, three years and so on), and accelerates your progress toward that purpose in a principled, human-centred way.

However, you can move no faster than the speed of relationships.

CHAPTER 17

Leadership at the speed of relationship

'In every deliberation, we must consider the impact on the seventh generation...'

GREAT LAW OF THE IROQUOIS

Following a long day at a conference discussing leadership trends we had been asked to gather at the top of the staircase at precisely 7 pm. As we stood talking to one another the sounds of a live orchestra emerged from the adjoining room. Where 90 minutes earlier had been a room of flip charts, whiteboards and work, we were astonished to find members of a leading symphony orchestra playing beautifully — each with a vacant chair beside them. CEOs more used to gathering around boardroom tables sat alongside violinists and cellists, and squeezed in beside trumpets and trombones. We looked and listened with wonder and awe as the conductor and musicians displayed their talent and their art.

One of my colleagues wondered whether the conductor added much value as a leader in such an illustrious group of world-class performers. The conductor answered by leading the orchestra through an exquisite rendition of a short piece from Vivaldi's *Four Seasons*. Then, in a simple and profound demonstration, he invited the musicians to perform the same music to the best of their ability without his leadership. With a gesture of his baton the conductor initiated the recital, which quickly degenerated into a chaos of unmodulated sound, ego and attitude, lacking cohesion, tempo, harmony and beauty in the absence of the conductor's shaping and unifying influence.

Leadership enhances individual capabilities by enhancing relationships. Leadership takes the talent that each person possesses and combines it with those of every other player on the team to create a symphony from a sound, order from chaos, focus from frenzy.

Navigating this chapter

The next two chapters are going below the journey line to reflect on the question of *Being: Who are you going to be on the way?* This is a question of culture, about which there is a vast array of very good research material. In these two chapters, however, I want to focus on a particularly human aspect: developing relationships and developing human-centred leaders.

This chapter considers the implications of relationships for leadership. Building on the earlier observation that a person is a relational being, we will look at leadership as a relationship, then consider four key leadership relationships:

- your inner circle
- your stakeholders — staff, shareholders, customers, suppliers …
- the communities in which you operate
- the next seven generations.

Leadership is relationship

The fact that a person is a relational being has profound implications for leadership. It means leadership starts with relationships and only then turns to activity. You cannot lead people if you are not in a relationship with them, and they with you. Anything less than a relationship requires a command and control model of leadership, or something more insidious such as brute force or bribery.

You cannot engage in effective long-term business with someone if you are not in a relationship with them. In the absence of a relationship you merely have a transaction, a brief exchange between two parties with little prospect of continuity.

Business touches people. Whether producing products or generating services, whether your customer is a corporation or an individual, successful business requires successful contact between at least two people. The key to success is recognising the humanity of the other, viewing them primarily as a person, rather than as a consumer, a purchaser, a prospect or a pay cheque.

Business is relational and proceeds at the speed of relationship.

Think about that carefully. Have you ever wondered why a deal fell over at the last minute — the potential client lost interest, or you got pushback from your staff, or your engagement or net promoter scores were down? Somewhere in there was a relationship failure (or many failures). In every one of these situations there is a person who has not been treated the right way in some regard. Sometimes you're not even sure what went wrong; however, you can start by looking at the relationships.

A relationship failure

I once spent months building a relationship with Chris, the regional manager of a global firm. Their Chairman had introduced us, with a view to providing mentoring support to Chris in his new, expanded role. We had met numerous times, understood the issues for Chris and documented all the details of our arrangements, including the engagement process. The mentor I recommended had considerable domain experience in the areas where Chris faced his biggest challenges, and their initial conversations had gone well. Late one Friday afternoon Chris indicated he was 'going ahead', so I immediately set in place our internal client procedures: confirming arrangements with the mentor, emailing Chris a confirmation note, advising our accounts department of the company and client details…

My sense of satisfaction was shattered about three hours later when my inbox exploded with emails from Chris. He was enjoying a social night out when *his* inbox received a slightly impersonal invoice from someone in our accounts department who he did not recognise with what seemed to be quite onerous payment terms. His emotional email to me expressed amazement that I could issue an invoice when we had yet to agree on

(continued)

A relationship failure *(cont'd)*

firm commencement dates or payment terms. He continued by laying out his opinion of the way we did business, concluding with a note that he was closing down communications between us.

I have been over this many times in my mind. Despite what I may believe about clear conversation and careful steps, one thing remains blindingly obvious: I got ahead of our relationship when I switched into process mode. And I rather suspect I had assumed a level of trust in the relationship that did not yet exist.

When you get ahead or behind in a relationship you have to rely on manipulation or coercion to hasten the outcomes you seek. For example, how many firms use money to motivate people when what they really want is recognition based on a relationship? Some employers find it easier to negotiate a bonus than to navigate a relationship and so believe they have done their job by agreeing on financial terms, yet they have failed in relationship terms. Sometimes a bribe is used to sidestep a relationship and make one party subject to the will of the other and so get people to do something they would not normally do. A financial inducement distorts the exchange from a human relationship to a monetary relationship that includes a form of bondage: one party is now indebted to the other in ways they do not yet fully appreciate.

The four leadership relationships

Human-centred leaders 'stand back' — or take a helicopter view — and identify all the human beings with whom they and their organisation interacts. They look at the moving parts of the enterprise primarily in human terms, rather than, say, in terms of the supply chain or value chain or voting bloc. They think about how Maya in the store engages with Josh when he buys new clothing and Dick when he makes a delivery. They think about Bharti who works from home producing unique pieces while she raises her two children.

Although a chief executive may not know names at this level of granularity, a human-centred leader recognises that these roles and positions are filled by real people going about their lives. This is a quite different view from that of a results-centred leader, who focuses firstly on what gets done and only later on who is getting it done.

Just as you personally have four key relationships (as discussed earlier), you also have four key leadership relationships (see figure 17.1). You can think of these as 'touch points', the people you touch as a leader. These include:

1   your inner circle
2   your stakeholders—staff, shareholders, customers, suppliers...
3   the communities in which you operate
4   the next seven generations.

Figure 17.1: four key leadership relationships

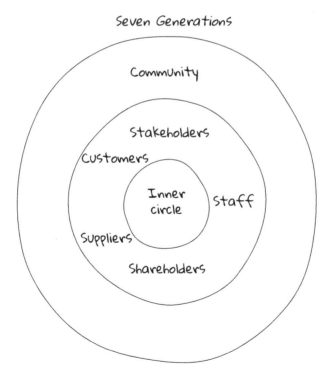

1: Your inner circle

Although Plato's advice to know yourself can be followed by devoting time each day to reflection, it is extraordinarily difficult to really know yourself as a leader. Just as golfers cannot see their own swing and springboard divers cannot see their true form, leaders cannot see themselves leading. You can only observe through the eyes and insight of others. No matter how often you encourage people to tell you the truth and be open, the power you hold in the relationship — however virtuously you exercise it — makes it very difficult for people to be completely honest. The information you receive is shaped by your demeanour and filtered through the self-interest of the messenger.

Confidants who are independent of the organisation keep you grounded in reality and focused on what matters.

'What do you tell people when they ask about having a mentor?' I asked Grant Blackley, the former CEO of Ten (one of Australia's leading free-to-air television channels) as we met in his office, with its wall of televisions always on in the background.[1]

'Mentors can play a crucial role in assisting CEOs to prioritise key issues whilst acting as a confidant and trusted guide,' he replied without a moment's hesitation, recognising the need to always stay on top of his game. He expanded on this by using the analogy of a player being selected for a national sporting team. 'They receive the team uniform, then meet the physiotherapist, the trainer, the high-performance coach, the dietician … The point is quickly made that they are good enough to make the team but they need to work hard to stay on it, using every resource available, because their competitors are working hard to beat them.'

Grant pointed out that being a CEO was like that — the appointment is just the beginning. Confidants, who help you stay true to yourself, are aware of your impact, and provide a sounding board for you to test and be pushed in your thinking, provide a key relationship for leaders.

2: Your stakeholders

Your relationship with those you work with in the enterprise is vital to success. They know whether you care or not. They know whether the relationship is about them or really about you and what you can gain from them. And if you do not have an effective human relationship with your staff and colleagues, then they are not engaged.

A 2008 study by the Department of Business in the UK found two-thirds of employees are disengaged, costing the UK economy about sixty billion pounds each year. The cost of not putting people first is astronomical — they don't engage, don't give discretionary effort, and almost certainly don't promote your firm or your services to other people. And all because of your failure to be a human-centred leader.

Beyond the firm, your stakeholders include your customers, suppliers and shareholders. Although I would like to think it is self-evident why these relationships matter, I never cease to be surprised by people who act in ways inimical to this.

3: Your community

When we consider the leader's relationship with the wider community I can do no better than remind you of Paul Polman's warning: business cannot prosper in a community that fails. His actions show his deep understanding of the importance of this relationship, and of balancing social outcomes with commercial imperatives.

Within these three circles — in particular the last — is a subset of distinct relationships that require active attention: connections with people who can expose you to new ways of thinking and acting, who can expand your view of the world, and who can inspire your growth and development. These are the relationships you cultivate when you 'get out and see the future'.

4: Seven generations

The fourth circle shifts your gaze from today into the distant future. It invites you to look far beyond the annual report, the five-year plan or the budget cycle to the 200-year legacy you will leave.

'The CEO is a guardian for future generations,' said Alan White, the former CEO of N Brown Group in the UK.[2] 'She plants the seeds of long-term growth on sound principles,' he continued.

The Iroquois appeal to consider the next seven generations when making decisions has been around since at least the 12th century. Seven generations thinking says, 'It stops with me'. Seven generations thinking refuses to rely on someone in 200 years' time to tidy up the residue of your actions. When you find yourself thinking that someone in the future can fix this problem, then you are abdicating your responsibility to those who follow. When you think someone else can remediate the land, or repair the national budget, or rebuild rundown infrastructure, you are ignoring your relationship with, and obligation to, future generations.

Human-centred leaders recognise the breadth and depth of their relationships, both geographic and temporal — across space and time. One of my clients has a simple test for any action: 'Will doing this create a problem for any person who replaces me in this seat?' It's a good question to ask.

Your relationships

Before you read on, take the time to draw up a quick list of the key relationships in each of the circles described in this chapter, and make a note also of the gaps:

- Who are the people in your inner circle, the trusted confidants who provide unvarnished feedback and on whom you can test your thinking?

- What are the key relationships in your enterprise? Who are the key customers, suppliers and shareholders you need to keep in touch with, and what is your plan for doing so? There are some you can immediately list by name, others by function, and still others by a question, since you don't know who they are.

- Who are the community leaders and influencers with whom you need to engage in the communities in which you operate?

- Where do you leave a footprint that extends beyond your lifetime?

You will by now have pages of names, including a few generic ones, such as 'New York customer #2' or 'Government representative in China'. Now ask yourself:

- What is the nature and quality of each of these relationships?

- Is the relationship satisfactory given the challenges before you?

- Is it satisfactory against the measure of being a human-centred leader?

- What needs to change or be done differently?

- What does your footprint look like to those it touches?

Human-Centred Leadership cascades from the board, through the CEO and executive team, into the organisation. Human-centred leaders make decisions with an eye on the purpose of the firm and the people who populate its world.

Human-centred leaders put relationships first. They put the human person at the centre of their thinking and ask what is in the best interests of that person, the people with whom they relate, the community to which they belong, the nation of which they are a part and the world we share. They always ask about the people affected by the decisions, and how to minimise negative impacts and maximise what is good.

They always think about developing their people. Their actions show that their primary role is to help people flourish and become all they can be. In this sense they focus first on creating high-touch environments as a precursor to high performance. They don't think in terms of Anjila's output, but in terms of what is good for Anjila. While thinking about global sustainability they are thinking about talent sustainability. While thinking about growth in the business they are thinking about growth in their people.

How do you do that? How do you create human-centred leaders? It's a good question, and perhaps the single most important responsibility of a leader.

CHAPTER 18

Developing human-centred leaders

'All your scholarship would be in vain if at the same time you do not build your character and attain mastery over your thoughts and your actions.'

MAHATMA GANDHI

Navigating this chapter

This chapter continues to look at who your organisation is on the journey, and considers your responsibility as a leader to build character and moral capability in your employees. It draws two main conclusions:

- People require moral as well as technical development, and you are a role model when people are not sure how to act.

- Organisations face a 'character challenge' since people join with little character formation. Business has an obligation to form leaders, both for the good of the person and to minimise moral risk.

People, technical *and* moral development

Since human-centred leaders integrate the technical and moral dimensions of leadership, they take people development to another level, a moral level. Human-centred leaders develop technical capability in their people, and they also develop character and moral capability. They recognise that people will face morally ambiguous situations and decisions that affect them and the organisation.

The risks associated with not developing moral competence are extreme. People who choose poorly could end up on the wrong side of the law. They could make choices that damage themselves, their relationships and their future. They could make decisions that undermine the reputation, financial results, strategic direction or even the viability of the firm.

Where are Barings and Enron today? What has been the fallout from the LIBOR scandal at Barclays and other firms? The Bank of America paid almost $17 billion to settle a charge of selling flawed mortgage securities.[1]

These scandals, failures and collapses were *all* the result of a person, or group of people, making poor moral choices. They had their genesis in moral, not technical, failure. There was no shortage of bright people doing very clever work and delivering wonderful short-term returns. There was a shortage of courageous people asking questions, such as whether this was the wisest way to act.

Trusting your people to do the right thing at all times is vital to the success of the enterprise you lead (and frankly to your health), but you need to know that trust is well founded. Since you cannot be in all places at all times, you need to be confident that your people will choose wisely and well when faced with complex, often morally ambiguous decisions. You won't be there to watch over every action — although you will have to sign off on the accounts, attest to their accuracy and truthfulness, and confirm that the company has not engaged in corrupt or illegal behaviour. Might it not be helpful to equip your people with a moral compass?

'You can never stop people like me,' said Nick Leeson. But he could have been stopped — when he first started work and was in desperate need of moral role models. He could have been stopped if the firm had prioritised people over profit, if the firm had learned to ask better questions ... and in particular if the firm had not assumed they could trust him.

In other words, you stop the Leeson effect by recognising that people join your organisation with a wide range of perspectives on what is right or wrong, and on what constitutes acceptable behaviour, which have been shaped by their own upbringing and experiences. And when they join your firm they will generally adapt themselves to the prevailing culture. In the absence of a strong moral compass they will model themselves on you—yes, *you*—because your behaviour sets the tone for the entire organisation, no matter how big or how dispersed. What you tolerate or accept, what you reward or reject, what you say and do, and the way you say it and do it, sets the standard for the organisation.

If you want to really take care of your people, you have to grasp your responsibility to help them make good moral choices in a morally challenging world, so they can grow in goodness, in humanity and toward the best version of themselves—and along the way ensure that your organisation has a positive impact on its customers, suppliers and community and the next seven generations.

You are a role model

'Who will lead us?', the question I continue to hear, is not about strategic or political or social leadership. It is about moral leadership, and contains within it the search for the new Mandelas.

As you will recall, I have suggested that *you are the new Mandela*. And you become this by becoming the best version of yourself, following a moral compass and becoming a person of moral stature, with a moral vision of what can be in the lives of people who look to you for leadership. When people look for leadership in your firm, they look first to you.

This means you have some questions to answer. What behaviours will you exhibit in yourself and allow in others? What will you do to help your people navigate the moral fog of the 21st century to become all they can be?

You cannot avoid these questions, I'm afraid. You have a responsibility to your country, company and community, and the individuals within these, to ensure your people are fit for purpose, that they have the tools and capability to figure out what is right, to stand up for what is right and to do what is right, guided by principles and purpose, directed toward Beauty, Goodness and Truth.

The character challenge

Remember John, the sports executive who recognised the link between elite performance and character? He had observed that people joining the team bring a wide range of moral perspectives and moral competence, and realised that character formation is crucial to success.

The military recognised the importance of character training many years ago, explained Major General Arthur Denaro as we talked in the library at the Cavalry and Guards Club in London. General Denaro is an imposing figure and a man with a lifetime of military experience, including in the UK Special Forces, as commander of a tank regiment during the First Gulf War and as Commandant of the Royal Military Academy, Sandhurst (RMAS). I listened intently to his rich insights about leadership under extreme pressure, and the relationship between character, values and mission success.[2]

General Denaro mentioned that self-interest and the lack of a social conscience among new cadets was one of his biggest challenges when he was Commandant at RMAS. He noticed that young cadets arrived with little consistent values or standards, and some with only vague ideas about the right or wrong way to behave. The General tackled this head-on in an informal conversation with each new intake during the first week after their arrival, talking with them about values of consideration and care for others, of trust, integrity and respect. He told them stories that demonstrated the behaviours he expected, and was very clear about the consequences of failure to abide by the values: instant dismissal. General Denaro explained that the focus of RMAS is on laying the foundations of leadership capability and character in future military leaders.

Business obligation to form leaders

Sports teams want to win. The military wants to win. They believe they need to develop character as the foundation for future leadership and future success. And they believe this is just as important as skill development.

'The corporation has a pastoral role,' said Dame Alison Carnwath as our conversation drew to an end. 'Pastoral' is an interesting term, with its overtones of sustainable farming practices. It conveys the idea of developing and caring for people and looking after them for the long term. In particular, it carries a sense of responsibility for character formation.

Business generally assumes this is not its responsibility and while it is happy to run ethics workshops, it avoids deeper character training. Unlike the military, it has given this little consideration. But if you recruit people based on character and then develop their character, you will require far less emphasis on ethics training. If you develop human-centred leaders who put people first, you will almost certainly accelerate results in an ethical manner.

Businesses will need to take responsibility for character formation if they want to succeed over the long term — in a way that balances profit with maximum positive impact on people and the planet. To assume the moral goodness of people joining the firm, and to focus on technical development without moral development, is fraught with danger. It exposes the firm to deep moral risk — that people inside your organisation will do what is good for them in a way that undermines your reputation, results or long-term survival.

The shortcomings of ethics training

Ethics training, as it's generally pursued today, can have four main failings:

1   It usually relies on case studies of well-known ethical failures with well-known outcomes. This fosters debate about what happened, rather than insight that can be applied to vastly different scenarios.
2   Presenters often rely on complex scenarios to highlight limitations in ethical thinking. For example, a trainload of passengers is about to derail unless you switch it to another line, but if you do an unwary worker walking across the tracks will be killed. What do you do?
3   It's a course rather than a lifestyle. Ethics training is usually driven by a compliance regime — a legal construct — and the need to ensure people have had the rules and expected behaviours explained to them.

(continued)

The shortcomings of ethics training *(cont'd)*

---

4   They often present two ethical theories — one based on rules and one based on outcomes — as if these are the only two approaches to ethics. A virtue-based ethics is much more helpful and avoids the shortcomings of these two approaches.

And since ethics courses usually operate without a perspective on Beauty, Goodness and Truth, they can fall foul of relativism, and equality of opinion and views. One young man remarked to me, after completing the (extraordinarily brief) ethics component of an MBA and sitting through a vigorous debate about the use of facilitation payments in a foreign country, that although he learned little about ethics he learned a lot about who not to do business with.

While ethics programs have an important place, they are a poor substitute for character formation. They rarely address the underlying question of the person making ethical choices, or put ethics in the context of human excellence and being the best person we can be. When firms start testing for character in their recruitment processes, and forming character in their development programs, they will minimise the need for ethics training and maximise the growth of their people as flourishing human beings.

One way you can develop character is by equipping your people with the kind of moral compass outlined in this book, so they can more easily choose the right path.

In addition to character, however, people need to understand how to navigate moral dilemmas or to make moral decisions, not just strategic decisions. This is a key skill for human-centred leaders.

CHAPTER 19

Moral reasoning

'Nothing in life is to be feared, it is only to be understood. Now is the time to understand more, so that we may fear less.'

MARIE CURIE

Have you ever found yourself in a conversation, or perhaps an argument, where you think the person on the other side of the table could just as easily be from another planet? Despite how clearly you explain your position, they remain blind to your insights? And have you noticed how they think the same thing about you?

Have you seen this in our elected political representatives, in the way they vehemently disagree with one another about often simple matters? While both sides claim they care and that they hold the moral high ground, those they care about continue to suffer.

Different people, whether your family, friends, work colleagues or fellow citizens, have *different ways of looking at and resolving moral issues*. Where some think in terms of black or white, good or bad, others see nuance and shades of grey.

Could I suggest that if you talked to a large number of people about the process they use to work through moral challenges you would be able to identify a number of very similar approaches? You could then form groups of people based on these observations. One set, for example, could consist of those who rely on external authority, while another could be those who figure things out for themselves.

Can I also propose that *the way in which individuals and communities think about moral issues is changing*? Not the conclusions they reach, but the way they go about reaching those conclusions. For example, while most people supported the actions of their leaders during the Second World War, one generation later many opposed the Vietnam War. What changed? In the 1940s most people commonly accepted and followed the edicts of their government, yet by the 1960s people openly challenged external authority—to the great surprise of those in authority. This post-war generation adopted a different approach to moral reasoning, to how they chose 'right' from 'wrong'.

The process of moral reasoning, at both personal and social levels, needs to be upgraded to cope with the demands of the 21st century. Although this is happening with some people, others are struggling to adjust. Some remain stranded at a level of reasoning that is inadequate for the challenges we face in the contemporary and emerging world. They need people such as you, who apply the principles of Human-Centred Leadership, to help them.

Navigating this chapter

The next two chapters look above the line on your organisational leadership journey at *Doing: What are you going to do to get there?* Whereas in Part II we talked about making wise decisions in your own life, now we look at making wise decisions as a leader. The aim of this chapter is to help you understand different ways of moral reasoning. To do that I will introduce you to the work of Lawrence Kohlberg, and explain the relevance of this for you and your leadership. The chapter is divided into two parts:

- 'Stages in moral reasoning', the bulk of the chapter, provides a crucial theoretical framework for understanding how people choose what they consider to be right, and how you can develop that capability. The examples help to explain the concepts.

- 'Moral reasoning at national and global levels' looks at how you can use these insights to look at what is happening within and between countries.

Stages in moral reasoning

Lawrence Kohlberg was a founder of developmental psychology in the early 1960s and remains one of the most influential thinkers in this field. Anyone who has studied psychology will be aware of Kohlberg's work, the impact of his thinking and the ways others have built on his theories.

I am only a tourist in this area, however, and so bring the perspective of someone visiting Paris for the first time. I enjoy its culture and history, the art and architecture, the scenery and the citizens. And yet I do not speak the French language, have only a rudimentary understanding of the richness of their history and culture, and see only houses where they see homes.

But just as unexpected aspects of Parisian life, or the beauty of Monet's *Water Lilies*, open new vistas before me, so too Kohlberg points me down new and interesting avenues of thought. Rather than looking at his thesis from the perspective of an academic or a theoretician, I explore and interpret it from the coalface of leadership. In this sphere I have found it to be enormously helpful for understanding people, people in community with one another, and their moral development. His theory provided both the rigour I sought, and something of a roadmap for the moral journey we are all on.

Summary of Kohlberg's six stages of moral development, grouped into three levels

---

Level 1: Pre-conventional: People 'see morality as something external to themselves, as that which … people say they must do.'[1]

- *Stage 1: Obedience and punishment.* People believe rules are unchanging and obey them in order to avoid punishment.

- *Stage 2: Individualism and exchange.* People become aware of their own point of view and tend to act in ways that serve their own needs—that is, self-interest begins to affect their decisions.[2]

(continued)

Summary of Kohlberg's six stages of moral development, grouped into three levels *(cont'd)*

Level 2: Conventional. Conventional morality assumes that the views or attitudes expressed 'would be shared by the entire community'.[3]

- *Stage 3: Interpersonal.* People are increasingly aware of social expectations and norms.

- *Stage 4: Maintaining social order.* People begin to consider the wider community when making moral decisions.[4]

Level 3: Post-conventional. People ask about the kinds of ethical principles that may be required to live effectively in a good society.[5]

- *Stage 5: Social contract and individual rights.* People begin to recognise the different views, values and beliefs of others.[6]

- *Stage 6: Universal ethical principles.* People internalise moral principles.[7]

Although Kohlberg talks about stages of moral 'development', you may find it helpful to think of each stage as a progressively more complex way of moral reasoning. One example of this is the point at which you realised that things are not simply black or white, that there are shades of grey and that you needed to consider a much wider range of inputs. In other words, you needed, and developed, a different way of thinking about moral matters.

Your moral reasoning ability grows and develops when something changes in your world, which is often accompanied by some kind of discomfort. One obvious example is when you first went to school. Your world expanded from that of parents and family members, to teachers, new friends and a wider community. You discovered that other people had different points of view and ways of seeing the world, although it probably felt like an extension of home rather than a foreign country.

Perhaps another example you would recall more clearly is when you first started work. Do you remember what it felt like to move from the relatively stable and secure world of family and school or university friends, to the very different world of work? You would have discovered, as I did, a wide range of very different people, motives, expectations and rewards. You may recall the uncertainty, the doubts, the excitement, the opportunity, the learning challenges ...

When your environment changes it provides an opportunity for growth, which can sometimes be uncomfortable. Your values and belief systems can be challenged. You may need to upgrade your knowledge, understanding and capabilities in order to operate effectively. You almost certainly will encounter new and different ways of moral thinking.

Kohlberg helped me understand that some people have a very straightforward approach to moral reasoning, along the lines of 'my parents taught me' or 'the Bible says' or 'the law says'. Others have deep insight into what appear to be competing value systems, combined with a robust personal system, and can bring new perspectives and wisdom to complex moral issues. This is what happens, for example, when someone like Mandela or King looks at oppression.

Someone who accepts and lives by an external code is not morally better or worse than someone who navigates moral complexities with apparent ease. One is not morally superior to the other, in the way we tend to think someone with a higher IQ is smarter than someone with a lower IQ. They just approach moral challenges in a different way. It is very important to recognise these differences and respect the different ways people operate. Also, someone who is comfortable with moral complexity (shades of grey) can still make very poor decisions and choices.

However, the complex range of moral challenges we face today means we need people with an appropriate moral reasoning ability. Just as leaders require a certain level of intellectual strength to deal with contemporary challenges, so too do you need a measure of moral horsepower.

Leaders face a range of complex moral dilemmas and decisions almost every day. They operate in a diverse, interconnected world, in a relentless cycle focused on maximising results and minimising risks across every domain. Failure to appreciate different moral frameworks, and different ways of moral reasoning, can be both a source of conflict and an obstacle to resolution when you try to reconcile differences.

If you find yourself, for example, operating in a community that believes in total unquestioned obedience to a religious figure or religious writings, then telling someone they are wrong or appearing to impose your antithetical views on them will be entirely unhelpful.

So, with that background, let's look at the stages of moral development in more detail, remembering that they are more precisely different ways of moral reasoning. Understanding these stages will help you recognise them when you encounter people operating at these levels, and will help you understand how to lead them from where they are. It will, that is, make you a better, more human-centred leader.

In the *first stage* people have complete confidence in authority figures such as their parents and generally do the right thing so they don't get into trouble. This is most common among pre-school children, who hold their parents in awe, and who also assume that everyone's view is the same as their own. Their worldview is as yet somewhat limited.

In the *second stage* people begin to be influenced by a wider set of authority figures, such as school teachers or community leaders. They continue to operate quite comfortably on the basic assumption that whatever they are told by those authority figures is completely and absolutely the truth.

It is possible to live your whole life in a good and productive way at stages 1 and 2. Most societies were like this until relatively recently in historical terms. Most people accepted the authority of kings and queens, of popes, presidents and parliaments, and obediently followed their directives.

Each stage, right up to stage 6, incorporates and transcends the previous. The first two stages provide a solid footing to your future moral platform, in the same way you need a deep and wide foundation to support a very high tower. Therefore, these first two stages are crucial. During these you 'learn' about authority—is it brutal or loving, for example? You begin to understand that you are a part of a community. You learn to share, to care and to live with others. You lay the foundations for empathy, which is a critical skill if you are to put yourself in someone else's shoes, and put people first.

Stage 3 is where it starts to get interesting. During the third stage you become more aware of your ability to decide who and what you will and will not believe, and how you will or will not act. Do you remember when you were a teenager how much you wanted to fit in, to not be different from your peers? You may also remember questioning the values and beliefs received from your parents and other authority figures, choosing to accept those that aligned with your developing values and beliefs and reject those that didn't.

Imagine you are carrying a backpack that has been filled with meaning and values inherited from your parents and immediate community. They put these in your backpack as both tools and gifts to help you through life.

In the third stage you realise that you are carrying someone else's 'belief system' and so reach into the backpack to have a closer look at its contents. Do you recall wondering what you believed, turning over different ideas in your mind, choosing to keep some and reject others? You made choices, for example, to accept or reject your parent's views on religion or sexuality. You realised that you could make your own decisions about what you hold to be true, or what you believe is right and good. While parents can easily interpret this as teenage rebellion, it is actually a crucial aspect of growth and development into an independent adult.

Regularly reassess your beliefs

Socrates said, 'The unexamined life is not worth living'. Set aside some time on a regular basis—say, once a year—to reach into your backpack and have a look at what you are carrying. Remove some objects and replace them with others. Remind yourself of the treasures within. And occasionally turn the bag upside down and shake out whatever might be hiding underneath everything else.

One consequence of reviewing your beliefs and values at this stage is that you find yourself in disagreement with others. The serious thought and effort you put into deciding what is 'right' led to the natural conclusion that someone who arrived at a different position must be 'wrong'. Since you cannot both be right, they must be wrong—and they are usually your parents and teachers. When a teenager, for example, concludes that 'God is not real' or 'morality is what I decide is right or wrong', then it is plainly apparent to them that anyone who disagrees with them is wrong. At this time in our life, at this stage of moral reasoning, we can draw only one conclusion.

During this stage people become very aware of their own power to choose, and can become an authority unto themselves. This is a dualistic time of black or white, either/or, with no room for paradox or ambiguity. It's a world of 'I'm right ... therefore you are wrong'.

Many people operate at this stage of moral reasoning and live full and flourishing lives, although if you find yourself in an argument with them it can be very difficult to persuade them to see other viewpoints.

I have heard it suggested that most organisational leaders operate at stage 3. This means their ability to see and appreciate other perspectives and points of view is limited. It also means their ability to lead effectively in a complex world is seriously compromised. Can you imagine the impact of this kind of thinking? Can you see this kind of thinking in your organisation? In your country? Can you see it in yourself? If you do observe it in yourself, then take time with people who hold very different views to you and try to discover the person who holds the view. Try to relate to them from a caring, human-centred perspective, rather than an ideological perspective. You don't have to find yourself in agreement, but you do have to be able to understand and respect their point of view.

As you continue to grow and develop, your awareness of others extends to a much broader social community, prompting your moral reasoning to be stretched yet again. This is the *fourth stage*, where you appreciate that doing the right thing is important for the effective operation of society. It's not just about you. You accept that in order for society to function well it is sensible to follow an agreed set of rules. Although those rules have an external origin and force, you make your own choice to follow them. You are not following them because, say, your parents told you to, but because you understand that particular ways of living promote harmony and a viable community. People at this stage experience 'rules' not as a restrictive burden, but as a liberating force that gives structure to their life. This is sometimes called a 'self-authoring' stage, capturing well the idea of designing your own life.

Here is a simple example of these first four stages.

I remember my father purchasing a new caravan and not having the correct licence plate as he towed it home. The dealer had supplied the relevant documentation to show proof of purchase and registration to any inquisitive law enforcement officer. As a young child (operating at stage 1), however, I was terrified that we could all go to jail for breaking the law. My worst fears were realised when a policeman noticed the non-compliant plates, pulled us over and asked my father to step out of the car. While I waited anxiously to be handcuffed, fingerprinted and marched off to the big house the adults quickly resolved the situation.

When I obtained my driving licence (and now reasoning at stage 3) I considered traffic regulations, such as speed limits, to be more of a 'suggestion' to help me make up my own mind. The signpost might say 60, but if my (assumed) ability and skill meant I could drive safely at 80, then was that restriction not unreasonable? And, in the arrogance of youth, I preferred that everyone else drove faster rather than slowing me down. Besides, I believed, I wasn't hurting anybody. At the time these self-centred perspectives seemed like quite reasonable points of view.

With the passage of time I realised that my behaviour was actually reckless and irresponsible, that there were many good reasons for having a traffic code, and that life went more smoothly for everyone when we followed it. (Although this observation suggests I was operating at stage 4, I would not want you to think this ability necessarily extended to all areas of my life.)

Can you see how a choice to drive at a speed that makes sense for myself and other users is a different kind of choice from one responding to fear of punishment? The outcome may be the same—driving within the speed limit—but the motivations are entirely different.

In the *fifth stage* you learn to live by moral principles. You begin to fully appreciate the complexity of living in a diverse society, and the tensions between different perspectives and systems, between the personal and the communal, between this group and that group. This is a 'self-transforming' stage.

Your worldview expands, you learn to respect those who hold different opinions, and become more comfortable with paradox and ambiguity. You can see and operate with massive complexity. You understand and accept that other good, rational, well-meaning people have a different perspective. You recognise that you don't hold a franchise on the truth, and you learn to live alongside those with whom you disagreed in the past. This is a shift from either/or, east *or* west, to both/and, east *and* west. When people and teams are able to operate at this level they collaborate and co-create effectively. Helping people reach this point through your influence is an important role for leaders.

At this stage you develop the ability to reconcile what appear to be divergent and opposing views, often in innovative ways, and recognise that the wider community needs to be part of decision making and the formulation of laws. Although this can sound slow and laborious to someone operating at a different level—who just wants everyone else to do as they want or do—it is crucial for the wellbeing and growth of society. It can also be a time of conflict with friends who continue to reason at a different stage. Your colleagues, for example, can be operating in a very 'black and white' world and have no appreciation of your shades of grey or world of colour. They can interpret your position as betrayal and 'selling out'.

Can you imagine, for example, how difficult it would have been for white people in America's South to support Martin Luther King Jr, either publicly or privately?

At *stage 6* you internalise and live your moral values deeply, recognising—and accepting—that at times these may be in conflict with the community of which you are a part. This may come at great personal cost. It can be observed in those people who cry out against injustice not because it breaks the law but because it injures humanity. This is the Wilberforce advocating an end to slavery or the Mandela calling for an end to apartheid. At this stage people do what they hold to be right because it is right, and are prepared to be punished for their views and actions. You can be ostracised, beaten, jailed, mocked, rejected ... and then with the passage of time the prophetic nature of your words and actions, and the stand you took, becomes evident to others.

And, by the way, the fact that someone may be able to reason at this level does not mean they are a saint, just as someone at stage 1, obeying rules to avoid punishment, is not a sinner. People at each stage can and do live exemplary lives. They can equally demonstrate quite atrocious behaviour. A powerful vision doesn't necessarily shed light on our own blind spots.

In other words, the internalisation of moral principles at a higher level of moral reasoning does not automatically mean someone is well rounded in every aspect of their character. It does not mean that they are perfect in any sense, and nor should we expect them to be. The hard work to become all you can be is an often bumpy journey.

Understanding these stages of moral development can perhaps assist you in leading others and yourself to grow in moral reasoning ability, but it will not show you how to grow in moral stature. That is the work of self-mastery we discussed earlier.

Moral reasoning at national and global levels

Kohlberg's theory can also help us make sense of what is happening at a global level. Whole countries demonstrate behaviour that indicates a particular stage of moral development. And many countries—and hence their citizens—are facing, and in most cases resisting, the need to transition to another level of moral reasoning.

Variations in moral reasoning ability are one of the most profound leadership challenges of the 21st century. It requires men and women of great moral stature and moral courage to resist entrenched self-interest, domineering pressure groups and reactive behaviour, to help forge a way forward for humanity. It requires human-centred leaders to overcome the challenges.

Some countries are operating at stage 1 or 2. Some may be in transition from stage 2 to stage 3. I think here of countries in the Middle East or Africa that have been dominated by dictators or religious leaders with the power to rule on every aspect of life. When this kind of leadership steps aside or is removed, and people are given free rein to form their own views, countries risk civil war, because whole swathes of the population begin to think for themselves but in dualistic ways—'we are right and hence you are wrong'. When this happens in cultures that resolve conflict in often bloody ways, civil war becomes almost inevitable. And the answer is not to return to dictatorial-style governments, but to rapidly increase exposure to the Beauty, Goodness and Truth of alternative perspectives, to help people grow in their moral reasoning capability.

And don't presume the West, or developed economies, are perhaps in some way morally superior, for they also need to develop their moral reasoning capability. Wherever individual countries and their leaders continue to hold that their way is the right way (that is, stage 3 reasoning at a national level), they will not be able to promote an effective global social order because of the underlying assumption that everyone else is wrong. This is the 'if you are not with us you are against us' mode of behaviour. No amount of dialogue and conversation can overcome this fundamental difference in moral reasoning. A simple shift to 'if you are not against us you are with us' can radically alter the landscape.

And as long as populist politicians and narrowcast media pander to—and reinforce—shallow interest groups (stage 2 reasoning among certain segments), those societies will experience increased partisanship and fragmentation, and decreased social harmony. The only way forward is into the discomfort of uncertainty, ambiguity and paradox, rather than retreating into simplicity and certainty.

Although much angst between people and nations manifests as polarisation or partisanship, it is often based on different ways of moral reasoning. Again, remember, not right or wrong, neither intrinsically good nor bad, but *different* ways of reasoning. Failure to take account of those differences is the source of considerable conflict.

* * *

The way forward requires human-centred leaders with enhanced moral reasoning ability. Not just business or political skills, not just vision and dreams, not just the ability to get stuff done, but rather, the ability to think about moral issues in an entirely different way, and then to help people cross what appears to be an abyss between their current and future ways of thinking.

CHAPTER 20

Moral decision making

The challenges posed by shifts and transitions, uncertainty and ambiguity, make it certain that those who follow you will face difficult, complex moral decisions. They will approach those decisions in a variety of ways, ranging from complete ignorance about—and even lack of interest in—their legal or moral obligations, to a well-developed and functioning moral compass. The future wellbeing of your company, country or community depends on your taking the time now to equip people for these challenges. Developing people includes developing their moral decision-making capability—an essential skill for human-centred leaders.

Navigating this chapter

This is the second chapter focusing on *Doing: What are you going to do to get there?* and in particular the moral decision-making aspect. This chapter provides some tools for helping you navigate your greatest strategic risk: moral risk. It offers a framework for decision making in the midst of moral ambiguity and complexity—for resolving moral dilemmas—and also provides examples of questions you can ask to determine the extent of someone's moral competence for leadership. It has three sections:

- 'The moral continuum' observes that people are located along a moral continuum, and that this can be divided into both what is legally permissible and morally proper. It also notes that, in the absence of guides, most people are looking for leadership.

(continued)

221

Navigating this chapter (cont'd)

- 'Preparing people to face moral dilemmas' tells the story of Ulysses and one difficult moral choice he faced, as a metaphor for the almost constant stream of difficult choices faced in leadership.

- I then offer a summary of the steps human-centred leaders follow when they are resolving moral dilemmas.

Finally you will meet Mike and see how he resolved a moral dilemma.

The moral continuum

Over the past few years I have asked many leaders how they resolve moral dilemmas, as a way of learning about their character and how they have become the person they are today. Their answers offer insight into their moral awareness, their moral reasoning and the influences on their moral framework.

Saints and sinners

Over time I noticed that people seem to inhabit a position across a moral spectrum or continuum, with 'saints' at one end and 'sinners' at the other (see figure 20.1).

Figure 20.1: the moral continuum

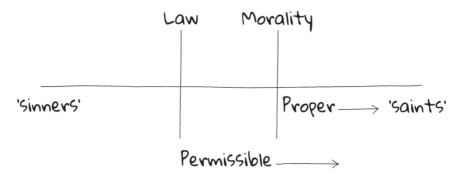

'I never have a moral dilemma,' said a professional woman in answer to my question. I was quite taken aback by this, wondering how that could be, and was further surprised to find she is not alone.

There is a small group of people who rarely encounter moral dilemmas. This appears to be for one of two reasons: either they have a very deep self-awareness and reliable moral compass that keeps them out of moral danger (the 'saints') or they are morally blind (the 'sinners'). I have heard stories of people engaged in fraud, deceit and immorality who are so deeply self-centred that they are oblivious to the terrible impact of their behaviour on others. To my amazement, these people are almost always deeply offended if challenged about their morality.

Clearly these moral giants and moral pygmies stand at opposite ends of a moral continuum. What lies along the continuum, between the good and bad ends? For many people, the law forms a dividing line. They want to stay on the right side of the law and conduct themselves in such a way as to avoid breaking the law. Although some people skate on thin ice, and try to push the boundaries, they still consider the law to be the dividing line between right and wrong.

Nick Leeson, whose fraudulent activity sank Barings Bank, understood this well.

'Behaviour exists along a continuum,' he said, 'with a good end and a bad end. And I've stood at both, and am probably now somewhere near the middle'. Nick's explanation of his role in the events leading up to the collapse of the bank demonstrated a legal, or rule-based, approach to moral decision making. And he was well aware that he had crossed the line.

'I broke the law and had to suffer the consequences,' he said. He knew he would get found out one day and would go to jail. On the day his fraud was discovered, as he rushed for the airport to take the first plane out of Singapore, he was frustrated when his wife wanted to return a rental video because she did not want to pay the fine.[1] I was struck by the contrast in moral behaviour: one did not want to return a video late and risk a small fine, while the other had just written a cheque that bounced a bank.

There is another dividing line on the moral continuum, however, and this is the 'moral' line. While the law enables you to ask the question 'Is this permissible?' morality invites you to ask, 'Is this proper?' People who stay on the right side of the moral divide employ a well-calibrated moral compass. The person who does what is proper can generally be confident they are doing what is permissible.

Is there a difference between legal and moral? Paying your employees a minimum wage fulfils your legal obligation. Paying them a wage that enables them to enjoy a reasonable standard of living, however, is your moral responsibility. In many societies it is legally permissible to engage in an extramarital affair, although most members of those societies consider this behaviour immoral.

Surely, some people argue, doing what's legal is enough? Is not the law a reasonable guide, without having to also consider what may be moral? Yes it is, but there are times when you just don't know or are unsure, and at those times you need a well-tuned moral sense of how to act. And your people, working in foreign environments, remote from head office, are going to need that moral compass.

Ian Bremmer, the geopolitical strategist mentioned earlier, kindly made time for me in a very busy schedule. Since he spends time with a range of world leaders I focused on one question: 'What kinds of moral dilemmas are being faced by the leaders you talk to?'

He immediately noted the challenges associated with encountering a wide range of business and political models by those who operate on a global scale.[2] While one person may believe their way is right, how do they resolve the conflict when confronted with other approaches that also claim to be right and can demonstrate success when doing so? Secondly, Ian noted the difficulty facing people with poorly constructed moral compasses who operate in countries where what is legal can be open to interpretation, rather than being obvious or defined. The combination of lack of internal clarity about what is proper and external frameworks that indicate what is permissible exposes people to moral and legal risk. What may be legal in one country can be illegal in another. What may be clear in one country can be unclear in another. In some countries friendship precedes commerce, while in others relationships excuse corruption. This difficulty is compounded in societies where traditional moral norms have lost favour and traditional moral guides, such as church and community leaders, have lost their authority.

Saints, sinners ... and swingers

What do your people do when they lack sound guides? The answer is they follow you. They copy your behaviour. Whereas people can learn what is permissible from clearly defined (albeit evolving) codes and canons, rules and regulations, they tend to learn what is proper from the example of others. This is what I hear when Alison Carnwath, or Major General Andy Salmon, or so many others, talk about the influence of upbringing. They learned how to behave from the example of strong role models.

In addition to the saints, sinners and morally upright, there is another group of people on the moral spectrum. They are not sure about the law *or* the relevant code of conduct. They are not 'bad' people and generally want to do the right thing. They lack a solid moral foundation, and when they are not sure how to act in a particular situation they make their decisions based on the way others act. This very large group can be found among colleagues and clients, in boardrooms and offices.

This group plays 'follow the leader' — and you have to hope it's the right leader. If you are appointing leaders, you need to choose wisely. While admitting he did the wrong thing, Nick Leeson believes the firm did not take full responsibility for their part in his downfall. They could have shown better leadership.

'At twenty I had ethics,' he reflected quietly. It is doubtful that he would have been able to articulate an ethical framework or moral compass at that time, and so would have been highly vulnerable to the culture of the organisation. When he made a mistake he was shown how to cover it up. When subsequent mistakes were made, he knew how to explain them away. Add to this a culture driven by greed and excess — at one stage the firm encouraged all traders to emulate Nick in order to make a lot of money — with little if any moral guidance, and you have a recipe for disaster.

The young Nick fell into a category of moral 'swingers' (not of the relationship type) and, unfortunately for him and so many others, chose the wrong side to alight from the swing. Like swinging voters, moral swingers are influenced by the latest opinion, the most attractive argument and a base appeal to self-interest. They are waiting to be led. I believe the absence of character formation places most people in this group (see figure 20.2, overleaf).

Figure 20.2: saints, sinners and swingers

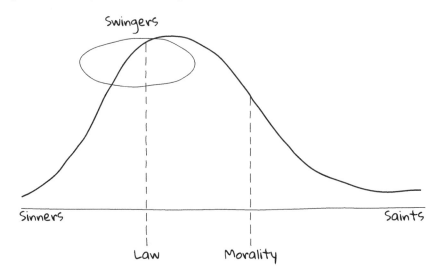

So how do you nudge people along the line toward moral greatness, toward the point where they can make wise moral decisions when no-one else is looking?

Help them develop their moral compass, then help them understand the reality of moral dilemmas and how to resolve them.

Preparing people to face moral dilemmas

When I ask people to talk about ways they have resolved moral dilemmas I start by quoting from Homer's story of Ulysses and his long journey back to Ithaca after the Trojan War.

During the journey Ulysses has to navigate the narrow straits of Messina. There is no other way home, and so he sets off, having been forewarned in a dream of what lay ahead: on the one hand is Scylla, the six-headed beast that lurks in the cliffs, and on the other, less than an arrow shot away, is the whirlpool Charybdis, which sucks down anything that comes within its clutches.

Sailing too close to the whirlpool risks losing the entire ship and crew, while sailing too close to the cliffs puts Ulysses within striking distance of the savage beast, exposing the sailors to grave danger. Faced with an agonising choice, and with his focus on their purpose—getting home—Ulysses chooses to risk losing some of his men rather than the whole ship.

A genuine moral dilemma occurs in that horrible moment when you have to make a choice between two unpleasant alternatives. Your character and reputation is shaped by the responses you make in those moments.

One CEO told me he constantly faced moral dilemmas in his global business, manifested in an endless stream of bigger and smaller choices. This is the pointy end of leadership. These are the hardest of decisions, upon which commentators, from the comfort of armchairs and the distance of history, can judge you harshly. You will always find someone who not only would choose differently but is happy to tell you why you are wrong. These decisions require courage.

The reality of complex moral decisions—and the certainty that there will be more—creates an obligation on you to prepare your people to face them. The Ulysses story can be a helpful starting point for a conversation (as can many other stories from classical literature):

- What would you do if you were Ulysses? Don't dismiss the question lightly. You cannot remain safe on the beach—you must launch your boat. There is only one way forward: through the straits, with danger on either side. There is no safe middle path. Some of your colleagues—and perhaps you yourself—will suffer. What will you do?

- What are the moral dilemmas you have faced? When have you found yourself between a rock and a hard place? What did you do? How did you weigh up and resolve the competing demands?

- Where are you, or your people, facing moral dilemmas at the moment (or where can you see them emerging)?

These questions should also be asked of Chairmen and CEOs before they are appointed, because only these answers will reveal their moral reasoning capability—and the impact they will have on the firm.

The resolution of moral dilemmas is one of the greatest tests of your leadership. It shapes you and shapes your business, government and society. Whether you resolve them in a way that strengthens your relationships, in a way that puts people first, goes to the heart of being a human-centred leader.

How do you make moral decisions when it seems there is no easy choice? Before I answer that question I should explain two other dilemmas that are not true moral dilemmas and so can cloud the discussion.

Two other dilemmas

Sometimes when people talk about a moral dilemma, the situation they describe is a decision either between right and wrong or between right and right.

Right versus wrong

When the choice you face is between what you know to be right and what you know to be wrong, you are merely facing temptation rather than a dilemma. This does not necessarily make it any easier to do what is right, as temptation by its very nature can be quite seductive, but there is usually little doubt about how you should act.

If, however, you are a little unsure about whether to do something, here are four quick tests you can use to help determine if something is wrong:

1   Smell it.
2   Broadcast your decision on the internet.
3   Tell a moral role model.
4   Ask about the relational impact.

I have always liked the 'smell test' as a simple guide to the rightness or wrongness of an act. Does it smell right or does it 'stink to high heaven', as people would say of a dodgy deal. You generally know a bad option when you smell it.

The problem with the smell test, however, is that some people lose their sense of smell as they age, or become acclimatised to their environment, so cannot smell excrement when it's sticking to their shoe or wafting in on the breeze. These are the people who become progressively inoculated to bad behaviour and no longer recognise the error of their ways, or of those around them. This is one of the benefits of good law, in that it provides boundaries for reasonable behaviour in social communities.

When your sense of smell fails, or you are picking up only a slight odour, try imagining the headline when your decision is broadcast on the internet, perhaps in a tweet that goes viral: 'CEO uses new investor funds to pay high interest to existing investors and enrich himself...' Would Bernie Madoff have behaved differently if he had known he would one day read the headline 'Ex-Nasdaq chair arrested for securities fraud'?

If you are not creative enough to generate a tweet, imagine telling your moral role model—someone you admire for their moral decency and integrity—what you have done just before the news breaks. What look would they give you? What would they say to you? What would they do in the same situation?

And finally, think in relational terms. How will this action impact other people, both near and far? Would you hate it if they did it to you?

I know when I face great temptation, when self-interest seeks satisfaction, applying a combination of these tests helps enormously. The presence of a bad odour and potential for a revealing tweet, a frowning friend or negative impacts on other people, can bolster my defences.

Right versus right

At other times you are faced with a choice between two morally sound and attractive options. Although this poses something of a dilemma, and can require a difficult choice, it is more specifically a question of judgement about which path you want to take toward your goal of human excellence. Should you choose this job or that job from between two offers? Should you focus on this service or that, on European or Chinese markets, on disability policy or unemployment?

In the absence of moral risk—one job would expose you to corruption, for example—these are questions for wise judgement about where to devote your time and energy in ways that align with your purpose or that of your firm or government. Questions for judgement are aided by the virtue of practical wisdom informed by justice and courage, so back yourself and make a decision. If you find out later it was a poor choice, fix the mistake, learn from it and move on.

This is not a moral dilemma, just a difficult decision. What do you do, however, when it *is* a moral dilemma? How can people make sound moral decisions in a morally ambiguous world?

How do you make morally sound decisions?

It's quite clear that leadership involves both technical and moral decisions, so human-centred leaders need to do well — and they want to do well — on the moral decision-making dimension. Those who navigate the dilemmas well seem to include the following elements in their process:

1   They have clarity about their purpose, principles and values and what are considered acceptable behaviours. They don't try to decide these in response to, and in the midst of, a moral crisis.
2   They stick to their principles, informed by virtues of wisdom, courage and justice, often in the face of much opposition.
3   They recognise and admit they are facing a dilemma. They don't ignore it, as Nick Leeson did, in the hope that it will sort itself out.
4   They have a commitment to uncovering what is going on, not covering it up. They are firmly of the view that sunlight is the best disinfectant.
5   They articulate the dilemma. They explain what it is — 'I had to make a choice between firing everyone on the list or ...' — and in the articulation realise they face a difficult choice with no easy answer.
6   They gather as much data and ask as many questions as possible in order to identify possible options. They go beyond asking, 'Is this right or wrong?', because that can be resolved by doing what's right. They try to discover options that minimise adverse impacts on people.
7   They seek wise counsel from as wide a group as possible.
8   They act decisively — and then review that decision after implementation or execution.

How a human-centred leader resolved a moral dilemma

Mike is one of the finest leaders I know. He is an outstanding professional and a deeply human-centred leader. At one time he was Country Manager of a global business that was acquired in a hostile takeover. Mike kept his position in the new firm, although 40 per cent of his former colleagues lost their jobs.

Three weeks into the new role Mike's day started with an email requiring urgent attention. It contained a spreadsheet listing one-third of his employees, with instructions to summarily dismiss them within 48 hours. The headcount reductions made no sense. His territory was the best performing region in the global business and their projections showed increased growth from a very solid sales pipeline.

'Even if we had to reduce headcount, there were people on that list who were standout performers,' said Mike. 'The business needed them if we were to look after existing customers and find new customers.'

The note instructed Mike to meet each employee at a nearby hotel in appointments staggered 12 minutes apart, to hand them a legal letter documenting their dismissal, and to explain that they were now locked out of the office and systems and would have their personal effects returned in a week.

Consider this situation for a moment.

Imagine you're Mike and you've just opened the email. Here's a list of the kinds of questions that arise when you look through the lens of Human-Centred Leadership, using a moral compass to take your bearings:

- What values matter to you?

  - Loyalty? To the company or the staff... or both?

  - Truth?

  - Integrity?

  - ...

- How will you behave in order to be true to your values?
- What does this situation tell you about the moral values, and so the moral culture, of this firm?
- Who are the people impacted by this decision and its implementation?
  - The managers above you?
  - The shareholders of the firm?
  - The staff—both those who remain and those who are going?
  - The families of the staff who are leaving?
  - Customers and suppliers who engage with those staff?
  - …
- How can this action be transformed so as to help people become the best they can be?
- Where can you discover beauty, goodness or truth in this situation?
- What can you do to add beauty, goodness or truth?
- What principles guide your actions?
  - Do no harm?
  - Don't do to others what you would hate if they did to you?
  - …
- Where are the conflict points between your principles and the organisation's principles?
- How can you abide by your principles and fulfil your responsibility to the firm?
- What might the virtues prompt you to do?
  - Take the time to reflect on humility … wisdom … courage … self-control … justice.
- What other questions need to be asked?
  - Do you have sufficient information and understanding?

- – Does the firm have sufficient data and understanding? Have they asked the right questions?
- What are the choices before you? Where are you doubtful or uncertain?
- Do you have a role model who you can emulate? If not, imagine what Gandhi, Mother Teresa, Mandela or King would do—and then 'act as if'.
- Are you clear about your intent?
  - – Do you want to be seen as caring and concerned while doing a difficult job, or callous and heartless?
  - – In the face of difficulty will you temporarily abandon a commitment to Human-Centred Leadership and become the messenger from head office?

Having taken your bearings in this way, test your thinking by putting yourself in the shoes of your staff who are about to walk in and get fired. Stand where they are standing.

- What are they working on at the moment?
- How long have they been with the firm?
- How will they feel about being invited to a mysterious meeting in a hotel?
- What will happen when people start to notice they have received similar email invitations?
- What will happen when people don't return from the hotel?

There are many, many questions you can ask to unpack a moral dilemma, all of which are helpful for learning, for growth and development, and for finding a resolution.

Doing exercises such as this should be a regular practice in your organisation for three reasons:

1 The operating environment is in an almost constant state of flux and change, so people will face challenges and issues that you, and others, have not yet encountered.

2 People get promoted and have to resolve more complex issues that come with increased responsibility.
3 New people join the organisation and you want them to become like you rather than the other way around.

Mike's response

Here's how Mike handled the situation.

'This is no way to treat people,' thought Mike as he digested the contents of the email. He was appalled by the inhumanity conveyed in the instructions.

'We should have been adding staff, not getting rid of them,' he told me with a shake of his head.

Mike immediately contacted head office to try to understand and influence the decision, but it had already been made and was not open for discussion. Although Mike received no explanation for the drastic action he was able to influence the firm to change some of the names on the list. (My view is that results-centred leaders in the firm said, 'Let's cut costs by x per cent' and drew a line through the headcount at that point.)

'I believed I had a responsibility to carry out the decision of the company to reduce headcount,' he said. 'But I refused outright to do it in the terrible way they suggested. And I also decided then and there that we had a significant lack of alignment in our values.

'I decided that I would give them an additional cost saving,' he said. He handed in his resignation soon after, when he had helped all but one of the people find new positions at other firms.

And to finish off this chapter... here's another dilemma for your consideration:

It's Friday lunchtime and the Group CEO has just confided in you about significant changes to the firm that will be announced after the market closes today. As both CFO and head of corporate affairs, you need to work on the necessary documents, while maintaining extreme confidentiality and discretion about this market-sensitive information.

While you are assembling your thoughts, Katie knocks on your door.

'I'm off to the bank in a couple of hours to sign the mortgage documents on our new property in San Francisco so we can move right in when I take up the new position,' she says. Katie's promotion to move across the country and set up a new division of the firm has been well publicised.

'The bank has asked for a letter from you confirming my appointment and remuneration structure. Here's a draft. Would you mind signing it if it's okay?' she asks as she places a document containing three short sentences in front of you.

The announcement in four hours' time will reveal that the firm has been taken over and expansion plans put on hold. Katie may not have a job in a month's time.

What will you do?

What would a human-centred leader do?

Conclusion: Human-Centred Leaders Change the World

The conversation during dinner with Anders ranged across trends and transitions, politics and the planet, leaders and leadership.

Low-level anxiety has been a constant companion through his life, and now shapes his views and outlook. While alert and engaged, his physical and emotional bearing display the tiredness that comes from a long life lived under constant threats and responses to those threats.

Anders grew up in Northern Europe in the shadow of the Russian bear and, as he described it, fear of an imminent atomic strike. As this peril faded a new planetary threat emerged in the shape of environmental degradation. He despairs about the future and has little confidence that humanity has the ability to avoid a looming catastrophe. This distress is compounded by a foreboding that today's youth will blame him and his generation for their poor decisions, that the world will descend into anarchy and he could find himself a target of the ensuing violence.

Although Anders is doing tremendous work to marshal people to action, his words and demeanour over dinner implied defeat and despair. His prognosis of a dystopian near future is influenced by a view that destructive forces are well organised, well funded and unstoppable in their relentless quest for profit or power at any cost. On the other hand, he believes any positive efforts for good are disorganised, disparate and generally discouraged. They lack leadership.

On this point we disagreed quite vigorously.

I see shifts but not permanent setbacks, challenge but not catastrophe, difficulty but not disaster.

My starting point is one of confidence in humanity and the future. While Anders displays a low level of anxiety I have a high level of hope.

Even if you accept his thesis that there are few global movements for good that are effective in the face of greed, corruption and entrenched self-interest, there are still countless grassroots organisations and activists responding to need where they see it. There is no shortage of men and women, families and communities, doing what they can in their part of the world to make it a little better. They may not be connected under the umbrella of a global brand, but they are deeply connected by the threads of meaning and purpose. They are each leaders in their own world, and this gives me hope.

I do, however, share Anders' view that we are at a pivotal moment in human history, at a moment that demands much of us.

It's time

Robert Kennedy's observation in his 'Day of Affirmation' address from half a century ago still rings true today: 'a great burden of responsibility is thrust upon this generation'. Your parents and grandparents responded to the pressing needs of their age—and now the baton has passed to you.

You stand on a firm foundation with a clear sense of purpose. You have the authority to lead from where you are. Now you have the burden of responsibility.

- What will be your contribution?

- What kind of world do you want to live in and leave?

- What will you do to ensure people are put first on every occasion and in every situation?

- What will you do to ensure that a moral foundation underpins the technical edifice of business, government and society?

- What will you do to ensure people are treated as human beings with inalienable rights, rather than as economic assets to be used solely for productive purposes?

Human-centred leaders engage with human issues. They don't point out the window at what needs to be done and who can do it; they look in the mirror and see there the person who will respond.

Intersecting trajectories

'What meaningful contribution can I make to the world in which I belong?' is one of the most compelling questions you will encounter. We have explored the answer to this question with regard to your own purpose and the purpose of the organisation you lead. As we finish this part of our journey together I would like to invite you to lift your gaze toward building not just a better business or institution, but a better world.

You discover your contribution to the world by aligning your personal and organisational purpose with a societal challenge. Finding this alignment creates a fulcrum to leverage the contribution of individuals and the enterprise of which they are a part in a way that transforms society.

Part II asked two questions in particular about the journey from Here to There: 'Where are you standing?' and 'Where are you going?' Having answered the latter by discovering your purpose, you then created a moral compass to keep you heading in the right direction. This direction establishes a trajectory for your life.

Part III talked about the parallel journey that takes place when you lead an organisation: identifying where the firm is standing today, and finding immense clarity on its purpose or where it is heading. You are only a steward of the organisation, tasked with looking after the wellbeing of its people and ensuring its continuity while you lead it for a part of this trajectory.

You make your greatest contribution as an organisational leader in the place where these two trajectories meet — that is, where your purpose, vision and values align with the purpose, vision and values of the organisation you lead. When these lack alignment you have two choices: *change* the organisation or change *the organisation*. In the former you bring about change where you are, in the latter you change where you are.

When you create alignment between these two trajectories your purpose and the purpose of the firm become entwined, creating greater momentum and lifting the trajectory of both. When you help each person in the firm discover their purpose, and their point of alignment with the firm, you accelerate this process.

Meanwhile there is another trajectory, which I referred to in Part I as the falling trajectory of human development. More broadly, it is the trajectory of human need, of social need. It is the trajectory of those challenges facing society that require someone to take responsibility. Some of these are broad, such as access to food, water and energy. Others are narrow, such as training young people in financial literacy. Although the list could be endless, finding the solution to almost every problem sits within someone's sphere of influence. Some of them are directly within your sphere of influence.

You have a moral obligation to respond to the particular challenges that intersect with your purpose and your organisation's purpose. This is how you can change not just the institution you lead, but the world you touch, at the point of touch.

When you discover the place where your trajectory and the trajectory of your organisation intersect with the needs of the world, you will find your ultimate point of contribution. You can then weave all three together on a new trajectory that changes the world (see figure E).

Figure E: changing the world

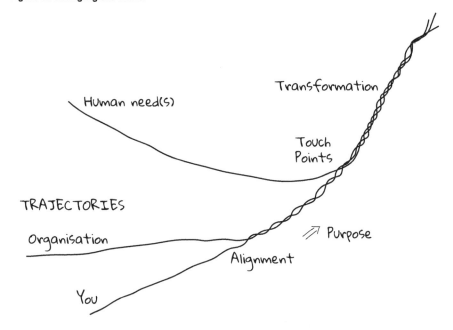

This means you face three crucial tasks:

- Master the foundations of Human-Centred Leadership (Part II).

- Master the art of being a human-centred leader in your country, company or community (Part III).

- Master the art of aligning yourself and your organisation with pressing social need at your point of influence — that is, find the touch points of intersection and then create alignment.

This is the kind of thinking exhibited by Paul Polman at Unilever when he recognised both the social impact and the social responsibility of the firm.

However, you don't have to be the CEO of Unilever or the President of your country—you just need to align your mission and purpose with the mission and purpose of a Human-Centred Organisation, and examine the points where these touch the community. To do so, consider the following questions:

- Where does the country, company or community of which you are a leader touch people in very direct ways—who are all the stakeholders? You have already considered this across the four key relationships in your own life and in the context of your leadership.

- What is the impact of that touch through seven generations—are people enhanced or diminished? Do they flourish or flounder? Are they enriched or impoverished?

- What are the needs of the people at your touch points?

  - These people are mothers and fathers, sons and daughters, going about their daily lives. They are not necessarily living in poverty without access to the basics of life. Look deeply, however, and question whether they require better access to food, water or energy, to better healthcare and education, to a more equitable wage. Compare them with yourself and what you enjoy or take for granted. Is there anything you can do, from your leadership position, to dramatically alter the trajectory of their lives?

  - In particular, ask about those who need you in some way, and hence where there could be an imbalance in power—employees deep in the organisation, workers in developing countries, communities who depend on your presence, for example. Make a habit of putting yourself in their shoes, because the power you have over them can prevent them from speaking freely and allow imbalance to creep into the relationship.

- What is your dream for yourself and your organisation and the positive impact it could have on the world?

  - Could you decide to halve your use of the world's resources, or ensure every family member of every employee is educated to the level necessary for their next job, or institute a 24-hour zero injury policy (that is, no injuries ever, even accidents or illness at home that might arise from work pressures). The opportunities for good are limited only by your imagination. Set some grand, aspirational goals and then invite your colleagues to join you in the quest. You might be surprised by the impact. You can change the world from your point of leadership. While charities and not-for-profits do very good work helping the poor or marginalised, you can make a difference to the infrastructure of a country, or the fair treatment of women, or cross-cultural understanding and harmony.

One day your children, and those who come after you, will ask what difference you made. Pointing to an improved share price, a healthy bank balance, a bridge named after you, staff engagement surveys or time in office is unlikely to satisfy the enquirer. What will satisfy them is the positive impact you had on the world when you had the opportunity to make that impact. Perhaps your children will never ask the question because they will know the answer. They will hear it when other people tell of your impact, of the difference you made in their life, of what the world was like before and after you passed through.

What stories will they hear?

The hinge of history

This is a pivotal moment in history, a moment when we need to make some very wise choices for humanity, for the kind of people we want to be and the world we want to live in and leave.

Does this historical moment matter more than any other? Perhaps not, but this is *your* moment, when your choices and actions will determine the shape of your world and tomorrow's world.

The question is not how to stop change and progress. This is no different from sitting foolishly with King Canute as the tide rushes in, believing you have the power to prevent the inevitable. Doing so fails to recognise the reality of the trends, transitions and shifts. The question, rather, is how to navigate the transitions. How do you shape the future? How do you shape the best possible future? And how do you lead others into that best possible future?

These are leadership questions. And they are moral questions.

It is not a fork in the road in front of you but uncharted waters that require skilled navigators. We are living in a fog of complexity, confusion and uncertainty, lacking clear guidance from legal or moral authorities that lag rather than lead. The economic, political, environmental and social risks confronting us are demanding and difficult.

But the more serious challenge is one of moral imagination, moral courage and moral leadership. It is the challenge of navigating the narrow moral passage between Scylla and Charybdis with confidence and clarity of mind and purpose against seemingly overwhelming odds. This requires men and women who have a firm foundation, a robust moral compass and outstanding professional competence, who effectively integrate the moral and technical demands of leadership while putting people first. It requires human-centred leaders.

Human-Centred Leadership places human beings at the centre of our thinking and acting. It recognises that to be human is to be in relationship with other people, both near and far, across time and space. It recognises that fostering and supporting conditions that allow human growth and development—human flourishing—is not just a good thing to do, but the right thing to do.

Human-Centred Leadership asks questions about the impact of our decisions and actions on the people involved, on those who inform the action and on those who will be touched by it. It gives political leaders a lens through which to view education policy and asylum seeker policy. It gives board directors a lens through which to assess risk and strategy, executives a lens through which to test execution and operations, and all of us a lens through which to evaluate our place in society, our contribution to it and our response to whatever challenges we perceive.

Why do I believe human-centred leaders make such a difference?

Because it's all about the people. It's people who created the world as we know it today, and people who will create the world of tomorrow. It's people with whom we engage in every activity.

And I don't want to lose that. When robots are driving our cars, doing our shopping, writing our blogs and articles, cleaning our homes and providing medical care ... what will be left for us to do? It won't be a question of what we do, though, but of who we are, of what kind of people we are, of how we relate to one another, how we care for one another.

We have to secure the foundations of a human-centred world before we find ourselves on the periphery. Human-centred leaders are the key. They are the moral force that will defend humanity.

It is time to humanise the enterprise of humanity. It is time to place leadership at the service of humanity—in business, government and society. It is time for Human-Centred Leadership. This is the key to success in the 21st century.

When Nelson Mandela died world leaders flocked to South Africa to pay their last respects to this great man. Obituaries overflowed with anecdotes and insights.

'Mandela's personal qualities,' wrote Rex Murphy in Canada's *National Post*, 'make him an icon of integrity and honour far beyond the bounds of his own country. What so much of the world actively hungers for in its public life, and so very rarely finds, is there in Nelson Mandela—leadership with moral force'.[1]

Mandela's moral force—his power to galvanise and inspire—underpinned his achievements, as it underpins those of all human-centred leaders. Where are the new Mandelas, though? Where are the men and women with the moral imagination, moral courage and moral leadership who will accept the burden of responsibility? The question remains, and perhaps grows more urgent with the passage of time: 'Where are the new Mandelas?'

You know the answer.

The new Mandela is looking at you in the mirror each morning.

You are the new Mandela ... and you are surrounded by people whose lives you can change when you show care and concern for them. Find those opportunities. Notice the people you touch, on whose lives you can have a positive impact. Make a decision now to let Beauty, Goodness and Truth shine, and refuse to settle for anything less. Have the courage to lead from where you are.

At the start of this book I suggested you write a note starting 'I am the new Mandela...' and answering the questions:

- What sort of person would you be?

- What impact would you have on the world?

- What big issues would you speak out about?

    And then...

- What would you need to do to become the best version of yourself—the new Mandela?

What did you write then... and what will you write now?

More importantly, what will you do now?

Endnotes

Chapter 1: The future and the future of leadership

1 Handy, C 2002, *The Empty Raincoat*, Arrow Books (originally published 1994)

2 Bremmer, I 2012, *Every nation for itself. Winners and losers in a G-Zero world*, Portfolio/Penguin, p. 3

3 ibid., p. 5

Chapter 2: Shifts 1–3: Technology

1 From 'Paradexity: the convergence of paradox and complexity' by Anthony Howard, Journal of Management Development, Vol. 29 Iss. 3, pp. 210–223 © Emerald Group Publishing Limited.

2 See Wright, R 2000, *Nonzero. The logic of human destiny*, Vintage, where he explains this insight and provides numerous examples through history

3 Howard, A 2010, 'Paradexity', op. cit.

4 Kennedy, J 2011, 'Amount of data in 2011 equal to 57.5bn 32GB Apple iPads', *Silicon Republic*, accessed 7 July 2014, www.siliconrepublic.com/ enterprise/item/22420-amount-of-data-in-2011-equa, 28 June 2011

5 ibid.

6 'A comprehensive list of big data statistics', accessed 7 July 2014, http:// wikibon.org/blog/big-data-statistics/

7 Pearson, I 2014, 'Fairies will dominate space travel', accessed 7 July 2014, http://timeguide.wordpress.com/2014/06/06/fairies-will-dominate-space-travel/

8 Björk, B-C, Roos, A & Lauri, M 2009, 'Scientific journal publishing: yearly volume and open access availability', *Information Research*, 14(1), paper 391, accessed 7 July 2014, www.informationr.net/ir/14-1/paper391.html

9 Howard, A 2010, 'Paradexity', op. cit.

10 ibid.

Chapter 3: Shift 4: Moral drift

1 Sandel, M 2009, 'Michael Sandel: A New Citizenship: 2009', *The Reith Lectures*, BBC Radio 4, 9 June 2009, accessed 1 July 2014, www.bbc.co.uk/programmes/b00kt7rg

2 ibid.

3 See Fallows, J 2012, 'Bit by Bit It Takes Shape: Media Evolution for the "Post-Truth" Age', *The Atlantic*, 29 August 2012, accessed 2 July 2014, www.theatlantic.com/politics/archive/2012/08/bit-by-bit-it-takes-shape-media-evolution-for-the-post-truth-age/261741/

4 Buck, T 2014, 'Crisis of trust as economic downturn in Spain ends', *Financial Times*, 24 June 2014, accessed 25 June 2014, www.ft.com/cms/s/0/671e1626-dc31-11e3-8511-00144feabdc0.html#axzz35dg58Fox

5 Adams, B 2014, 'Gallup: Congress is pretty much the worst thing we track — seriously, it's awful', *Washington Examiner*, 19 June 2014, accessed 20 June 2014, http://m.washingtonexaminer.com/gallup-congress-is-pretty-much-the-worst-thing-we-track-seriously-its-awful/article/2549961

6 Abbas, M 2013, 'UK poll points to mistrust of clergy, lack of moral leadership', 31 March 2013, accessed 3 April 2013, www.reuters.com/article/2013/03/31/us-britain-poll-christianity-idUSBRE92U03I20130331

7 Smith, G 2012, 'Why I Am Leaving Goldman Sachs', *The New York Times*, 14 March 2012, accessed 10 May 2014, www.nytimes.com/2012/03/14/opinion/why-i-am-leaving-goldman-sachs.html?pagewanted=all&_r=1&

8 'Can we still be friends with Facebook after its controversial "emotions" experiment?', accessed 30 June 2014, www.news.com.au/technology/can-we-still-be-friends-with-facebook-after-its-controversial-emotions-experiment/story-e6frfrnr-1226972831122

9 'Facebook admits it made an error by "communicating badly" with users after its emotion study went public', accessed 3 July 2014, www.news.com.au/technology/online/facebook-admits-it-made-an-error-by-communicating-badly-with-users-after-its-emotion-study-went-public/story-fnjwmwrh-1226975741888

10 'ATM Dispenses Extra Cash in Scotland, Huge Line Forms as News of Error Spreads Via Twitter, accessed 3 July 2014, www.huffingtonpost.com/2012/11/19/atm-dispenses-extra-cash-huge-line-news-twitter_n_2159581.html

11 ibid.

12 McCurry, J 2009, 'New Zealand couple flee after finding £4m in their bank account', *The Guardian*, 22 May 2009, accessed 2 July 2014, www.theguardian.com/world/2009/may/21/new-zealand-millionaires-flee-westpac

13 ibid.

14 Beswick, A 2012, 'Runaway millionaires sentenced', 24 August 2012, accessed 2 July 2014, www.3news.co.nz/Runaway-millionaires-sentenced/tabid/423/articleID/266656/Default.aspx

Chapter 4: The convergence and crossover of 'man' and machine

1 Wilson, R, 'What is the homo economicus?', accessed 11 July 2014, www.investopedia.com/ask/answers/08/homo-economicus.asp
2 Pearson, I 2014, private conversation
3 Love, D 2014, 'Scientists Are Afraid to Talk About The Robot Apocalypse, and That's a Problem', accessed 19 July 2014, www.businessinsider.com.au/robot-apocalypse-2014-7
4 White, A 2014, 'G20 urged to unleash women's potential', accessed 19 July 2014, www.theaustralian.com.au/business/g20-urged-to-unleash-womens-potential/story-e6frg8zx-1226992757876

Chapter 5: Becoming the best version of yourself

1 www.firstpeople.us/FP-Html-Legends/TwoWolves-Cherokee.html, accessed 3 February 2014, modified to incorporate elements from two versions
2 Bahrampour, Tara 2014, 'Romanian orphans subjected to deprivation must now deal with dysfunction', 30 January 2014, accessed 30 July 2014, www.washingtonpost.com/local/romanian-orphans-subjected-to-deprivation-must-now-deal-with-disfunction/2014/01/30/a9dbea6c-5d13-11e3-be07-006c776266ed_story.html
3 ibid.

Chapter 6: Foundations of leadership

1 Treanor, J 2012, 'Barclays chief Bob Diamond takes home £17m in pay, shares and perks', accessed 22 July 2014, www.theguardian.com/business/2012/mar/09/barclays-chief-bob-diamond-pay
2 'Barclays AGM: 31.5% reject remuneration report', accessed 22 July 2014, www.theguardian.com/business/blog/2012/apr/27/barclays-protests-live-agm-bob-diamond
3 ibid.
4 'Parliamentary Commission on Banking Standards — UK Parliament', accessed 22 July 2014, www.parliament.uk/bankingstandards
5 Carnwath, A 2014, private conversation, London

Chapter 7: In search of Beauty, Goodness and Truth

1 Quinn, B 2014, 'Alice Herz-Sommer: pianist and oldest known Holocaust survivor dies aged 110', accessed 23 July 2014, www.theguardian.com/world/2014/feb/23/alice-herz-sommer-holocaust-survivor-dies
2 Dunne, T 2008, 'Method in Theology', accessed 10 April 2014, http://users.wowway.com/~tdunne5273/Lonergan-Method%20in%20Theology.pdf
3 ibid.

Chapter 9: A life of virtue

1 See Plato, *The Republic*, Book Four; see also http://plato.stanford.edu/entries/plato-ethics-politics/#2.2, accessed 16 October 2012

2 McKay, B 2013, 'What Is Character? Its 3 True Qualities and How to Develop It', accessed 1 January 2014, www.artofmanliness.com/2013/06/25/what-is-character-its-3-true-qualities-and-how-to-develop-it/

3 Moore, M 2013, 'Riot after Chinese teachers try to stop pupils cheating', accessed 8 June 2014, www.telegraph.co.uk/news/worldnews/asia/china/10132391/Riot-after-Chinese-teachers-try-to-stop-pupils-cheating.html (italics mine)

4 'Dozens suspended in Harvard University cheat scandal', accessed 2 February 2013, www.news.com.au/world/dozens-suspended-in-harvard-university-cheat-scandal/story-fndir2ev-1226567299425

5 Koziol, M 2014, 'Lawyer who smuggled notes down trousers for ethics test struck off roll', accessed 8 June 2014, www.smh.com.au/nsw/lawyer-who-smuggled-notes-down-trousers-for-ethics-test-struck-off-roll-20140607-39pwh.html

Chapter 10: Five virtues for effective living

1 Salmon, A 2013, private conversation

2 Salz, A 2013, 'Salz Review. An independent review of Barclay's Business Practices', April 2013, http://online.wsj.com/public/resources/documents/SalzReview04032013.pdf, p. 9

3 Collins, J 2001, *Good to Great, Why some companies make the leap ... and others don't*, Harper Business, p. 20

4 'Humility key to effective leadership', accessed 3 January 2014, www.eurekalert.org/pub_releases/2011-12/uab-hkt120811.php

5 Moore, P 2013, private conversation

6 Swannell, R 2013, private conversation

7 Leeson, N 2013, private conversation

8 'Hewlett-Packard fined $3 million for misleading customers', accessed 29 July 2014, www.news.com.au/national/hewlettpackard-fined-3-million-for-misleading-customers/story-fncynjr2-1226675031958, 5 July 2013

9 Collins, B 2013, 'Meet the Iraqi Refugee Who Tried to Repay Over $18,000 In Welfare Money After He Became a Success', accessed 29 July 2013, www.businessinsider.com.au/this-former-iraqi-asylum-seeker-tried-to-repay-centrelink-more-than-18000-after-he-became-a-success-2013-7

Chapter 11: Making wise decisions: thinking well

1 See Howard, A 2012, 'The thinking organisation', *Journal of Management Development*, volume 31, issue 6, pp. 620–32, for a longer, more detailed explanation of this process.

2 Lonergan, B 1972, *Method in Theology*, The Seabury Press, pp. 4–24, 1979 edition

Chapter 12: Making wise decisions: choosing well

1   Parliamentary Commission on Banking Standards 2013, 'An accident waiting to happen: The failure of HBOS', www.publications.parliament.uk/pa/jt201213/jtselect/jtpcbs/144/144.pdf

2   Cohen, R 2012, 'Seeking an imperfect compromise', *The New York Times International Weekly*, 16 June 2012, quoting Rabbi Hillel

Chapter 13: Navigating life with a moral compass

1   Holleran, M 2013, private conversation, New York

Chapter 14: Human-Centred Leadership

1   Baer, D 2014, 'How Changing One Habit Quintupled Alcoa's Income', accessed 18 August 2014, www.businessinsider.com.au/how-changing-one-habit-quintupled-alcoas-income-2014-4

2   ibid.

3   'Unilever Sustainable Living Plan', accessed 18 August 2014, www.unilever.com.au/sustainable-living-2014/unilever-sustainable-living-plan/

4   Carrington, L 2013, 'Global Vision', in Business Reporter, distributed with *The Sunday Telegraph*, July 2012, accessed 19 August 2014, http://engagegroup.co.uk/wp-content/uploads/2013/05/Employee-engagement-special-report1.pdf

Chapter 16: Your organisational purpose

1   Stengel, J 2012, *Grow: How Ideals Power Growth and Profit at the World's Greatest Companies*, Virgin Books

2   'About Us | Academy for Global Citizenship', accessed 26 August 2014, agcchicago.org/school/our-mission/

3   'American Financial Group, Inc. (AFG)—Operating Philosophy', accessed 26 August 2014, www.afginc.com/phoenix.zhtml?c=89330&p=operatingphilosophy

4   'General Electric (GE) mission statement 2013 | Strategic Management Insight', accessed 26 August 2014, www.strategicmanagementinsight.com/mission-statements/general-electric-mission-statement.html

Chapter 17: Leadership at the speed of relationship

1   Blackley, G 2008, private conversation

2   White, A 2007, private conversation

Chapter 18: Developing human-centred leaders

1   'Bank of America to Pay $16.65 Billion in Historic Justice Department Settlement for Financial Fraud Leading up to and During the Financial

Crisis', accessed 20 November 2014, www.justice.gov/opa/pr/bank-america-pay-1665-billion-historic-justice-department-settlement-financial-fraud-leading

2   Denaro, A 2010, private conversation

Chapter 19: Moral reasoning

1   Crain, WC 1985, *Theories of Development*, Prentice Hall, p. 118, accessed 29 September 2014, http://faculty.plts.edu/gpence/html/kohlberg.htm

2   Cherry, K, 'Kohlberg's theory of moral development', accessed 30 June 2014, http://psychology.about.com/od/developmentalpsychology/a/kohlberg.htm

3   Crain, op. cit.

4   Cherry, op. cit.

5   See Crain, op. cit.

6   Cherry, op. cit.

7   ibid.

Chapter 20: Moral decision making

1   Leeson, N 2013, private conversation

2   Bremmer, I 2013, private conversation

Conclusion

1   Murphy, R 2012, 'Rex Murphy on Nelson Mandela: Where have all the leaders gone?', *National Post*, 21 July 2012, accessed 28 August 2012, http://fullcomment.nationalpost.com/2012/07/21/rex-murphy-on-nelson-mandela-where-have-all-the-leaders-gone/

Bibliography

Abbas, M 2013, 'UK poll points to mistrust of clergy, lack of moral leadership', 31 March 2013, www.reuters.com/article/2013/03/31/us-britain-poll-christianity-idUSBRE92U03I20130331

Adams, B 2014, 'Gallup: Congress is pretty much the worst thing we track — seriously, it's awful', *Washington Examiner*, 19 June 2014, http://m.washingtonexaminer.com/gallup-congress-is-pretty-much-the-worst-thing-we-track-seriously-its-awful/article/2549961

Baer, D 2014, 'How Changing One Habit Quintupled Alcoa's Income', www.businessinsider.com.au/how-changing-one-habit-quintupled-alcoas-income-2014-4

Bahrampour, Tara 2014, *Romanian orphans subjected to deprivation must now deal with dysfunction*, accessed 30 July 2014, www.washingtonpost.com/local/romanian-orphans-subjected-to-deprivation-must-now-deal-with-disfunction/2014/01/30/a9dbea6c-5d13-11e3-be07-006c776266ed_story.html

Beswick, A 2012, 'Runaway millionaires sentenced', 24 August 2012, www.3news.co.nz/Runaway-millionaires-sentenced/tabid/423/articleID/266656/Default.aspx

Björk, B-C, Roos, A & Lauri, M 2009, 'Scientific journal publishing: yearly volume and open access availability', *Information Research*, 14(1), paper 391, www.informationr.net/ir/14-1/paper391.html

Bremmer, I 2012, *Every nation for itself. Winners and losers in a G-Zero world*, Portfolio/Penguin

Buck, T 2014, 'Crisis of trust as economic downturn in Spain ends', *Financial Times*, 24 June 2014, www.ft.com/cms/s/0/671e1626-dc31-11e3-8511-00144feabdc0.html#axzz35dg58Fox

Carrington, L 2013, 'Global Vision', in Business Reporter, distributed with *The Sunday Telegraph*, July 2012, http://engagegroup.co.uk/wp-content/uploads/2013/05/Employee-engagement-special-report1.pdf

Cherry, K, 'Kohlberg's theory of moral development', accessed 30 June 2014, http://psychology.about.com/od/developmentalpsychology/a/kohlberg.htm

Cohen, R 2012, 'Seeking an imperfect compromise', *The New York Times International Weekly*, 16 June 2012, quoting Rabbi Hillel

Collins, B 2013, 'Meet the Iraqi Refugee Who Tried to Repay Over $18,000 in Welfare Money After He Became a Success', www.businessinsider.com. au/this-former-iraqi-asylum-seeker-tried-to-repay-centrelink-more-than-18000-after-he-became-a-success-2013-7

Collins, J 2001, *Good to Great, Why some companies make the leap ... and others don't*, Harper Business

Crain, WC 1985, *Theories of Development*, Prentice Hall p. 118, accessed 29 September 2014, http://faculty.plts.edu/gpence/html/kohlberg.htm

Dunne, T 2008, 'Method in Theology', accessed 10 April, 2014, http://users. wowway.com/~tdunne5273/Lonergan-Method%20in%20Theology.pdf

Fallows, J 2012, 'Bit by Bit It Takes Shape: Media Evolution for the "Post-Truth" Age', *The Atlantic*, 29 August 2012, www.theatlantic.com/politics/archive/2012/08/bit-by-bit-it-takes-shape-media-evolution-for-the-post-truth-age/261741/

Handy, C 2002, *The Empty Raincoat*, Arrow Books (originally published 1994)

Howard, A 2010, 'Paradexity: the convergence of paradox and complexity', *Journal of Management Development*, vol. 29, issue 3, pp. 210–23

Howard, A 2012, 'The thinking organisation', *Journal of Management Development*, vol. 31, issue 6, pp. 620–32

Kennedy, J 2011, 'Amount of data in 2011 equal to 57.5bn 32GB Apple iPads', *Silicon Republic*, www.siliconrepublic.com/enterprise/item/22420-amount-of-data-in-2011-equa, 28 June 2011

Koziol, M 2014, 'Lawyer who smuggled notes down trousers for ethics test struck off roll', www.smh.com.au/nsw/lawyer-who-smuggled-notes-down-trousers-for-ethics-test-struck-off-roll-20140607-39pwh.html

Lonergan, B 1972, *Method in Theology*, The Seabury Press (1979 edn)

Love, D 2014, 'Scientists Are Afraid to Talk About the Robot Apocalypse, and That's a Problem', www.businessinsider.com.au/robot-apocalypse-2014-7

McCurry, J 2009, 'New Zealand couple flee after finding £4m in their bank account', *The Guardian*, 22 May 2009, www.theguardian.com/world/2009/may/21/new-zealand-millionaires-flee-westpac

McKay, B 2013, 'What Is Character? Its 3 True Qualities and How to Develop It', www.artofmanliness.com/2013/06/25/what-is-character-its-3-true-qualities-and-how-to-develop-it/

Moore, M 2013, 'Riot after Chinese teachers try to stop pupils cheating', www. telegraph.co.uk/news/worldnews/asia/china/10132391/Riot-after-Chinese-teachers-try-to-stop-pupils-cheating.html

Murphy, R 2012, 'Rex Murphy on Nelson Mandela: Where have all the leaders gone?', *National Post*, 21 July 2012, http://fullcomment.nationalpost.com/2012/07/21/rex-murphy-on-nelson-mandela-where-have-all-the-leaders-gone/

Pearson, I 2014, 'Fairies will dominate space travel', accessed 7 July 2014, http://timeguide.wordpress.com/2014/06/06/fairies-will-dominate-space-travel/

Plato, *The Republic*, Book Four; see also http://plato.stanford.edu/entries/plato-ethics-politics/#2.2

Quinn, B 2014, 'Alice Herz-Sommer: pianist and oldest known Holocaust survivor dies aged 110', accessed 23 July 2014, www.theguardian.com/world/2014/feb/23/alice-herz-sommer-holocaust-survivor-dies

Salz, A 2013, 'Salz Review. An independent review of Barclay's Business Practices', April 2013, http://online.wsj.com/public/resources/documents/SalzReview04032013.pdf

Sandel, M 2009, 'Michael Sandel: A New Citizenship: 2009', *The Reith Lectures*, BBC Radio 4, 9 June 2009, www.bbc.co.uk/programmes/b00kt7rg

Smith, G 2012, 'Why I Am Leaving Goldman Sachs', *The New York Times*, 14 March 2012, www.nytimes.com/2012/03/14/opinion/why-i-am-leaving-goldman-sachs.html?pagewanted=all&_r=1&

Stengel, J 2012, *Grow: How Ideals Power Growth and Profit at the World's Greatest Companies*, Virgin Books

Treanor, J 2012, 'Barclays chief Bob Diamond takes home £17m in pay, shares and perks', www.theguardian.com/business/2012/mar/09/barclays-chief-bob-diamond-pay

White, A 2014, 'G20 urged to unleash women's potential', www.theaustralian.com.au/business/g20-urged-to-unleash-womens-potential/story-e6frg8zx-1226992757876

Wilson, R, 'What is the homo economicus?' www.investopedia.com/ask/answers/08/homo-economicus.asp

Wright, R 2000, *Non Zero. The logic of human destiny*, Vintage

Index

Connect *with* WILEY ▶▶▶

WILEY
Browse and purchase the full range of Wiley publications on our official website.

www.wiley.com

Check out the Wiley blog for news, articles and information from Wiley and our authors.

www.wileybizaus.com

Join the conversation on Twitter and keep up to date on the latest news and events in business.

@WileyBizAus

Sign up for Wiley newsletters to learn about our latest publications, upcoming events and conferences, and discounts available to our customers.

www.wiley.com/email

Wiley titles are also produced in e-book formats. Available from all good retailers.

WILEY

Learn more with practical advice from our experts

Doing Good by Doing Good
Peter Baines

Above the Line
Michael Henderson

The Social Executive
Dionne Kasian-Lew

From Me to We
Janine Garner

Extraordinary Leadership in Australia & New Zealand
James Kouzes and Barry Posner with Michael Bunting

Stop Playing Safe
Margie Warrell

Lead with Wisdom
Mark Strom

Winning the War for Talent
Mandy Johnson

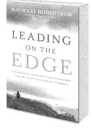

Leading on the Edge
Rachael Robertson